DRAMA THERAPY

DRAMA THERAPY
Concepts and Practices

By

ROBERT J. LANDY, Ph.D.

Associate Professor of Educational Theatre
Director of the Drama Therapy Program
New York University
New York, New York

CHARLES C THOMAS • PUBLISHER
Springfield • Illinois • U.S.A.

Published and Distributed Throughout the World by

CHARLES C THOMAS • PUBLISHER
2600 South First Street
Springfield, Illinois 62717

© *1986 by* CHARLES C THOMAS • PUBLISHER

ISBN 0-398-05176-3

Library of Congress Catalog Card Number: 85-17231

With THOMAS BOOKS *careful attention is given to all details of manufacturing and
design. It is the Publisher's desire to present books that are satisfactory as to their physical
qualities and artistic possibilities and appropriate for their particular use.* THOMAS
BOOKS *will be true to those laws of quality that assure a good name and good will.*

Printed in the United States of America
SC-R-3

Library of Congress Cataloging in Publication Data

Landy, Robert J.
  Drama therapy.

  Bibliography: p.
  Includes index.
  1. Drama—Therapeutic use. 2. Psychotherapy.
3. Drama in education. I. Title.
RC489.D72L357   1985   616.89′1523   85-17231
ISBN 0-398-05176-3

INTRODUCTION

Since the human potential movement in the 1960s and 1970s, new forms of psychotherapy have proliferated like the many heads of hydra. After more than a decade of primal, meditative, and confrontational therapies, why should there be yet another form—drama therapy? Hasn't this new breed actually existed for a long time in the form of psychodrama? How is drama therapy different from psychodrama, and why should another of the arts be separated out from the generic—creative arts or expressive therapies—to establish its own turf as had music, art, and dance therapy? Is there a place for drama therapy at a time in Western civilization marked by a return to fundamentalist religions, an obsession with computer-generated information, even in relation to therapy, a compulsive stockpiling of nuclear weapons, and a faith in psychotropic medication to combat mental illness? Even if a need could be demonstrated, are there jobs and appropriate client populations for drama therapists, given a general retrenchment in the mental health field and resettlement of the mentally ill within their communities?

Although the reader will be challenged to draw his own conclusions, these and many other difficult questions will be addressed in the following chapters. Drama therapy is new as an academic discipline and psychotherapeutic profession, although its roots are as ancient as the earliest known healing rites. It has yet to establish clear concepts, practices, and research methodologies. It is, in fact, in its early stages of development, marked by the establishment of an American organization in 1979, The National Association for Drama Therapy, and the British Association for Dramatherapy, established in 1977; the publication of descriptive and scholarly articles in such journals as *The Arts in Psychotherapy*; and the development of training programs, such as those at New York University, Antioch University, San Francisco, the Creative Psychotherapy Center in New Haven, and SESAME in England.

Although other books and anthologies concerning the therapeutic application of drama have been published recently, this text is the first to examine drama therapy as a discipline. In Part I, a context for drama therapy will be established in relation to other fields and other psychotherapies. Further, the term *drama therapy* will be defined in terms of its objectives, rationale, and training procedures.

In Part II, the conceptual basis of drama therapy will be examined, tracing its interdisciplinary sources and delineating important concepts gleaned from related fields. A theoretical model of drama therapy will be offered, based on the source material. The most widely practiced techniques of drama therapy will be examined in Part III, including psychodramatic practices and projective techniques. The focus of Part IV will be appropriate populations and settings for drama therapy including school, clinical, and other community settings. In Part V, we will look at research past, present, and future, and conclude with observations based upon the significant role drama therapy can play in fostering balance within individuals and among peoples.

An understanding of a new field is often associated with the work of individual practitioners and theorists. Although this book will incorporate the thought and practice of several drama therapists, it represents this author's present view of the field, which is in a constant state of evolution.

The orientation presented in this book favors the non-theatrical; that is, the drama therapy experience is viewed as best served by spontaneous improvisational enactment rather than the performance of scripted material to an audience. The terms *drama* and *play* will be seen as largely synonymous, both referring to a spontaneous process of enactment involving an imaginative projection of the self onto a character or object. In drama and play therapy, there is not, for the most part, an actual audience present.

The term *theatre* will be used to refer to the act of producing a play to be performed for an actual audience. The attention in theatre is directed toward a finished product which exists within a given time frame.

For many years, theatre artists have intuited the therapeutic effects of drama and theatre, the psychic healing that occurs as a by-product of the play, rehearsal, and performance experience. This book attempts to articulate what those theatre artists have intuited. This is not a book about drama in therapy, the limited uses of drama within an essentially non-dramatic form of psychotherapy. Rather, it is about drama therapy, a discipline in its own right with interdisciplinary roots, a theoretical base, a series of viable techniques, and a body of developing research.

This book is a start toward synthesizing a complex body of material into the paramaters of a new discipline. Drama therapy, like the production of a classical play, must be subject to various and changing interpretations to avoid a stasis and fixed status.

This author's interpretation will be biased toward the art form of drama/theatre and the spontaneous, improvisational moment within the art form. It will be based in the premise that the act of creating or re-creating reality in terms of one's inner vision is essentially a self-affirming act, an act of psychological healing.

Throughout the book, the masculine pronoun "he" will be used for stylistic reasons only. It is the author's hope that within this and other developing disciplines, a non-sexist attitude will prevail.

R.J.L.

ACKNOWLEDGMENTS

The inspiration for this book springs from my years at the Adams School, 1967–1971. I remember my colleagues and students with great fondness and respect.

In the organized profession of drama therapy, several individuals, through their writing and practice, continue to be important influences on my thinking, particularly David Johnson, Gertrud Schattner, Eleanor Irwin, and Renée Emunah.

The following people in related fields continue to do work that I greatly admire and that informs my own: Barbara Hesser, Susan Perlstein, Judith Gleason, Akhter Ahsen, Peter Pitzele, Bradley Bernstein, Richard Courtney, Gavin Bolton, and Dorothy Heathcote.

Sue O'Doherty and Roberta Zito provided invaluable assistance in preparing and editing the manuscript. I am most grateful for their critical readings, advice, and friendship.

Finally, many of the ideas and experiences in this book could not have been formulated without the trust, intelligence, and courage of my students at NYU.

CONTENTS

PART II. THE CONCEPTUAL BASIS OF DRAMA THERAPY

Chapter

PART III. THE TECHNIQUES OF DRAMA THERAPY

Chapter

PART IV. THE POPULATIONS AND
SETTINGS FOR DRAMA THERAPY

Chapter

PART V. RESEARCH IN DRAMA THERAPY

Chapter

DRAMA THERAPY

PART I
DRAMA THERAPY IN CONTEXT

Chapter One

ESTABLISHING A CONTEXT
FOR DRAMA THERAPY

DRAMA IN EDUCATION, RECREATION, AND THERAPY

Drama

Drama, derived from the Greek, *dran*, literally means a thing done. From both a historical and developmental perspective, drama is a process of enactment that appears to be unlearned and indigenous to all human life. Dramatic action is not simply doing something in the world. When one sits at a desk moving a pen across the paper, one is not necessarily engaged in dramatic action. For drama to occur it is necessary for the actor, one who acts in everyday life, to distinguish between either one aspect of the self and another or between self and non-self. This distinction is most clear in theatre, where an actor plays the role of a character who is not himself. It is less clear in everyday life, because many of the distinctions made through play and drama remain unconscious. A child at play, for example, in impersonating a parent, does not consciously say: "Now I am going to act out the role of my mother and feed my doll like my mother feeds me." Rather, he assumes the role of mother spontaneously. From the child's point of view, there is often no distinction at all between the two roles. That is, as he plays mother, he becomes mother, just as the actor trained in the method technique becomes his role through an identification with his character.

Drama is not only a separation of self and non-self but also a separation of realities. Dramatized reality is different in space, time, and consequence from everyday reality. The child playing with his dolls in the role of mother might, for example, feed the doll for fifteen seconds, then become distracted by another toy and leave the role of mother behind. There is not a chronological sequence to dramatized events that necessarily corresponds to the reality of everyday events. The child behaves as the mother in some ways but not in others. His actions in feeding the doll do not have the same consequence as the mother's actions do in feeding an actual baby. Furthermore, the child easily transforms his play space from a room in his house to a field or a spaceship or another imaginary environment. Dramatic play in everyday life, then, does not follow the classical dramatic unities of time, place, and action. Rather, dramatic play follows the psychological realities of the person at a given stage of development. The child at play lives simultaneously in two realities: that of the everyday, the actual; and that of the dramatic, the representational, the fictional.

Everyday reality is transformed into drama through an act of the imagination. The child is able to conceive of himself as mother through creating a mental image of mother and seeing not only how mother behaves but, at a deeper level, how she feels, thinks, and judges. That mental image of the mother who is good or bad, who is gentle or harsh, is projected outward, becoming the dramatized role of mother played out by the child in his own unique ways.

Examples of drama in everyday life are at least as old as the first appearance of human life on earth. Generally speaking, the more complex the brain and the structure of consciousness—that is, the more one is able to symbolize and to recognize distinctions between self and nonself—the more complex one's drama becomes.

At the early stages in the developmental history of a human being, drama is undifferentiated and based in reflexive and imitative action. As the human being becomes more cognitively complex and able to engage in symbolic and projective thinking, his drama reaches a more mature form.

With the development of systems of worship and ritual early in history, the indigenous drama of everyday life began to take on symbolic forms and serve specific purposes. To ensure a good harvest, a productive hunt, or a victorious battle, celebrants would role-play the elements, animals, gods, enemies. In role, they would enact ritual dramas in preparation for the actual event. Through the drama, they would symbolize their hopes for a good crop or a victorious battle and their fears of hunger and defeat.

With further differentiation of institutions of law and war, religion and healing, education and recreation, drama became a further means to an end. Most often that end was education.

Drama in Education

Early dramatic education was not institutionalized; that is, a boy learned how to be a hunter naturally, imitating and playing out the hunter role. However, with the advent of feudal society, drama entered the institutions. The church was the first to apply drama to education. As early as the tenth century, the *Quem quaeritis trope,* relating the story of Christ's resurrection, was introduced into the morning prayers on Easter day. A trope was part of the liturgical text written for special holy days to accompany the church music. The significance of the *Quem quaeritis trope* is that for the first time the text was intended to be performed rather than simply chanted. In it, we find an early form of a dramatic scenario instructing the monks and later the secular mime how to assume dramatic, liturgical roles (Chambers, 1903). Through the dramatization of the resurrection of Christ, many illiterate parishioners learned of the story of Easter and thus participated more fully in the symbolic events of the Mass.

The early history of dramatic education has been well documented elsewhere (Courtney, 1974). Since the 1930s, drama has become an accepted means of education in many schools in the United States, the United Kingdom, and other countries. It is generally taught in two basic ways. The first is as a self-contained subject. That is, students study the art of drama and/or theatre. Secondly, drama and theatre is used as a method to teach other subjects, most notably, history and English.

Teaching History Through Drama

Teachers generally choose one of two methods of teaching history through drama. In the first approach, students enter into the historical context of a particular time, i.e., the American Revolution. Through their immersion in the cultural experience of eighteenth century dress, movement, cuisine, philosophy, music, art, theatre, and politics, the students re-create a sense of that time. And through assuming the roles of known and imagined historical characters of the revolutionary period they learn about the events, motivations, ideas, and life-styles of people in eighteenth century America.

A second way of teaching history through drama involves a more internal approach. Rather than assuming the external trappings of mid-eighteenth century America, students explore the political, social, cultural, and biographical documents of the time, then search out related dilemmas in their own experience in the contemporary world. Through dramatization, they enact a scene of, for example, a group of townspeople in Virginia attempting to decide whether or not to go to war with the British. Using their knowledge of the history combined with their subjective point of view, the students create a spontaneous drama focused in the exploration of the more universal notion of revolution. Following such an improvisation the group might discuss their thoughts of breaking away from an oppressive institution, looking at examples both from history and from their own experiences.

Teaching English Through Drama

In the late 1960s, the teaching of English was deeply influenced by the work of James Moffett. Among other things, he posited drama, the moment of direct experience, as "the base and essence" of the English curriculum from kindergarten through college (Moffett, 1968). For Moffett, the learning of language is based upon the child's ability to play with sounds and words, rather than to learn the rules of grammar. As the child engages in open-ended, spontaneous dialogue with others, incorporating their language as he incorporates their roles, he comes to understand the means of linguistic communication.

Reading and writing skills can be directly taught through speech and dramatization. Many difficulties and blocks in writing can be overcome if the students begin to generate speech spontaneously, through improvisation, without the mechanical concern of writing it down. In the role of another who speaks in a certain way, the student has the opportunity to create a particular style and form of language. The speech created through this kind of simple role playing can be transcribed by a tape recorder or an older student skilled at writing. The speech can then be replayed or read back to the student who, in consultation with the scribe, further develops and edits his written piece.

The kind of writing most applicable to this approach seems to be creative, personal writing. However, a role-playing approach can also be applied to more objective forms of expository writing. This approach would involve several steps, including the presentation of an issue, a translation of the issue into particular roles and experiences familiar to the student, a playing out of the particular roles, and, finally, the writing of an expository piece based upon the role-playing situation.

As an example, a sixth grade teacher might wish to have his class write an expository piece about the dumping of nuclear waste in a particular community. After introducing the issue, he would help each student create the role of a member of that community with a particular point of view, i.e., an irate middle-class citizen, a mollifying politician, a defensive corporate executive. The roles can be reversed, with students taking on points of view that contradict their own. As an intermediate step, students can research the issue through readings and interviews with actual community members. Following the role playing and research, students can speak or write down their thoughts and feelings from the point of view of one character. Finally, they can be asked to create an expository piece, far removed from their first-person dramatizations, yet based upon their role playing and research.

Reading can also be taught through drama. Again, the approach involves encouraging the student to personalize the text so that it is not seen as a forbidding object. One method used with much success is that of reader's theatre. Though performance based, it involves a process of transforming narrative into drama. The students work with a published story, creating a script by breaking it down into spoken dialogue. They add further dialogue, narration, sound effects, and props. Next, they distribute the roles among themselves and, finally, perform their dramatization of the story to an invited audience of peers and teachers. Though the performance orientation can be problematic in terms of competing for the best roles and focusing too much attention on the need to please an audience, the students are able to personalize a text and vitalize it through their dramatic action. A further problem in using reader's theatre is that of trivializing a complex piece of literature. When this occurs, the teacher/director needs to intervene to help the students stretch their ability to play with speech, thought, and language, and find a balance between their interpretation and the integrity of the text.

Theatre-In-Education

Drama is not only applied to the teaching of history and English but can be viewed as a central element throughout the curriculum (Courtney, 1980). Through experiments in theatre-in-education (TIE), subject matter as diverse as evolution, sex role stereotyping, and child abuse has been explored within schools (Landy, 1982). TIE involves a trained group of actor/educators who create a piece of theatre based upon an educational issue and intended for a particular school audience. The TIE piece is performed for the students who participate in the drama by directly interacting with the performers either during or after the dramatization.

Goals of Drama in Education

Given the many and varied applications of drama to education, it is difficult to specify concrete goals. The statements of goals published most often in the standard creative drama texts tend to be general and redundant. The educational psychologist, Benjamin Bloom, and his colleagues published specific behaviorally based models for cognitive and affective learning (Bloom et al., 1956, Krathwohl et al., 1964). Their work has been extended by Ann Shaw (1968) and Linaya Leaf (1980) into the domain of creative drama learning.

Dramatic education is an aesthetic education, a learning through art and play. To specify its goals behaviorally is problematic, because many of the qualitative changes that occur through drama are internal and non-observable. In attempting to specify internal processes behaviorally, Bloom et al., as well as Shaw and Leaf, subscribe to a philosophical position that claims that all learning can be seen, tested, and measured. But can it? The meaning of a dramatic experience does not necessarily manifest itself immediately, and dramatic learning is not necessarily attached to a specific content. The child who plays the role of Benjamin Franklin during a dramatization of the American Revolution might not learn many facts about Franklin. What then might the dramatic experience have taught him?

For one, he might have learned how to better engage in dramatization. Also, he might have learned something about the relation of thought to action, of research to role playing. That is, the more he knows about the life and times of a historical character, the better he will be able to speak and act from that character's point of view; conversely, the more he enters into the role play, the more information he needs to add substance to his characterization. This action based upon research and the research based upon action might well be vital to the process of learning how to learn.

Finally, he might have begun to learn to speak, and think like a person of great practical and scientific wisdom. These educational goals are of a higher order than the knowledge of a set of facts about Franklin in eighteenth century America.

The goals of drama in education can be seen as:

1. learning about drama,
2. learning about learning, and
3. learning about thinking and speaking.

It is difficult to evaluate these skills in a simple behavioral way. One's learning would have to be observed over time, looking at the development of skills in dramatization, self-directed learning, thinking and speaking.

The larger notion of drama in education is that, like play, it is a natural means of learning that begins long before formal schooling. If the teacher can apply the natural processes of role playing and dramatization to learning across the academic curriculum, then he has harnessed a powerful method of education. Dramatic learning is not the acquisition of new tools, tricks, and exercises but, rather, their elimination in order to model the process that infants use to make sense of the world: that of play.

Drama in Recreation

The word *recreation* has the same implication as drama. It is a re-creation of reality, a making over in play what one has experienced in everyday life. Like drama, recreation implies two realities: that of the everyday, the actual, and that of the representational, the fictional. Recreation also implies revitalization, respite from a day of study or work. Even Sigmund Freud, who was known to work six days a week from early morning until late at night, needed to take a three-month vacation each summer in order to revitalize his energies, libidinal as well as intellectual.

At the heart of the recreational experience is play, of which much has been written in recent years. There are diverse theories of play which view it in the context of evolution, objects and tools, society and culture, and symbols (Bruner, Jolly, Sylva, 1976). In the theoretical literature, we also find a diversity of aims realized through play, including: discharge, exercise, meta-communication, mastery, novelty, problem solving, cooperation, and creativity. As we shall see in Chapter Three, the psychoanalytically based theories which view play as a symbolic representation of unconscious feelings provide a direct link to drama therapy.

The media of children's play, i.e., toys and dolls, are, for the most part, inherently dramatic. Exceptions include quiet games, such as chess and checkers, and competitive sports. Dramatic play, as defined by Richard Courtney (1974), is play that involves impersonation and/or identification. Further, in the use of puppets, masks, dolls, costumes, and makeup, dramatic play also involves the process of projection, as the child endows the object with properties of himself and represents his view of reality through his projective play.

Dramatic play generally has a spontaneous, improvisational quality. The flow of action is determined by the attention and imagination of the players at any given moment. There is a structure to children's play that obeys the subjective experiencing of the child rather than the logical, sequential thinking of adults. Peter Slade (1954), the British child drama expert, refers to five to seven-year-old children at play as "acting in the round," that is, moving spontaneously in any direction around their bodies according to their wills, rather than the rules of any game.

Dramatic play is a natural re-creational process for the pre-school child requiring no adult interventions. At times, children's play will be directed toward adults; but children will also spend time each day in solitary play, either imagining an audience of parents or quite unaware of any onlooker.

As children begin to attend school and participate in community life, they discover recreational opportunities planned by adults. Drama is incorporated in many community institutions. Since the 1930s, influenced by Winifred Ward in America and Peter Slade in England, a number of American and British elementary schools have incorporated drama not only within the school curriculum but also after school. After-school dramatic activities include theatre games, creative drama experiences, and theatre performances. In Britain, farsighted community planners have transformed desolate and neglected property into "adventure playgrounds," community spaces where children are encouraged to participate in creative drama and theatre, as well as other art forms.

The recreational dramatic play of adolescents, adults, and seniors is often of a different order than that of children. The developing adolescent might easily view the use of puppets, masks, and costumes as "kid stuff." At the adolescent stage, recreational drama turns either inward, as fantasy, or outward, as theatre. An example of an internal dramatic re-creation would be: following an unsatisfactory, humiliating encounter with an adult authority figure, a fourteen-year-old girl replays the scene in her mind; only in the re-creation she assumes the power and humiliates the adult. In this instance, the girl uses mental imagery to transform reality and feel in control. The re-creational imaginative experience can also take on the function of previewing a potentially difficulty encounter yet to come. This internal re-creational process is spontaneous and occurs in the natural forms of fantasy, wish, daydream, and dream.

The most widely practiced outward form of recreational drama for adolescents as well as adults and elders is the making of theatre. Unlike the young child who has a psychological need to "act in the round," the developing adolescent needs to focus his creative energy in one direction: towards an audience who can offer a very direct form of validation. After-school and community theatre have many recreational values as participants work cooperatively toward a common goal and test out their abilities to design, write, direct, act, sing, and dance. The main difficulty occurs when the players view the process as other than recreation and focus their attention on competing for leading roles and facile praise from the audience. As long as the theatre experience remains joyful and focused upon the experience itself, it can prove valuable as recreation. It requires a sensitive director to balance the cooperative, joyful moments with the competitive, narcissistic ones.

A form of recreational theatre for elders that has proven most valuable is that of life history theatre. Life history theatre is based on Robert Butler's notion of life review (1963), in which a person examines his past life as a whole, in order to make sense of it. In the South Bronx and other New York settings, Susan Perlstein and her colleagues have developed many life history plays based on Butler's notion of life review. Perlstein's organization, Elders Share the Arts, is devoted to "destroying sterotypes, altering the way elderly people perceive themselves, reducing the fear of aging, recognizing the beauty of each stage of life, while reinforcing the 'resources this society shuts off in its flight from death'" (Lippard, 1984). The life history plays are generally created by the actors themselves, through improvisation and discussion, and are centered upon significant past experiences. Following the performance of the plays to peers, friends, and interested others, audience members participate in dialogue with the actors, sharing similar experiences from their lives.

Much of recreational theatre for adolescents, adults, and elders is not as ambitious as the concept of life history theatre. The content of the plays, presented in recreational settings, tends to be more superficial and less connected to the lives of the players. However, the production of more conventional, scripted plays can be valuable if the players are willing to re-create and explore authentic aspects of their experience through an identification with their characters. Given the loneliness and isolation experienced by many elders confined to institutions, a less lofty, yet no less significant recreational aim of theatre can be that expressed by an eighty-seven-year-old man in the Jewish Home and Hospital for Aged in New York City: "Theatre is important to me because it keeps me busy. There's such a thing as lonesomeness. How do you overcome lonesomeness? By doing something interesting" (Landy, 1982).

Other community institutions that use theatre recreationally with adult populations are the church and the synagogue. Since the 1950s, the church and the synagogue in America have been major environments for community theatre. Some of the productions are religious in nature, including original ritual dramatizations and such literary offerings as T. S. Eliot's *Murder in the Cathedral.* But many of the productions are only tangentially religious, focusing rather on political and social issues, such as racism, sexism, war and peace. Several church-based community theatres, as part of the early off-Broadway theatre movement in New York City in the 1950s and 1960s, transcended the aim of theatre as recreational and became a major aesthetic force in the avant-garde theatre movement. At the Judson Poet's Theatre of Judson Memorial Church, the director, Reverend Al Carmines, dealt frequently with significant social issues (see Landy, 1982). He and others retained the notion of theatre as re-creation only in the sense of representing certain social issues and aesthetic visions of reality. Their aims were certainly not the conventional recapitulation of the status quo but, rather, a more radical exploration of the issues and symbols of everyday life.

Theatre has also been applied to prison settings for recreational purposes. Part of the rationale is to relieve the boredom of the everyday prison routine and help inmates renew a sense of hopefulness. However, like life history theatre for elders and avant-garde socially relevant theatre performed in churches and synagogues, much of prison theatre also has a more social and political purpose. When Herbert Blau brought his San Francisco production of *Waiting for Godot* to San Quentin in the mid-1950s, it was clear that the inmates understood the essential existential message of a play that has baffled middle-class audiences ever since it was first performed. They knew about passing the time with mundane rituals. They knew about hope deferred. They knew about messengers that came and went with no reprieves, no promises. Since that moment, other theatre groups have performed in prisons throughout the world. More significantly, prisoners have begun to create their own theatre. We will examine several examples of theatre in prisons in Chapter Ten.

Herbert Blau's work in San Quentin was about the more political implication of theatre as recreation. Those influenced by his example, those struggling for a more humane penal system, view re-creational theatre as a reconstruction of reality, so that it can be seen with new eyes by performers and audiences alike.

Drama in Therapy

Drama therapy, itself, incorporates the aims of educational drama and recreational drama but is greater than the sum of the two. It is about learning and it is about renewing and re-creating, but it also incorporates aims of theatre artists, psychoanalysts, developmental psychologists, and sociologists. When the first anthology of readings appeared in this new field in 1981, the editors, Gertrud Schattner and Richard Courtney, called their book, *Drama in Therapy.* Why not drama therapy? Is the use of the preposition merely incidental? It is probable that neither editor yet saw a coherent field. Although they collected papers documenting the use of dramatic techniques within the psychotherapeutic process, they were unwilling to take that next step and commit themselves to the view that drama therapy existed as an independent form of therapy. Their book was some years in the making and their thinking began back in the mid-1970s. Since that time, drama therapy as a profession has grown substantially, as evidenced in research and publications and the growth of academic training programs and professional organizations.

The direct predecessors of drama therapy are those forms of psychotherapy that employ dramatic techniques and processes. The primary examples of drama in therapy occur within such action-oriented approaches as Gestalt, psychodrama, and play therapy. Practitioners in these areas have drawn extensively upon role-playing techniques and spontaneous, creative processes to help clients express and resolve problems. Although they employ dramatic processes, they are not, for the most part, trained in the art form of drama/theatre. Thus, they are practitioners who use drama *in* therapy. Their work, as well as that of other more conventional psychotherapists, provides source material for the new field of drama therapy. In the following pages we will examine that work.

DRAMA THERAPY IN RELATION TO OTHER PSYCHOTHERAPIES

Although older forms of psychotherapy have changed and newer forms have evolved to meet contemporary needs, certain basic models provide a comparative spectrum of approaches most widely practiced. In establishing a context for drama therapy, we will look at those essential models that have the most relevance to the new field. They include: the psychoanalytical model of Freud, the analytical model of Jung, the biofunctional model of Reich, the existential model of Laing, the humanistic model of Rogers and Perls, the psychodramatic model of Moreno, the behavioral model of Skinner, and the family therapy model of Satir.

Psychoanalysis

Psychoanalysis, in its pure Freudian form, is in many ways obsolete. The structure of the cool, distant analyst sitting behind a patient who free-associates while lying on a couch is now uncommon. Since the 1930s, Freudian technique and theory have been modified substantially. The therapist tends to be more of a partner in the session, less distant and cool. The client does not necessarily recline but may engage the therapist directly. The dilemmas of his life might take a more immediate focus than a purely historical perspective. And the four or five times a week schedule has been reduced, in many cases, to one or two sessions per week.

Today, Freud's model can be viewed as psychoanalytic psychotherapy (see Kovel, 1976). The main tenets of both classical psychoanalysis and psychoanalytic psychotherapy are: the emphasis upon the inner, unconscious life of the client and the effects of repressed emotions; the prominence of infantile sexual experience in the determination of present behavior; the notion of action in everyday life as symbolic and often defensive; and a view of the therapeutic interaction as based in transference, a dramatic representation of past psychological issues.

Technique

Psychoanalysis is primarily a verbal therapy. The client sits or reclines and speaks to the therapist, who is for the most part a listener, reflector, and interpreter. However, the mode of talking about what happened, a narrative mode, often becomes an experiencing of what is happening, a dramatic mode. That is, when the client reaches a point of feeling, as, for example, he confronts the therapist upon whom he has transferred the role of father, he is then engaged in a kind of psychoanalytic dramatization. Because of the centrality of transference, the psychoanalytic technique is very much based in the relationship between therapist and client. One implication of this is that the therapist needs to explore his counter-transferential issues, that is, his own feelings and associations toward the client.

His technique further involves an analysis of the client's resistances, including transference, that block his ability to review repressed material. Through the classical technique of free association—the spontaneous verbalization of thoughts and feelings—or through a contemporary version using more directed verbalization, the therapist leads the client toward a resolution of the transference neurosis and a view of the infantile dilemma that has determined his present dysfunctional behavior.

Goals

The main goal of psychoanalysis is a change of consciousness, a movement from repression to expression, rather than a change of behavior. As the psychoanalyst, Joel Kovel (1976), states: "The goal is to promote a self-reflective process and to take it to the point where the individual can continue on his or her own." In psychoanalysis, the client directs his own therapy. The therapist helps him explore the roots of his neurotic patterns and understand the historical conditions that have led to his dysfunctional behavior. The emphasis is on understanding and seeing oneself more clearly in relation to one's past. Many analysts assume that a corresponding change of behavior will occur, but, as behavior is not their direct aim, they focus their attention on the symbolic, inner life of the client.

Clients

Psychoanalysis is generally a long-term therapy involving a commitment of considerable time and money. It is for the most part not indicated for a psychotic, non-verbal client population. It is more appropriate for treating neurotic, verbal clients and those who generally need to look at recurring problems in their lives.

Through the work of Anna Freud, Melanie Klein, Margaret Lowenfeld, Virginia Axline, and Erik Erikson, many of Freud's notions have been applied to therapy with children. Based in the assumption that a primary language of children is play, and that through their play disturbed children enact a symbolic representation of their conflicts, play therapists help the children come to terms with their disturbances through that medium.

Implications for Drama Therapy

As related to drama therapy, psychoanalysis provides an understanding of the dramatic dialectical process in terms of the notion of defensive techniques. To defend against a fear of acting out his unfulfilled needs for sex, love, and power, a person represses these needs and constructs an elaborate series of psychic walls. To protect himself from expressing his own anger, he projects his anger onto another. To protect himself from feeling weak and powerless, he identifies with a strong role model and imitates the external behavior of the model. And to protect himself from confronting the object of his love and/or hate, he re-creates another in its image through transference and acts toward the therapist, for example, as he would wish to act toward his mother. The three defensive techniques of projection, identification, and transference, as we shall see later, provide an important part of the conceptual framework of drama therapy.

Freud's most significant contribution not only to drama therapy, but also to the totality of twentieth century thought, is the concept of the unconscious (Freud, 1943). The notion of behavior as virtually determined by a storehouse of unexpressed feelings and dark instinctual longings for sex, love, and power has had a profound effect upon most all intellectual disciplines. This notion applies most clearly to drama therapy as it achieves a visible form through symbolization or representation in language and action. The adaptation of the psychoanalytic technique to play therapy with children is based in the notion that the unconscious can be viewed as the client enacts his repressed feelings through symbolic means. And, through the repetition of the repressed issues in play, the child can achieve a degree of liberation from the tyranny of the unconscious.

The notion of the unconscious is at the heart of the aesthetic experience. The maker of art, whether a professional artist or client in a creative arts therapy, is one who gives form to a feeling state. That form, expressed through movement, sound, or visual imagery, embodies a symbolic representation of the unconscious. Thus, through the aesthetic form, the inner life of the artist or client can be viewed. In a therapeutic context, the creations of the client can serve as a way out of the darkness of repression and toward the light of integration.

And finally, in his tripartite model of the personality as id, ego, and superego, Freud provides an image of balance that, as we shall see, is crucial to the drama therapy model. Health is determined by a psychic system of checks and balances and an ego that mediates between the instinctual demands of the id (the pleasure principle) and the demands of the outside world (the reality principle). Neurosis and psychosis can be seen as imbalances among the elements—a dominating id leading to impulsive behavior, a dominating superego leading to compulsive behavior. In relating this model to the actor on stage or in everyday life who needs to find a balance between self and role, we find a powerful means of diagnosing and treating dysfunction.

Analytic Psychology

Freud's colleague, C. G. Jung, went beyond the master by founding a technique based upon a notion of a cosmic consciousness that transcends individual psychological experience. Jung's concept, the collective unconscious, viewed individual experience as linked to universal experience, to the history of the human race. According to Jung, the behaviors, dreams, and fantasies of people are symbolic re-creations of a universal human experience whose hidden meanings, once analyzed, explain the nature of reality. The mind, then, becomes a kind of transcendent phenomenon imprinted with the wisdom and culture of the ages. Through its symbolic representations, it reveals archetypes or universal images and myths that recapitulate the crucial metaphors of man's existence (Jung, 1964).

Jung's second break from Freud's orthodoxy was an attention to the future, to growth and the realization of creative potential — so crucial to later models of Gestalt and Rogerian therapy. Jung further extended this notion toward the human desire for rebirth.

Jung postulated eight basic interacting concepts as structures of the personality. The first is the ego, or the conscious mind, containing perceptions and conceptions of the self and world. The second, the personal unconscious, is an intermediate link between the ego and the collective unconscious. It contains material that is available to consciousness but which, like that of Freud's preconscious, has been partially repressed. The collective unconscious, with its archetypes of universal experience throughout the evolutionary spectrum, is a link between all human beings, between man and nature, and between man and the supernatural. The fourth personality structure, the persona, is the mask or role that one wears in relation to the social world. It is the social archetype through which one presents himself in everyday life.

In postulating an essential human androgeny, Jung identified two further archetypal structures of personality: the anima, or female part of the biological male, and the animus, or male part of the biological female. Further, Jung identified the dark, animal-like, instinctual part of the human being as the shadow archetype. And finally, Jung offers the concept of self as the core of the personality, containing all the other structures and providing a unity and wholeness to the personality. The self as archetype represents man's movement toward integration and actualization.

As in Freud's model, Jung saw these structures as interactive and striving toward balance. The dialectic and conflict between structures was seen by Jung as essential in fostering a creative existence.

Jung's system was an erudite and eclectic one that incorporated many aspects not only of psychology but also of religion, anthropology, fine arts and literature, mythology and the occult.

Technique

Jungian analysis, like psychoanalysis, is primarily a verbal therapy, although Jung added an imagery-based technique, that of active imagination. Through this expressive technique, the client builds upon a dream image, for example, allowing it to unfold spontaneously through a creative, expressive process. In exploring the transformations of the image through movement or drawing, the client reveals his unconscious archetypes to the therapist. Through the further technique of amplification, the therapist helps the client to see how his imagery connects to his everyday life, as well as to the larger scheme of transpersonal experience. The therapist works both backward, toward the historical causes of a problem in the individual's past or the racial/cultural past, and forward, toward the individual's goal of integration. The Jungian analyst tends to be more active and play a more oracular role than his psychoanalytic cohort. Since the client's neurotic issues are viewed by the therapist as located in a larger cosmic sphere rather than within one's personal history, the client tends to feel less responsible for causing his neurosis and more responsive to the therapist's interpretation of his dilemma.

Goals

The goal in analytic psychology is to empower the client to view his life as a confluence of fully developed, differentiated, and interactive personality structures. Further, the analyst helps the client achieve a level of individuation, a psychic wholeness, based in an integration of personal history, collective human experience, and future strivings toward actualization.

Clients

Jungian therapists would claim that analytic psychotherapy is suitable for all types of emotional disturbances—neurotic, borderline, and psychotic. In practice, the Jungian model seems to apply most to those creative, intuitive individuals, accepting of the transcendent approach, who seek to find deeper meaning and purpose in their lives. It is unclear how effective Jungian therapy has been for psychotic and borderline patients, who need to focus more on everyday reality and personal consciousness than on cosmic consciousness.

Implications for Drama Therapy

Jung built upon the concepts of Freud, developing, for example, an understanding of transference and projection in terms of his own system. However, defensive techniques were not central to his therapy. The unique feature of Jungian analysis that relates directly to drama therapy is the emphasis upon the intuitive, creative aspects of the human being, the parts that participate in re-creating myths and archetypes through internal dramatizations found in dreams, reflections, and fantasies. Jung's dreamwork is especially suited to drama therapy in its personal view of the dream as part of the scenario of one's life and its universal view of the dream as a kind of classical drama that embodies the essential themes of human existence.

Further, Jung's notion of active imagination, of translating images into expressive forms, provides a model for all the creative arts therapies. In extending the structures of the personality into the dramatic archetypes of persona and shadow, anima and animus, Jung further provides a model for drama therapy as a means of working through mask and role, through dialectic and representation.

The personal account of one's own life history, and the universal quality of fairy tales, myths, and legends, are aspects of drama therapy practice. As such, their understanding and analysis can well benefit from Jung's seminal work in analytic psychology.

Biofunctional Therapy

Reichian therapy, like Freudian psychoanalysis, has changed much since the death of its founder. From the model developed by Wilhelm Reich, the field has evolved into bioenergetics, associated with the work of Alexander Lowen (1967), and other body-oriented therapists. The common factor in all the biofunctional approaches is the attention to the healing of emotional problems through the body. Unlike Freud, Reich was not interested in exploring mental states as the focus of neurotic patterns, but rather physical ones.

Consequently, Reich developed a psychotherapeutic approach that was essentially nonverbal and directive. Because the therapist played an active, directive role, there was less opportunity for transference, which had little place in Reich's work. There was, however, a strong verbal component to his early work in Europe involving what he termed *character analysis*. For Reich (1961), character was a physiological mask, a defense against the full expression of one's potential and one's potency.

Technique

In therapy, Reich would indicate, then analyze, a client's resistances as manifested in observable physical conditions, i.e., a stiff neck, folded arms, a fixed smile. Through a verbal analysis of the resistances, called body armor, Reich proceeded to uncover a client's character.

Later, as he focused more directly on the manipulation of the body through massage and breathing techniques, Reich depended less upon the verbal analysis. Toward the end of his tumultuous life, Reich's experiments focused upon the cure for cancer and other organic diseases through orgone treatment, a balancing of somatic energies within a controlled environment.

Goals

The goal of Reichian therapy becomes a letting go of the body armor in order to achieve complete orgasmic potency, a full flow of sexual energy. The Freudian cognitive goal of understanding and the Jungian transcendent goal of wholeness did not appeal to Reich. For him, mental illness was a blockage of sexual energy that, once released, would restore healthy functioning.

Clients

Reichian, biofunctional therapies are most appropriate for neurotic or alientated individuals who manifest their problems through sexual dysfunction and visible muscular tension. There is much potential value in working with more severely disturbed individuals through some of the breathing and expressive techniques; however, such methods as deep massage and body manipulation could well be too threatening for a psychotic person. Although Freud, Jung, and Reich all had extensive experience with psychotics, their techniques are not generally indicated today in the treatment of psychotic disturbance.

Implications for Drama Therapy

Reichian therapy has a direct link to the expressive, creative arts therapies. For one, it leans heavily upon non-verbal experience as essential in the treatment of mental illness. With its biological base and emphasis upon movement and body alignment, it is perhaps most directly relevant to dance and movement therapy. The notion of character as defensive has a particular relevance to drama therapists who work constantly with roles and characterization.

In acting for the theatre, one would not perceive the taking on of another character as defensive. The actor creates a character as a means of communicating with an audience. But applied to the drama therapy session, Reich's notion can serve diagnostic as well as treatment purposes. Working from a Reichian perspective, the drama therapist would examine how the client uses a role to mask a part of the self and defend against full expression. For example, a rather timid client defending against his aggressive tendencies might choose to enact an aggressive character in a role-playing situation. The discrepancy between the presentation of self in role and out of role can aid the therapist in analyzing the client's dilemma. Further, by encouraging the expression of the aggressive part of himself, the therapist can help the client become aware of how his everyday character as timid defends against the aggressive tendencies which have been repressed.

Finally, the Reichian notion of blocked energy needing physical release relates to a dramatic understanding of catharsis. The safe release of aggressive or sexual energy in drama therapy is often accomplished through the dramatic projective techniques. In understanding catharsis as applied to drama therapy, the notion of a balance of psychic energy is crucial.

Existential Therapy

Existential therapy, which became popularized in the 1960s through the work of Rollo May (1969) and R. D. Laing (1967), is predicated on the notion that "no one can begin to think, feel or act now except from the starting point of his or her own alienation" (Laing, 1967). Mental illness for Laing is not a function of the individual psyche but an artifact of living in a family or society that fosters madness in those who cannot conform to the alienated condition. Existential therapy, in viewing the individual as alienated from self, family, and society, seeks to help him achieve a sense of responsibility, conceptualized by Martin Buber as an ability to respond (Buber, 1937), through the interaction with the therapist and/or the therapeutic community.

Technique

The technique of existential therapy, though for the most part based in a one-to-one verbal interaction, takes on a more radical form in Laing's experiments with therapeutic communities. At Kingsley Hall and more recent therapeutic communities in London, Laing broke down the conventional social/political structures that separate client and therapist, powerful and powerless. All residents of the therapeutic communities, whether mentally ill or not, whether therapist or client, participate equally in the business of maintaining an everyday existence as a community. Through group therapy sessions, issues of everyday life are discussed and resolved without reference to any pathology, unconscious processes, or muscular armor. Laing's central metaphor is politics. Mental illness is political as is every other facet of contemporary life, and the way to resolve it is to alter the conventional political dynamics between the governed and the governors. The Laingian therapist to a great extent participates in the process with the client, engaging himself at times in a voyage in and out of madness. There is no attention to the psychological or biological basis of psychopathology. All therapy occurs in the moment—the direct, unmediated here-and-now that has become the basis of Gestalt and other humanistic therapies.

Goal

The goal of Laing and his followers is to provide the mentally ill with a responsive support system so that they may confront their problems, take their "dark voyage through madness," and re-emerge as more whole, more responsible for their existential condition, and more responsive to their community.

Clients

Laing's clients have tended to be schizophrenics—those individuals with severe, psychotic symptoms. Rejecting the labeling of the mentally ill by the psychiatric establishment, Laing has proceeded to treat his clients within the confines of a therapeutic community. His notion of mental illness differs radically from the mainstream, as he views it as socially defined rather than as biologically or psychologically determined.

Generally speaking, existential therapy, as practiced on an individual or group basis outside of a therapeutic community, is most applicable to the alienated individual who seeks a means of establishing more authentic social relationships and learning how to take more responsibility for his existential dilemma.

Implications for Drama Therapy

Laing's connection to theatre was firmly established in the late 1960s when The Living Theatre included a line from his work, *The Politics of Experience* in their apocalyptic play, *Paradise Now* (Laing, 1967): "If I could turn you on; if I could drive you out of your wretched mind; if I could tell you, I'd let you know." The line became a chant, repeated over and over again, representative of the Laingian notion of madness as a visionary experience, of the dark voyage through schizophrenia as essential in a culture gone mad. Since that time Laing has written many quasi-dramatic poems and parables that characterize the existential realities of interpersonal and political experience in an expressionistic, non-linear flow of words and images.

Laing's playful, symbolic use of language and imagery to characterize existential reality relates well to poetry therapy which proceeds primarily through verbal imagery. As in the example of The Living Theatre, Laing's poetics can also provide the basis for a kind of liberationist drama.

Laing's redefinition of the role of the therapist and of the relationship between client and therapist also has implications for drama therapy. In that the drama therapist often engages in role playing with the client, he works within the structure of a responsible (ability to respond) relationship. Through the role-playing, the power structures and role hierarchies of everyday life can be explored as the therapist works to guide the client into a more responsible, less alienated state of being.

In its attention to the present, subjective experience of clients and its movement away from analysis, existential therapy sets the stage for a more overtly dramatic therapy: that of Gestalt.

Rogerian and Gestalt Therapy

The human potential movement of the 1960s led to the development of a number of psychotherapeutic approaches. Most forms, whether individual or group, verbal or expressive, subscribed to a characteristically American positivism. Freud's theories were viewed as too pessimistic and dark. Existential thinking was closer in intent with its emphasis on personal responsibility, dialogue, and present time orientation. However, the philosophical roots of existentialism are in the work of Kierkegaard, Heidegger, Husserl, and Sartre. Their image of man as alone, alienated, and despairing proved also too gloomy for the American positivists. They turned, rather, to a more optimistic philosophy, grounded in the early work of John Dewey (1966) and William James (1948) but exemplified most directly in the non-directive therapy of Carl Rogers (1961).

Rogers viewed man as having a core self that is basically whole and good. He de-emphasized the unconscious as a primary psychological concern. Like Laing, Rogers insisted that the therapist establish an empathetic relationship with his client and offer him unconditional positive regard, that is, total affirmation. The Rogerian therapist becomes a mirror that reflects back to the client that which he puts out to the therapist. If that reflection is positive, based in the affirmation of client by therapist, then the client will see himself in a positive light.

Of the subsequent approaches based in the ideas of Rogers and the ideals of the human potential movement, perhaps the most fully realized was Gestalt therapy. Like Rogers, Frederick Perls, the founder of Gestalt therapy, took a positivist position and worked from the image of the self as potentially whole and good. Perls minimized the demonic and unconscious psychic forces, working instead with surface behavior, the obvious, and staying firmly rooted in the present, the here-and-now.

Technique

Perls' technique was intended to be primarily a non-verbal and emotional one. As he said many times: "The real communication is beyond words" (Perls, 1969). However, in practice many of Perls's techniques involved quite a bit of talk. Perls leaned heavily upon dramatic techniques which were in many ways similar to psychodramatic techniques developed by his predecessor, J. L. Moreno. For example, Perls often used an empty chair which represented another or a part of oneself with whom the client has unfinished business. Through a dialogue with the empty chair in the here and now, the client expresses his feelings toward that person/part. Emotional expressiveness is of primary importance in Gestalt therapy and many therapists work toward large cathartic moments.

Perls also engaged in much dream work, again using a dramatic approach by having a client take on the roles of various characters or objects in his dream. For Perls, the dream represents various split-off parts of the self, and in playing out those parts, the client reclaims them and moves toward an acceptance of himself as a whole.

Gestalt therapy tends to be fairly brief in duration, generally not lasting longer than three months. Often, it is considerably shorter when based in intensive workshop experiences that in some instances include less than twenty hours of therapy.

Goals

The main goal of Gestalt therapy is to help the client perceive himself as an organismic whole, with complete integration of his cognitive, affective, and motor functions. Further, as implied in the "Gestalt prayer"—"I do my thing and you do your thing"—the therapist works to help the client learn to take responsibility for his own life as an individual separate from the therapist or other authority figure.

The Clients

The clients in Gestalt therapy have been generally highly verbal, rational, intelligent individuals seeking a greater ability to feel. Gestalt therapy became an education of the feelings. Perl's denial of dark, unconscious forces and emphasis upon the obvious and visible made Gestalt a popular therapy for those otherwise uninclined to seek psychotherapy. In that it leaned heavily upon expressive experience, Gestalt has also been popular among artistic individuals and groups. With its emphasis upon intense emotional, cathartic experience, it is generally unsuitable for more disturbed individuals.

Implications for Drama Therapy

Gestalt is closely related to drama therapy in its practice. The technique of the empty chair, the enactment of dreams, and the general emphasis upon movement and spontaneity place it fully in the realm of drama. Philosophically, however, Gestalt is not as close. In its denial of transference, historical experience, and dialectical struggles between the unconscious and conscious forces of the psyche, it moves away from the essence of drama which is inherently about tensions between past and present, conscious and unconscious, self and role.

Psychodrama

Psychodrama, developed by J. L. Moreno in Vienna in the early twentieth century, goes much further than Gestalt into the heart of the theory and practice of drama therapy. In fact, drama therapy would be difficult to conceptualize outside the context of Moreno's pioneering work (Moreno, 1946, 1959). Far from reducing drama to the obvious and explicit, Moreno clearly saw the deeper representational, social-psychological nature of the dramatic experience. His career was nothing less than extraordinary. He developed not only an early notion of improvisational drama, which he called "therapeutic theatre," but also a seminal formulation of group psychotherapy. Perhaps his most significant innovation was the application of role playing to psychotherapeutic practice. For Moreno, then, psychotherapy became a dramatic technique. The client was called "protagonist" and the therapist was called "director." Drama was the central rather than peripheral element of the therapy. Like the Gestalt and existential therapists, Moreno focused on a present-time frame, the moment of spontaneity. He did not negate the Freudian notion of the unconscious and the importance of early developmental experience, but these elements were not central to his theory.

Far beyond his Viennese and American colleagues, Moreno moved into the social sphere in developing the fields of sociodrama and sociometry. Never one to resist grandiosity, Moreno had intended to do no less than transform human society into a less repressed, more humane world through his sociodramatic techniques.

Technique

The technique of psychodrama, to be discussed in greater detail in Chapter Six, is generally a series of role-playing situations based upon the interaction between four elements: a director who is the therapist, a protagonist who is the client, auxiliary egos who are significant others in the client's life, and doubles who are the inner voices of the protagonist. Through the interaction of these players, the protagonist explores a problem in his life within a group setting. There is a fifth important element to the psychodrama: that of the group or audience members who participate in the psychodrama through an identification with the protagonist's dilemma and a sharing of their own life experiences during the closure. At times, the audience members participate in the drama by playing roles of doubles and auxiliary egos.

The sociodramatic technique incorporates the same structure, although instead of playing a personal role, the protagonist assumes a collective role of, for example, men, women, blacks, whites.

Goals

Moreno's most grandiose goal was to endlessly trigger off psychodramas and sociodramas, replacing the sentimental, manipulative television soap operas with his techniques. Seeing psychodrama as a link between psychoanalysis and behaviorism, Moreno aimed toward making behavior visible and measurable, then reintegrating that behavior within the protagonist's psyche. Further, Moreno focused upon developing an individual's capacity to act spontaneously, to discover adequate responses to new situations and novel responses to old ones. On the social level, he aimed toward healing the repressions and oppressions of groups of people.

Clients

Throughout the history of psychodrama, the technique has been used with various types of clients—children and elders, the psychotic, neurotic, mentally retarded, physically disabled, and the generally healthy. Much of psychodramatic work is verbal in nature. However, psychodrama also incorporates such expressive, non-verbal activities as movement, art, and music.

Since it is a cathartic and potentially volatile form of therapy, the technique requires a population that can tolerate highly charged emotional expression. Although based often in fantasy, psychodrama has been used with schizophrenic populations as a way to provide a reality-based enactment. Success has also been documented with populations of alcoholics, drug addicts, and prisoners.

Implications for Drama Therapy

As psychodrama is the most dramatic of therapies, the question arises: How, then, is it different from drama therapy? As we shall see later, it provides both a theoretical source for drama therapy and a series of techniques widely used by drama therapists. It is quite similar to drama therapy in its use of role playing, spontaneity, fantasy, and representational experience. However, drama therapy encompasses other dramatic and theatrical media, such as puppets, masks, theatre performance, storytelling, and story dramatization. Drama therapists, unlike psychodramatists, are required to train in creative drama and the dramatic arts, as the basis of their work is the creative experience of making dramas.

Psychodrama has had a long and distinguished history and has influenced not only drama therapy but also the fields of psychology, theatre, sociology, and education. Although drama therapy and psychodrama are different in the training of practitioners and application of techniques and processes, the distinctions break down at the most basic level, as both are centered in the experience of role playing and dramatic action.

Behavioral Therapy

The behaviorist approach to therapy is one that turns away from the internal, imaginative life of clients, focusing rather on their observable behaviors. *Behaviorism*, a term coined by the American psychologist, J. B. Watson, embraced the psychologically oriented work of Ivan Pavlov in conditioning and reacted against the more subjective, intuitive approaches of Freud and Jung. The prominence of behavioral therapy in America can be attributed to the trend in the behavioral sciences to measure the visible effects of psychotherapy.

More than other therapists, the behaviorist looks to the environment — those forces outside the individual that determine behavior. The notions of unconscious experience, imagination, self and role, responsibility and fantasy are minimized and often non-existent in behavior therapy. They are replaced by the concepts of stimulus and response, habit, drive, cue, and reinforcement. A central focus in behaviorism is on learning theory. According to the researchers Miller and Dollard (1941), the conditions for learning include a subject who wants something (drive), notices something (cue), does something (response), and gets something (reward).

Technique

The practice of behavioral therapy has been highly influenced in twentieth century America by B. F. Skinner (1969) and Joseph Wolpe (Wolpe and Lazarus, 1966). It is generally a short-term therapy in which the therapist, having diagnosed a problem as manifest in particular symptoms, prescribes a series of corrective tasks for the client. The relationship between therapist and client is not a primary concern in the therapy, as there is no attention to issues of transference and countertransference.

Joseph Wolpe's most widely practiced technique is that of systematic desensitization. Used primarily in treating phobias and anxiety conditions, it concerns the development of a hierarchy of tasks. The therapist begins by introducing a low level task that arouses minimal anxiety and that is simple for the client to achieve. He proceeds toward more difficult ones that gradually approach the fearful level of the phobic condition.

B. F. Skinner's approach is that of operant conditioning: a modification of the environment to bring about desired responses on the part of the client. The therapist attempts to discover, through a process of trial and error, the appropriate reinforcements that will encourage positive and discourage negative behavior. Reinforcements can be both negative, as in punishing animals who respond incorrectly to a stimulus through a series of shocks, or positive, as in rewarding an autistic child who establishes eye contact with a therapist with candy. Skinner has extended his theories both to a vision of social living through behavioral engineering in his Utopian novel, *Walden II,* and to global politics in his book, *Beyond Freedom and Dignity.* To Skinner, then, behaviorism is not only a therapy but a social and political philosophy, a global prescription for the ills of contemporary society.

Goals

The goal of behaviorism is to extinguish undesirable behavior—anxiety, depression, phobias, and masochistic tendencies—and to replace it with desirable, positive behavior. In many ways, it is the therapist who will decide which behaviors are desirable and which are undesirable, although the behavioral options are to a large extent socially determined.

Clients

The kinds of clients best treated behaviorally are those with severe symptoms who do not respond to the more in-depth therapies. The most widely used treatment for autistic children tends to be behavior therapy, given its systematic approach and unrelenting use of reinforcement. It is also used frequently for treating sexual problems, phobic behavior, and other dysfunctions that become manifest in specific behavioral symptoms.

Implications for Drama Therapy

Although the behaviorist position of objectifying behavior and minimizing subjective experience is not consistent with the more phenomenological position of the creative arts therapies, there are several areas of research that relate directly to drama therapy. The most important of these concern behavioral research into the dramatic processes of imitation and identification. Although many of the behavioral explanations of imitation are rather mechanistic, O. H. Mowrer (1960) offers a two-factor theory which accounts not only for reinforcement but also for satisfaction, a more internal construct, as a condition for imitative behavior. Further, Mowrer postulates that imitation is based upon identification, which he sees as an emotional, internal process of empathy. In discussing the infant's learning of language, Mowrer draws upon the dramatic notion of representation (1960):

> In a very primitive and rudimentary sense, they are trying to represent the mother, i.e., make her present again, in an autistic, quasi-magical way. . . . But then, as the infant thus learns to make conventional word sounds, the *second* stage of word functioning emerges. Now he utters a specifically meaningful word which serves, literally, to represent the mother, recall, recapture, recreate her. . . . Now, instead of merely playing with words, the infant makes them work.

This notion of taking on the role of mother and speaking as she does is extended even further by Bandura and Walters, who view role playing as an effective means of behavioral therapy (1965): "Role playing may be a particularly effective means of producing behavior change, since . . . the role player dependently accepts the assigned role and then is usually reinforced by approval for reproducing the behavior of the model."

Unlike Moreno and Freud's early notion of the cathartic effects of role playing, Bandura and Walters believe that through direct or vicarious role playing one identifies even further with the role model. In their studies of aggressive behavior, they found that rather than catharting and thus reducing aggression, the subjects engaged in continued aggressive behaviors when they identified with aggressive role models.

Although the behaviorist approach is in many ways limited in application to the expressive therapies, it does offer another perspective on such representational processes as imitation, identification, and role playing. And, most important, in its focus upon the influences of the environment upon behavior, it provides a further understanding of how and why the total person functions.

Family Therapy

Psychoanalytic-oriented therapies postulate that at the root of a neurotic problem is a disturbed relationship to one's family which occurred at an early stage of psychosexual development and is based in one's fantasy of the family, filtered through the murkiness of unresolved oedipal wishes. Family therapy, a radical departure from that point of view, looks at the present, reality-based interactions among family members. Unlike more conventional therapy, it works with several members of the family at once and is concerned with a group that will maintain its identity outside the therapeutic environment. Family therapy is not as much about projection as about individuals playing the role of self in relation to others playing their reality-based roles. It is an interactive therapy based to a great extent in the interpersonal theory of Harry Stack Sullivan (1953). It combines elements of Gestalt in its here-and-now orientation, behaviorism in attending to observable processes and reinforcement strategies, and psychodrama in working through role playing. Its current practice is heavily influenced by the work of Virginia Satir (1967), who writes: "When one person in a family (the patient) has pain which shows up in symptoms, all family members are feeling this pain in some way." Thus, family therapy concerns the interdependent relationships among all members of a family.

Technique

There are many forms of family therapy, but we will look primarily at the seminal work of Virginia Satir. Satir works generally with a married couple and their child or children. She begins by compiling a family life chronology or history. The process involves eliciting statements from the clients as to the courtship of the mates, the family background of the husband and wife, the child's view of his parents, etc. Questions are addressed to each family member present. Although the therapy sessions are highly verbal in nature, Satir carefully studies the non-verbal behaviors of the family members and helps them interpret their actions.

She also uses more dramatic role playing and game techniques. For example, in asking mother to play the role of father and vice versa, she employs a psychodramatic technique of role reversal. Through an elaborate series of family systems games and communication games, Satir uses improvisational techniques to further explore the family dynamics. One example is the rescue game involving a family triad: one in the role of the agreeable one; another in the role of the disagreeable one; and a third in the role of the irrelevant one. Through improvisation, both the therapist and clients look at how family members attack and rescue one another. Satir (1967) helps the players progress from rescue games toward growth vitality games characterized by open dialogue among the players, thereby moving "from a pathological system of interaction to a growth-producing one."

The role of the family therapist, according to Satir, is a highly active one, mediating between all family members, clarifying issues, and providing a mature model of communication.

Goals

Satir's goal is to move from pathological relationships to growth-producing ones. Her model of growth is based on a dynamic process of interactions among family members. In working toward her goal she examines observable behavior and language, attempting to change behavior and attitudes through focusing upon the communication among family members.

The Clients

The clients in family therapy can include any family group, whether a more conventional husband, wife, and child, or less conventional homosexual mates with or without children. The family group might be a nuclear one or a more extended one. The one member who is seen by the others in the family as responsible for the family problems is called the *identified patient.* This person might exhibit neurotic or psychotic symptoms. The family therapist works with both mild and severe forms of emotional disturbance within the context of the family. His focus is not only on the identified patient but all members of the family who, like the identified patient, bring much pain with them into the psychotherapeutic session.

Implications for Drama Therapy

Family therapy theory and practice are highly relevant to drama therapy. The family structure is a major focus of drama therapy, especially in the extended dramatization, to be discussed below. The notions of interpersonal theory, systems and communications theory are also important for drama therapists who need to look at the group dynamics inherent in all improvisational action.

In a broader sense, the family can be seen as a metaphor for any ongoing drama therapy group. In fact, one excellent theatre group of ex-offenders is called The Family. In a drama therapy group, the participants constantly re-create family roles and patterns which they project onto their improvisational roles and/or transfer onto others in the group, including the therapist. Through their role playing, the clients examine their issues with family from a safe distance, since the actual family members are not present.

Drama therapists also work at times with actual families, examining the interactions between spouses, parents, and children as they engage in a common dramatization.

Drama therapy, then, relates in some ways to all of the major psychotherapeutic approaches, each of which presents a unique and significant image of man motivated by one or more of the following: biological instincts, universal and transpersonal symbols, a core self that is essentially whole and good, a state of alienation and aloneness, reinforcements and environmental contingencies, and social interactions. The one psychotherapeutic theory most oriented toward drama is that of Moreno's psychodrama, which views man as essentially dramatic and spontaneous in nature, as able to learn how to live better with himself, within his family and community through a process of role playing.

Significant applications of drama therapy theory and practice can be gleaned from each of these perspectives. Although a drama therapist might be essentially trained as a psychodramatist, psychoanalyst, or

Gestalt therapist, it is still incumbent upon him to understand how the other disciplines function and how their concepts and practices further contribute to the dramatic process of healing.

THE RELATION OF DRAMA THERAPY TO DRAMA
AND THEATRE BY, WITH, AND FOR THE HANDICAPPED

Since the early 1970s, the national consciousness has been raised as to the needs of the handicapped or disabled individual. A publication arising from the White House Conference on Handicapped Individuals defined that group as follows (1978):

> A handicapped individual is one who has a physical or mental impairment or condition which places him at a disadvantage in a major life activity such as ambulation, communication, self-care, socialization, vocational training, employment, transportation, adapting to housing, etc.... The physical or mental impairment or condition must be static, of long duration, or slowly progressive.

In 1975, through Public Law 94-142, The Education for All Handicapped Children Act, handicapped children were assured access to a free public education, incorporating not only conventional curriculum subjects but also related services which include the creative arts.

This act and further legislation have enabled an increasing number of disabled people to attain experience in drama and theatre. At the same time, public awareness of the plight of the disabled Vietnam veteran has been heightened by dramatizations such as the film *Coming Home*, the play, *Sticks and Bones*, and the theatre piece, *Tracers*. These factors have contributed to the evolution of many drama/theatre groups by, with, and for the handicapped. "By" indicates theatre performed by handicapped actors. "With" indicates drama/theatre created with or within a group of handicapped people. "For" implies theatre performed to an audience of handicapped viewers. These developing groups based in schools, community organizations, and theatres often incorporate improvisation and non-performance dramatic activities. Most, however, have leaned heavily upon theatre experiences.

A great many special theatre companies, both professional and amateur, have begun or increased their activities since the mid-1970s. This national phenomenon includes such groups as: the National Theatre of the Deaf in Chester, Connecticut, a professional theatre organization in which both hearing and deaf actors perform original and classical plays for hearing and non-hearing audiences; Theatre Unlimited in San Francisco, California, in which developmentally disabled actors perform original theatre pieces for able and disabled audiences; The Rainbow Company in Las Vegas, Nevada, which also features original theatre pieces performed by physically disabled actors and conducts drama workshops with developmentally and physically disabled school children; the Happiness Bag Players in Terre Haute, Indiana, in which able actors perform original theatre pieces in schools and community organizations for developmentally disabled children; and the National Theatre Workshop of the Handicapped in New York City, which trains physically disabled individuals to become professional actors for general audiences.

Furthermore, community organizations have incorporated activities for the disabled into their recreational drama programs. Examples include a community-based program aiming to develop body awareness for physically and developmentally disabled children at the Recreational Center for the Handicapped in San Francisco; a hospital-based program aiming to develop social skills for an adult psychiatric population at Creative Alternatives of Mount Sinai Hospital in New York City; and a theatre program at the Alan Short Center, Arts for the Handicapped in Stockton, California, aiming toward training adult mentally retarded individuals in acting as well as socialization.

Two other special groups that have benefited substantially from participation in drama/theatre experiences are prison populations and the elderly. It is debatable whether to include these groups under the general label of handicapped. However, the former, often the product of a harsh environment, is at a disadvantage in a major life activity, that of free access to work, play, or life-style; and the latter manifests a physical condition that is inevitably progressive, that of aging. Drama/theatre experiences for prison populations and the elderly will be discussed further in Part IV.

In the area of deafness, the work of the National Theatre of the Deaf is only the tip of the iceberg. Not only have such alternative theatre groups developed as the Little Theatre of the Deaf and the New York Deaf Theatre, but educational drama and theatre has been incorporated within many elementary, secondary, and university curricula.

With such a proliferation of drama/theatre groups and activities in relation to special populations of actors ("by" and "with" the handicapped) and viewers ("for" the handicapped), many diverse and at times conflicting goals have arisen. In reviewing literature published between 1957 and

1979 in relation to the work of these and similar groups, Linaya Leaf organized the stated goals according to fifteen categories. The top three categories, representing the most frequently cited goals, included self-goals (i.e., self-understanding, self-development, and self-awareness); social goals (i.e., social interaction and cooperation); and "therapeutic values," a phrase coined by Leaf (1979), which includes the aims "to channel emotions into constructive uses" and "to achieve relief from anxiety and conflict resulting in behavior change." That is to say, most writers in the field viewed the goals of drama/theatre in relation to handicapped individuals as generally therapeutic on a personal or social level.

In comparison, the last three categories, representing the least cited goals, included entertainment, increased awareness of the environment, and potential careers for handicapped persons. The middle-range goals, although primarily educational (i.e., cognitive, verbal and non-verbal learning) also included political and aesthetic aims.

It is difficult to generalize about the work in this area, not only because such a diversity of goals and kinds of drama/theatre experience exists but also because of the diverse needs of different disabled individuals.

Further, there seems to be a contradiction between a statement of goals that tend to favor growth and developmental processes, primarily attributed to non-performance drama activity, and the current practice which largely favors audience-centered theatre activity. This is not to say that drama and theatre are mutually exclusive concepts. On the contrary, drama and theatre are closely interrelated. Yet, this interrelationship is often ignored by those who vehemently favor one aspect of the drama/theatre process over the other. Despite paying lip service to the values of the dramatic process, some adhere to a practice mirroring that of the commercial theatre which exists to sell a product through the attractive means of "star" personalities. At this level of consciousness, the more therapeutic, educational, and recreational goals of drama/theatre by, for, and with the handicapped become severely compromised.

There are many, however, who attempt to realize therapeutic goals through drama/theatre work with the disabled. But often, as we shall see in Chapter Ten, these people are not drama therapists. They are, rather, theatre artists, teachers, and recreational leaders who use dramatic, aesthetic means to achieve therapeutic ends.

There is an important distinction to be made between the terms *therapeutic* and *therapy.* Eleanor Irwin (1979), a prolific researcher and drama therapist at the Pittsburgh Child Guidance Center, refers to a therapeutic experience as: "Any experience which helps an individual to feel a greater sense of competence." For Irwin (1979), therapy is "a specific form of intervention, to bring about intrapsychic, interpersonal, or behavioral changes." Those who have subscribed to the therapeutic goals cited by Leaf are, for the most part, working through a creative process to foster a greater sense of self-awareness, sociability, and well-being within and among their group members. They tend to be, by profession, individuals primarily trained in the drama/theatre discipline. Although sensitive to the therapeutic needs of their groups and well versed in the drama/theatre techniques, they tend not to be drama therapists.

Drama therapists, like drama/theatre leaders of disabled groups, also work through the media of drama and theatre to achieve therapeutic goals. However, their training and their application of the techniques are different. Drama therapists often focus directly upon psychological and social concerns and are prepared to deal with their own counter-transferential issues. Further, drama therapists, in working to help clients discover healthy functioning through creative activity, evaluate the outcome in terms of the well-being of the client, rather than the success of the product.

Therapy can be defined, then, in terms of the training and aims of the therapist, the expectations of the client, and the interaction of therapist and client in moving toward healthy functioning. Many disabled individuals undoubtedly realize therapeutic benefits by participating in drama/theatre groups led by sensitive individuals. However, these therapeutic benefits, the raw substance of the creative process, are often secondary to the prime task of making theatre and are not consciously understood by the leaders, nor fully integrated by the actors. The drama therapist aims to make explicit that part of the creative process which is implicitly healing and to translate it into specific concepts and practices.

Among the many stories that have circulated in the wake of the Vietnam war is one concerning a young veteran, emotionally disabled from his experiences in Southeast Asia. Following his return, he sat at home all day with no motivation to work, study, play, or seek any connection with the outside world. Although involved in conventional psychiatric treatment, he experienced little change. One day, a friend urged him to look into a drama group consisting of other veterans. Although reluctant, he did go and became a regular member of the group, which worked primarily through improvisation and built theatre pieces based upon the experiences of the group members. Over time, the man's behavior began to improve. He began to participate in the world, seeking further education, work, and social activities. But, for lack of funds, the drama group folded. The man became despondent and his emotional condition deteriorated. He began to audition for other theatre groups, but, given the intense competition, he was repeatedly rejected. He withdrew more and more from social contacts and became depressed and suicidal. His family became equally desperate. Having become discouraged with conventional psychotherapy, they did not know where to turn. A concerned relative intuited that drama therapy might help the young man. However, at that time the field was in its infancy and the family did not know where to seek such therapy.

The ending of the story is unknown, since it was told anonymously some years ago and there was no opportunity for follow-up. The point is that drama/theatre can have a powerful therapeutic effect for a disabled person, even when it is not led by a drama therapist. The director/leader of such groups should be aware of the power and healing potential of his medium, but use it within the limits of his training. The danger does not lie in the close relationship between therapeutics and aesthetics but in the easy connection between special theatre and the more conventional theatre that aspires to Broadway, that is highly competitive and oriented toward the salability of a few chosen star performers and popular themes. In that the young veteran could not find a therapeutically oriented drama/theatre experience outside of the veteran's group, he felt abandoned, not only by the general society, but also by the one medium that could creatively and therapeutically transform his inner emptiness.

When performance-oriented groups working with the disabled confuse their aims with those of the commercial theatre, their therapeutic value will be diminished. Like drama therapy practice, drama/theatre by, with, and for the handicapped should be neither too competitive nor too audience centered. Its effectiveness may well lie in the notion that the successful creation of dramatic imagery can only be validated at the deepest level by the creator. And like the drama therapist, the sensitive leader of disabled drama/theatre groups can work toward helping individuals develop internal means of self-validation through the dramatic process.

This discussion is not intended to be limited to the issues of the disabled. Similar issues arise in recreational or educational drama/theatre by, with, and for the general population. Further, in that the above definition of handicapped is so broad as to include most all of us at some points in our lives, the issues become clearly universal ones. The main issue concerns a clarification of the goals and objectives of drama/theatre directors and leaders. Although these objectives might be implicitly therapeutic, they differ from more explicit intentions of drama therapists. In the following chapter, we will examine those intentions.

Chapter Two

TOWARD A DEFINITION OF DRAMA THERAPY

OBJECTIVES OF DRAMA THERAPISTS

The term *objective*, as opposed to the terms *aim, outcome,* or *goal*, has the implication of behavioral change. Behavioral change refers to that which is external and directly observable. In speaking of drama therapy objectives, we will take a broader approach than simply classifying behaviors. The terms objectives, goals, aims, and outcomes will be used synonymously to mean the general or specific, visible or invisible changes in perceiving, thinking, feeling, speaking, moving, relating, role playing, and valuing that can occur through drama therapy. These changes may be in awareness or understanding—that is, one may view one's relationship to oneself, to others, or to one's social/political environment differently. Or they may be in action or interaction—that is, through the process of therapy, one may begin to act differently in the world toward self, other, and community. The connection between change in awareness and change in action is complex. Most therapists would hope that one implies the other, that a change in understanding would lead to a corresponding change in action and vice versa. But this is not always the case. Psychoanalysts work toward making the unconscious conscious, but, from the client's point of view, once that goal is realized, it does not necessarily translate into action in the world. Conversely, behaviorists work toward behavioral change. But simply changing his behavior does not always lead the client to a corresponding change in awareness.

Objectives of understanding, action, and interaction can be formulated by both therapist and client. The therapist's goal will be very much dependent upon his theoretical orientation. As the theoretical training of the drama therapist is likely to be eclectic, he might well specify diverse goals in response to diverse situations. This can be problematic if the drama therapist subscribes to conflicting models. For example, let us look at the difficult issue of dealing with aggression in therapy. The early work of Breuer and Freud (1936) as well as the work of Moreno in catharsis suggests that if the client can release his repressed anger or hostility, he will regain a sense of equilibrium and repose. That is, through assuming an aggressive role, one can release aggressive tendencies. However, the behavioral model of Bandura and Walters implies that through an imitation of an aggressive model (that is, through acting aggressively himself), a client does not rid himself of aggression but rather increases his capacity to act aggressively. If the therapist sees validity in both the cathartic model and the behavioral model, what will his position be in regard to treating aggressive clients? As we shall see later, there is a third model, that of distancing, which re-examines the concept of catharsis from a social-psychological perspective and provides a solution to the problem of enacting powerful emotions in therapy.

The point is that if the drama therapist is conflicted as to which psychotherapeutic model to apply in formulating objectives, it is possible that he needs to discover a new or more comprehensive model which reflects the creative, expressive nature of drama therapy. Objectives which ignore this crucial reality will compromise the therapist's work in a modality that is inherently dramatic. As a statement of goals is interdependent with the techniques one uses to realize those goals (that is, as the ends are inseparable from the means), a therapist who works through the media of drama/theatre needs to formulate goals that are based in the art of drama/theatre.

The setting of specific objectives in drama therapy is also, to a great extent, dependent upon the nature of the client. In working with elders through the process of life history plays, for example, a specific goal might be to help individuals see a connection between past and present and to discover a sense of purpose and dignity in the present. However, a general, more philosophical goal of drama therapy, applying to all clients, is, simply stated: to increase the client's repertory of roles and his ability to play a single role more fully. Implicit in this statement is the notion of a change in awareness and behavior at both the personal and the social levels. A wide repertory of roles implies choice and flexibility, the ability to change one's behavior in relation to differing people and circumstances, i.e., to be a son to a father, a student to a teacher, a worker to a boss.

Many emotionally disturbed and developmentally disabled individuals do not have a wide repertory of roles and thus become locked into a fixed and rigid pattern of behavior played out in each social encounter.

Through realizing the objective of increasing his repertory of roles, the client will move toward two distinct goals: the social, behavioral goal of interacting with others more appropriately and with greater flexibility, and the personal, conceptual goal of viewing himself as a more complex, less rigid person, able to confront new social encounters less fearfully.

The ability to play a single role more fully implies increased flexibility of thought and behavior while being, for example, a son, a student, a worker, or a friend. A totalitarianism of consciousness may exist within the mind of an emotionally disturbed person, dictating how he should behave in role. Drama therapists aim to increase the dimensions of the role so that it is not oppressive, so that the client can view himself as a son who can express a range of emotions, think a range of thoughts, and perform a range of actions both within the boundaries of that role and in relation to the complimentary role of parent. Implicit in this objective is a change in consciousness from seeing oneself as confined to limited behaviors and thoughts in role, to developing a self-concept as, for example, a son who can relate to a parent in a variety of ways. Further, this objective implies a change in behavior as one moves from limited, passive movement and affect in role, to more flexible, active expressiveness.

Specific objectives in drama therapy are highly variable. In working with a particular group of adult psychiatric patients in a day treatment facility in California, for example, drama therapist, Renée Emunah (1983), lists the following objectives: "increasing social interaction, facilitating the release and control of emotions, changing nonconstructive behavioral and role patterns, developing spontaneity, imagination, and concentration, bolstering self-esteem and self-confidence." Emunah's aims are both personal and social, both conceptual and behavioral.

Even more specific objectives might be necessary in work with a more severely psychotic population such as non-verbal autistic children. With this group, attention to behavioral objectives might be most efficacious, as the children require a highly structured approach in daring to take even a small step out of their psychotic states. Such limited behavioral objectives as establishing eye contact or mirroring the movements and sounds of the therapist might initially be most appropriate.

An understanding of the physiological, psychological, sociological, and environmental dimensions of a special population is essential in formulating goals. Goals must be flexible, allowing for individual differences and for the possibility that a mentally retarded or psychotic child has been wrongly labelled or simply can perform at a higher level than expected.

The setting of objectives in drama therapy need not follow the educational models of Bloom et al., and the beginning drama therapist need not compose therapeutic lesson plans with stated behavioral objectives. However, he does need to think through and develop a therapeutic strategy that is based upon a knowledge of the client and a commitment to change that is behavioral as well as conceptual, personal as well as social.

In many cases, the client sets the goal and the therapist follows. An elder, for example, might well make it clear that what he needs is to be seen in the world and to feel that his life has had and will continue to have meaning. If the drama therapist does not hear that message and instead imposes a list of objectives for increasing social skills, personal spontaneity, and the like, he might well be sabotaging his own sessions.

RATIONALE FOR APPLYING DRAMA TO THE TREATMENT OF CLIENTS

"Drama is a metaphor. Its meaning lies not in the actual context nor in the fictitious one, but in the dialectic set up between the two." This statement, written by Gavin Bolton (1979) in reference to drama in education, contains a powerful understanding of drama. The metaphor of world as stage and self as performer has been used widely by poets, playwrights, priests, philosophers, and politicians for centuries, and most recently by social scientists. For the sociologist Erving Goffman, the self is performed and reformed in everyday life. For the philosopher Martin Buber, human interaction is characterized by dialogue. For the generals, the battlefield is a theatre of operations.

Psychotherapy, too, can be seen as a dramatic representation of everyday life. The most dramatic of therapies, Gestalt and psychodrama, literally use role playing to re-enact dreams or episodes from one's past. Psychoanalysis, the most verbal of psychotherapies, works through a representational process of transference where the therapist and client unconsciously cast each other in a dramatic role.

Clients are treated through drama, in part, because through their play and past dramatizations they have created a dysfunctional image of themselves in the world. In drama therapy, they re-create that image so that it can be reviewed, recognized, and integrated, allowing a more functional self to emerge. The dialectical nature of drama as moving between a fictional and actual context provides a way of looking at not only the conceptual basis of drama therapy but also the practical.

Drama therapy is not a gimmicky, trendy therapeutic modality. At its best, it does not impose hollow exercises and unnatural situations upon its clients. It is as natural to children as play and to adults as role playing. Although it can be highly verbal, it is not limited to talk. It incorporates sound, movement, imagery, and sensation. The most artificial aspects of drama therapy occur in the use of more theatrical devices, i.e., puppets and masks, costumes, props, and makeup. However, when the theatricality points to an actual context and illuminates it, it ceases to be artificial and superficial.

Another reason for applying drama to therapy concerns the traditional therapeutic function of theatre. The ritual and healing aspects of theatre performance have been demonstrated throughout history. The theatre has been an institution for socially sanctioned emotional release, thought and debate, recreation, as people take a respite from everyday problems, and revolution, as people are propagandized or educated by participating in a particular dramatized point of view.

In drawing forth the feelings, thoughts, and beliefs of an audience, the theatre has employed many devices, including stylized acting and design, costumes and props. In applying these devices to drama therapy, the therapist uses the stylization as a distancing device which can reveal the actual needs and problems of the client. The theatre artist projects a fiction through his role which will induce in the audience a willing suspension of disbelief. The drama therapist's job is to examine the projection and look behind the fiction. That is not to say that the aim of the drama therapist is to strip the character bare, as is seen in Ronald Harwood's play, *The Dresser.* In this play, the character, Sir, takes off his royal costume, wig, and makeup to reveal a pitiful old man. Rather, the therapist works to help the client view the dialectic between the mask and the face, the persona and the person.

The image of theatre is one of a constant shift of perspective between the fictional and the actual, both for the actor, who creates a role that is balanced between himself and another; and for the audience member, who may view aspects of himself in terms of the dramatized characters. The style of performance, whether expressionistic or realistic, will affect the actor and viewer's ability to identify with characters. In a like manner, the degree of stylization in drama therapy will determine the client's distance from his dilemma.

Theatrical devices, along with the more natural play and representational drama of everyday life, provide the substance of drama therapy. They are applied to the treatment of clients because they are powerful means of looking at the complexities of human existence, a state of being that once consciousness develops is perpetually dialectical, poised between the life of the imagination, the fictional, the subjective, and the life of the everyday, the actual, the objective.

TRAINING THE DRAMA THERAPIST

In 1985, several training programs exist at various stages of development in the United States and England. Most are located in universities; some are associated with private institutions or individuals. The most fully realized programs are those at Antioch University in San Francisco, which offers an M.A. in psychology with a concentration in drama therapy, and at New York University, offering an M.A. in drama therapy and a Ph.D. in educational theatre with a concentration in drama therapy. Such prominent American drama therapists as David Johnson of New Haven, Connecticut and Gertrud Schattner of New York City train students privately. Important training in movement and drama is offered in England at SESAME, directed by Marion Lindquist.

Most training programs offer a diversity of practical and theoretical experiences in the fields of drama/therapy, psychotherapy, and psychology. Although the National Association for Drama Therapy is in the process of establishing standards for training, specific requirements have not been finalized as of this writing.

In a recent paper (Landy, 1982), a model for training was offered based in the graduate program at New York University. The model focused upon four areas:

1. The self, involving the development of personal creativity and psychological awareness;
2. The client, involving an understanding of various disabled and able populations in relation to their environments;
3. The techniques, involving a range of drama/theatre and psychotherapeutic practices;

4. The theory, involving interdisciplinary concepts and philosophical considerations.

The Self

The first issue in training involves looking at oneself as a drama/theatre artist. This is an important issue, because some people believe they can enter the field of the creative arts therapies without necessarily being artists. The position here is that the drama therapist needs to practice the art form competently. A fundamental assumption of drama therapy is that the creative process of making drama has a therapeutic effect upon the creator. In order to fully understand this, the trainee needs to experience the creative dramatic process. If he finds that there is no personal therapeutic value in his creative work in drama/theatre, then he should examine the implications. Is he resistant to the dramatic process? Is he in the wrong training program? Is he in the wrong field? If these issues remain unexplored, he will undoubtedly transfer his ambivalence into his work as therapist.

Some will enter drama therapy training with little experience in drama/theatre, like many in the field of psychodrama. But unlike psychodramatists, who are not required to train in the dramatic arts, drama therapists are required to master the fundamentals of theatre performance and improvisational drama.

In developing the creative self, the trainee should achieve a competence in acting, directing, and dramatic writing. The trainee should not only study these areas from an academic perspective but should master the practical skills of acting, directing, and writing.

It is difficult to define competence in these areas. A competent actor or director is not necessarily measured by the quantity of his credits or reviews. Competency in these areas is a more qualitative issue. That quality can be measured in performance in selected projects in school, community, or professional theatres. The evaluators, outside experts or oneself, would attend to such issues as the ability to search for novel solutions to old aesthetic problems and to confront new aesthetic problems with a degree of inventiveness, as well as the ability to master basic technical skills in performance, technical theatre, and direction. A further measure would be the effect of the creative experience upon self-concept, implying that competence refers not only to the finished product but also to one's process of working creatively and one's ability to view oneself more clearly through that process.

The trainee should also achieve a level of competence as a player and director of improvisational drama and dramatic play. Again, he needs to see how his own play and drama affects his self-concept. As a leader of drama and play, he needs to become aware of his own personal style and issues of leadership as he works creatively with groups of children, adolescents, and adults.

In that most academic drama therapy programs exist at the graduate level, it would be beneficial for the trainee to have mastered the above drama/theatre competencies previous to entering the program. While in the program, he should further develop his creative abilities and reflect upon the corresponding issues of self-concept. These and similar competencies relating to self-awareness are not intended to be static but rather active processes of exploration that continue throughout one's work as a trainee and practicing drama therapist.

The second issue in training the self involves the development of psychological awareness through a process of psychotherapy. It is commonplace for students to go through a variety of psychotherapy training programs without ever having been a client. However, in order for a trainee to fully appreciate how the process works and to begin to become aware of his own needs and issues that may well become transferred onto the client, he should fully experience the role of client. His personal therapy can take many forms. For one, through his training he will be exposed to drama therapy groups. But outside of the classroom setting, he should also seek a therapist who is oriented either toward the creative arts or a more traditional psychotherapeutic approach. The value of working with a Freudian or Jungian-based analyst is that both examine in-depth the issues of transference and unconscious processes.

The Client

The second area of training involves an understanding of the client in the context of his environment. Drama therapists have been working with the following client populations: the emotionally disturbed, the gifted, the developmentally disabled, the physically disabled, the hearing impaired and the blind, the speech impaired, the elderly, and the sociopathic. Recently, drama therapists have included among their clients individuals without special disabilities who are in need of exploring specific problems or more generally in re-examining their lives.

Disabilities are often interrelated, i.e., mental illness can combine emotional, social, and developmental difficulties; physical disabilities often incorporate emotional ones. Thus, the drama therapist needs to be aware not only of the range of disabilities but also of the interconnections. Further, the drama therapist needs to be aware of the limitations of labels which affect the relationship and expectations of both the client and therapist.

The trainee needs to look at special and normal populations within an ecological framework (that is, within the context of their environments) because of the profound effect that environment can have on behavior and awareness. It is important that the trainee understand both the environment the client has come from and the one in which he presently lives. In that many clients live in institutional settings, the trainee needs to become familiar with institutional life and its effects upon those individuals.

In learning about special populations, students need to do considerable fieldwork, interacting with different groups and participating in life within their environments. The practical experience can be supplemented with appropriate coursework and research. It is impractical for trainees to achieve an in-depth experience with all the populations treated in drama therapy. However, through fieldwork placements, research projects, and more in-depth internships, trainees can become familiar with the issues of several populations within their social environments.

It is also important for the student to observe and work with clients of various ages and various stages of development. An in-depth internship should be planned so that the student works with two populations, each of a different disability and environment, and each of a different stage of development, whether child, adolescent, adult, or elder. At present, the internship requirement at New York University is 780 hours, a requirement consistent with that of psychodrama training.

Techniques

The third area of training includes an understanding and application of drama/theatre and psychotherapeutic techniques of treatment. Although borrowing techniques from Gestalt therapy, psychodrama, and other practices, the drama therapist bases his work most fully in the media of the dramatic arts—play, improvisation, storytelling and story dramatization, and theatre performance. The trainee needs to understand the dimensions of play as it relates to therapy. He also needs to understand his role as therapist in relation to the player/client. The way he plays his role, whether as observer or player, directive or non-directive leader, will be based in that understanding.

The techniques of improvisation are numerous. The trainee needs to learn the range of activities including short-term drama exercise in sensory awareness, transformation of objects, mirroring, sounding and speaking, movement and pantomime, among others, and more extensive role playing involving both real and imaginary situations. He also needs to know how to use the more stylized techniques of puppetry, mask, makeup, props, and costume. For a long-term group of clients, the extended dramatization, devised by Gavin Bolton and Dorothy Heathcote, is also valuable. This technique endows the client with a role and a series of responsibilities within a thematically based drama, which he acts upon throughout an extended period of time.

Another important area of training is that of storytelling and story dramatization. The trainee needs to learn to read stories, tell stories, lead dramatizations of stories, and understand the importance of myth, fairy tale, legend, and fable in the lives of clients. In learning the technique of life review theatre, the trainee has a further means of using the story as autobiography.

Theatre-in-education (TIE) is another technique that can be useful in drama therapy. In creating performances based in an area of social, political, or educational concern, the TIE team can investigate significant issues with a particular targeted audience. In mastering the technique of TIE, drama therapy trainees can work toward applying it to the problems of special populations.

Finally, trainees need to know the principles and practices of formal theatre performance, especially acting and directing. These areas are useful not only in viewing the self as a creative artist but also in helping clients achieve therapeutic goals. The trainee should be aware of the limitations of theatre performance and of the general danger of sacrificing the integrity of the therapeutic process in favor of a polished product. But if theatre performance is the chosen medium for a group of people who are ready to express themselves to an audience (i.e., a group of elders working through a life review technique or a group of prisoners dramatizing a script concerning prison life), then the trainee needs to understand both how to use theatre techniques and how to reflect upon the issues of performance that will inevitably arise.

The trainee should be encouraged to view drama therapy techniques as interactive. Theatre production employs improvisational techniques; life history plays and TIE use both improvisational and theatre techniques.

Further, drama therapy techniques should be discussed in relation to the needs of particular populations and to the abilities and preferences of particular therapists. A therapist may favor theatre performance; but if the need of his group of emotionally disturbed children is to examine narcissistic issues and to build inner means of approval, then theatre performance might be too stimulating for that group. Many issues need to be considered in choosing appropriate techniques of drama/theatre. These include: the purpose and value of the technique as it relates to needs of a particular individual or group; the abilities and needs of the therapist; the needs or demands of the administrator of an institution; and the nature of the institutional environment.

Theory

The fourth area of training involves an understanding of theoretical concepts that relate practice to theory and that respond to the question: Why drama therapy? The theoretical perspective will be interdisciplinary in nature, responding not only to the two most obvious components of drama therapy—that of drama/theatre and that of psychotherapy—but also to the related areas of play, education, sociology, and ritual. In that the field is still young, the conceptual basis of drama therapy is in great need of clarification. The trainee should examine the concepts and theories that are most relevant to the dramatic nature of drama therapy. As we have seen, drama therapy exists within a general context of education, recreation, and theatre, and within a psychotherapeutic context of prominent theoretical models. This context, as well as the issues of objectives and rationales, must be clear to the trainee.

Some have argued that the drama therapist needs a single psychotherapeutic model which informs his work and gives him a lens through which he can view the psychotherapeutic process (Irwin, 1979). However, drama therapy can be viewed as an eclectic form that draws from many models and yet is, in itself, greater than the sum of its parts. If this is so, then the drama therapy trainee does not need to begin or follow up his specialized drama therapy training with further training in an established psychotherapeutic technique, for drama therapy can be seen as a psychotherapeutic model in its own right, theoretically eclectic, conceptually based in those processes that are inherently dramatic. In training, the student needs to examine appropriate theoretical issues and engage in directed research to test out the efficacy of theory in relation to practice.

A model curriculum for a master of arts in drama therapy might include the following courses:

In Psychology:	Theories of Personality
	Developomental Psychology, infant through elder
	Abnormal Psychology
In Counseling and/or Psychotherapy:	Clinical Issues and Practices in Psychotherapy
	Individual Counseling or Psychotherapy
	Group Counseling or Psychotherapy
In Drama/Theatre:	Survey of Dramatic Literature
	Styles of Acting, Directing, and Writing for the Theatre
	The Theory and Practice of Dramatic Play
	Drama and Theatre in Education
In Drama Therapy:	Practices and Concepts in Drama Therapy
	Drama Therapy for the Emotionally Disturbed (to be alternated with other selected populations)
	Psychodrama and Sociodrama
	The Theory and Practice of Improvisation with Special Populations
	The Theory and Practice of Projective Techniques
	Internship and Supervision
	Model Drama Therapy Group

Supplementary courses might include the practical study of acting, directing, and playwriting for those deficient in the area of theatre production. Further elective courses can be included in the areas of art, dance, or music therapy (when available) and in the area of special education of a particular disabled population.

Following the completion of such a curriculum, it would be expected that the drama therapist has acquired the following competencies:

In Psychology:

1. An understanding of the major theories of personality and how they apply to psychotherapeutic practice.
2. An understanding of normal human development from infancy through old age, including the major developmental theories.
3. An understanding of the causes and effects of abnormal behavior from a psychological, sociological, and ecological point of view.

In Counseling and/or Psychotherapy:

1. An understanding of clinical issues, protocols, and treatment strategies within a psychiatric hospital, treatment center, or related setting.
2. A familiarity with diagnostic and evaluation procedures and an ability to recognize the basic types of emotional, developmental, and physical disabilities.
3. The ability to lead a psychotherapeutic session on a one-to-one basis.
4. The ability to lead a psychotherapeutic group.
5. An understanding of issues of transference and countertransference within individual and group therapy sessions; the ability to view and analyze one's effect upon a client.
6. An understanding of group dynamics.

In Drama/Theatre:

1. A general understanding of the history of dramatic literature.
2. An understanding of the major styles and theories of acting, directing, design, and writing in the theatre.
3. An understanding of the use of such dramatic media as puppets, masks, makeup, lights, props, and costumes.
4. The ability to act in a play, direct a play, and write brief dramatic pieces.
5. An understanding of the anxieties associated with performance.
6. An understanding of stage settings and how they affect thought, sensation, and movement.
7. An understanding of pantomime and movement.
8. The ability to execute non-verbal actions on stage.

9. An understanding of the play of children, especially dramatic play.
10. The ability to play as an adult.
11. An understanding of adolescent and adult play within the context of history, culture, and environment.
12. An understanding of the theory and practice of drama/theatre in education and recreation.
13. The ability to act in and lead improvisations.
14. An understanding of the theory and practice of TIE.
15. An ability to create a TIE experience.

In Drama Therapy:

1. An understanding of the relationships among drama therapy, recreational drama, and educational drama and theatre.
2. An understanding of drama therapy in relation to other models of psychotherapy.
3. An understanding of the dramatic basis of drama therapy.
4. An understanding of the major objectives and techniques of drama therapy.
5. An ability to view issues of self through participation in a drama therapy group.
6. The ability to work with children, adolescents, adults, and elders through drama therapy.
7. The knowledge of working with groups of able, developmentally disabled, physically disabled, emotionally disturbed, and related populations through drama therapy.
8. The ability to lead two or more such groups at two or more age/developmental levels.
9. An understanding of the interdisciplinary conceptual basis of drama therapy.
10. An understanding of appropriate research problems, methodologies, and means of evaluation.
11. The ability to engage in drama therapy research.
12. The ability to use psychodramatic, sociodramatic, and projective techniques in treating clients.
13. The ability to work as part of a psychotherapeutic treatment team within a clinical setting.

14. The ability to make preliminary diagnostic and evaluative judgments.
15. The ability to view and analyze the transferential and counter-transferential issues that arise while leading drama therapy sessions.
16. An understanding of "the therapeutic personality" and the ability to work toward developing it.

The last point (the development of the therapeutic personality) is an especially significant one. Without it, all the knowledge and technical expertise of the drama therapist is rendered meaningless. The therapeutic personality is difficult to describe because, first, it is an ideal and, secondly, it is not simply one series of attributes. The ideal drama therapist, with a fully developed therapeutic personality, can be seen as demonstrating a combination of personality functions, characterized by C. G. Jung (1968) as feeling, thinking, intuition, and sensation. At the feeling level, he would be able to empathize with clients' dilemmas and become a human being in their eyes through presenting himself as capable of expressing his own emotions and needs. Like the Laingian existential therapist, he would be willing to enter into his client's experience. At the thinking level, he would be able to maintain a certain professional distance, perform diagnostic and analytical tasks, and help a client reflect upon his enactments. Further, he would help the client plan realistic strategies to cope with everyday life.

At the intuitive level, the therapist would draw upon his expressive/creative abilities and help the client move toward insight as he engages in the process of therapeutic dramatization. He would work spontaneously in the here-and-now, responding in kind to the client's expressive actions.

At the level of sensation, the therapist would be grounded in reality, able to see the client's expressive imagery clearly. He would be further able to separate out his countertransferential issues from the actual issues of the client.

The therapeutic personality, then, can be seen as an ideal entity with interactive aspects of feeling, thinking, intuition, and sensation fully developed. Other attributes would include an ability to listen and to fully validate each client's needs and issues, to suspend moral judgments, to be aware of transference and countertransference issues and move toward their resolution, to be able to take risks, to assert one's role of leader without being exploitative, to believe that positive change is possible and to work toward that end without fostering false hopes and expectations.

Although an ideal, the notion of the therapeutic personality can serve as a model, a standard against which one can measure one's development as a drama therapist. The therapeutic personality cannot be taught in the same way as the competencies listed above. But it can be learned and developed as one practices the art of drama therapy and as one is willing to be self-critical and risk looking at those personality traits that block the search for authenticity and relationship.

DRAMA THERAPY IN CONTEXT

What then is drama therapy? Several attempts at definition have already been made. The British Association for Dramatherapists offers the following (1979): "Dramatherapy is a means of helping to understand and alleviate social and psychological problems, mental illness and handicap; and of facilitating symbolic expression, through which man may get in touch with himself both as *individual* and *group*, through creative structures involving vocal and physical communication."

The National Association for Drama Therapy states in its brochure: "Drama therapy can be defined as the intentional use of drama/theatre processes to achieve the therapeutic goal of symptom relief, emotional and physical integration and personal growth."

To that definition, David Johnson adds (1982): "Drama therapy, like the other creative arts therapies (art, music and dance), is the application of a creative medium to psychotherapy. Specifically, drama therapy refers to those activities in which there is an established therapeutic understanding between client and therapist and where the therapeutic goals are primary and not incidental to the ongoing activity."

These definitions take into account the creative and expressive nature of drama therapy and the psychotherapeutic goals of drama therapists. The British stress the populations to be treated. The Americans stress the organismic and humanistic nature of drama therapy in referring to the primary aims of emotional and physical integration and personal growth.

A complex discipline, like a complex work of art, defies simple definition and summary. Rather than proposing a new definition of drama therapy, let us again look at the field in context. Drama therapists aim to reach goals that are essentially dramatic in nature. A general goal might be to help others increase their repertory of roles and their ability to play a single role more effectively. Specific goals are very much dependent upon the nature and needs of the client. Although therapeutic in nature, the goals often bear resemblance to educational and recreational drama goals. Further, drama therapy relates in some ways to many major psychotherapeutic theories, viewing the client as embodying a confluence of conscious and unconscious processes of mind, body, feeling, and intuition.

The context enlarges even further as we look at drama therapy concepts and practices from within the field, from the point of view of drama therapists. In the following chapters, such a context will be provided in terms of concepts, practices, and research strategies that inform the work of drama therapists.

PART II
THE CONCEPTUAL BASIS
OF DRAMA THERAPY

Chapter Three

THE INTERDISCIPLINARY SOURCES
OF DRAMA THERAPY

In his seminal theoretical study, *Play, Drama and Thought*, defining the nature and intellectual background of drama in education, Richard Courtney examined many related disciplines, including: play, psychoanalysis, psychodrama, sociology, social anthropology, and theatre. Courtney focused upon an elucidation of the dramatic process within the theoretical structures of these disciplines and pointed out certain interactional elements among them. He concluded (1974) that dramatic education, later called developmental drama, "is the basic way in which the human being learns—and thus is the most effective method for all forms of education."

Like Courtney's model, drama therapy has roots in several disciplines: anthropology, psychology and psychotherapy, sociology and theatre. We will focus on the following aspects of each: in anthropology— play, ritual, and healing; in psychology and psychotherapy—play therapy, psychodrama, psychoanalysis, and developmental psychology; in sociology—symbolic interactionism; and in theatre—performance theory and educational drama and theatre. Each has been chosen because of its direct conceptual connection, not only to the dramatic process but also to that part of the process that implies a healing, therapeutic function.

PLAY AND PLAY THERAPY

Although a wide range of play theories has developed, a certain commonality exists. The common denominator is the dramatic nature of play in the sense of drama as a dialectic between the actual, everyday reality and the imaginative one. The child or adult at play is exploring the former context through the latter. The play context is an imaginative and spontaneous one, characterized by its quality of transforming objective reality into subjective imagery. Courtney distinguishes between dramatic play and general play in stating that the former is based in role-playing and identification.

Most play theorists reiterate the dramatic, representational nature of play. For Erik Erikson (1940), the play world is a scaled-down, miniature representation of everyday life, a microcosm of the macrocosm. For Piaget (1962), the child assimilates the outside world into his mind and tests out that knowledge back in the world through the related dramatic processes of play and imitation. And for Freud (1908), the play of the child represents the "first traces of imaginative activity." According to Freud, the child at play moves between levels of reality and fantasy, symbolizing his unconscious through his play action.

Melanie Klein and her colleagues (Klein, Heimann, Isaacs, and Rivière, 1952) have viewed spontaneous, make-believe play as an early form of imaginative, "as if" thinking.

Theories of the origins and functions of play differ considerably. For Freud (1908), play originates in the unconscious and functions as a means of acting out repressed energy repeatedly in order to master reality. For Piaget (1962), play originates in the developing cognitive schema and functions to assimilate new experience. For Johan Huizinga (1955), play is genetically based and functions as a means of perpetuating the human race. Other theories view play from an emotional perspective, functioning as a means of catharsis (Breuer and Freud, 1936); from a physiological perspective, serving a recreational end (Mitchell and Mason, 1948); and from a sociological perspective, functioning as a means of socialization and cooperation (Opie and Opie, 1969; Bruner and Sherwood, 1975).

For Peter Slade (1954), play marks the beginning of all dramatic activity for the infant. Slade distinguishes between two types of play: personal play and projected play. Personal play is the more active and physical of the two, characterized by movement and role playing. Projected play is more inner directed, relating to the child's exercise of his imagination.

For Slade, the play of children serves several functions: catharsis, self-awareness, social interaction, and the discovery of rhythm, movement, and creative speech.

Dramatic play or creative play in general is distinct from forms of goal-directed, competitive play exemplified in sports and games. Our focus is upon the creative forms of play that serve the functions mentioned by Freud, Piaget, Courtney, Slade, and others. From these theorists, several common characteristics of creative play emerge:

1. It is a spontaneous, improvisational activity rather than a calculated, scripted one.
2. It is symbolic, imaginative activity expressed through movement, speech, and/or thought.
3. Many forms of play have a projective nature in which the player's thoughts, wishes or needs are projected outward onto the world.
4. Play exists in a representational context. In enacting issues within the play world, the player comes to know something of the larger world outside.
5. A player often takes on and plays out the role of another character, thus dramatizing his experience.
6. Play is not directed toward an external goal (i.e., completing a task or making money); rather, it is directed toward less tangible, more personal or social goals (i.e., mastery or competence).
7. Play is an essential psychic reality of all human beings that might be genetically based.
8. Play represents a confluence of thought and action, of conscious and unconscious processes.

Freud's notion that child's play is comparable to the creative activity of the artist has been reiterated by many psychologists and educators (Klein, Heimann, Isaacs, and Rivière, 1952; Kris, 1953). Like the artist at work, the individual at play transforms reality into new forms through an act of the imagination and through a physical action in the world. And like the artist, he uses playful means to create order out of confusion and ambiguity.

The played creation, like the artistic creation, can be seen as an artifact of an individual's unconscious, as a visible form of the invisible construct, the mind. And the child at play, like the artist, uses his play to achieve a degree of mastery and control over a large reality that is often perceived as masterful and controlling.

Play Therapy

A natural development from the free-association, verbal technique of Freud was a treatment of children using the non-verbal method of play. The analysis begins with the symbols the child has created in his play.

The therapist's role is to help the child gain a mastery of his reality as it is represented in play. The child creates his play structures with toys, puppets, masks, and other objects. He becomes, first, a sculptor and designer who builds a symbolic world. Then he becomes a performer who takes on and plays out selected roles of objects and people within his representational world.

An example of play therapy in a hospital setting is in the use of dolls, puppets, and medical objects to help children with severe medical problems cope with their fears of painful procedures, surgery, and powerful doctors. The therapist presents several dolls or puppets and a variety of medical instruments to the child. The instruments can include syringes, stethescopes, and intravenous tubes. He then encourages the child to choose a doll and/or puppet and play with it. As the child plays at injecting a doll or examining it with the medical instruments, the therapist helps him take on the role of the doctor. The therapist might speak for the child as doctor or for the doll as patient, helping the child feel in control of the situation through an identification with the powerful doctor figure or express his own fears through an identification with the helpless patient figure.

At times, the play action can become violent. An example might be the child decapitating a doll. In identifying with the supreme power of the doctor as aggressor, the child is able to express his rage or his ultimate fear of being violated. The therapist would try to interpret the need of the child and allow him to express his feelings within the safety of the play situation, where, unlike the everyday world, violent actions do not necessarily have negative consequences.

Often, in play therapy the child will repeat the same action until he feels that he has mastered a troubling piece of reality. This representation is based in Freud's notion of the repetition compulsion, where a highly charged situation is enacted over and over until the subject feels he has gained control over that which had been controlling him.

Like play in general, play therapy is spontaneous, representational, symbolic, and dramatic in nature. It can begin with children as young as two years old (see Klein, 1932). Although based primarily in the psychoanalytic model, play therapy is explicitly dramatic in its re-creation of the everyday world with dolls, puppets, toys, and objects.

The play of children exemplifies the most pure state of dramatic activity, the unmediated projection of self outwards onto the world and the concomitant assimilation of the world within the self. The ability to dramatize, to exist simultaneously within the two realities of the imagination and the objective world, marks a significant development in the growth of human consciousness. Dramatic play, as an early form of being, provides a visible shape for unconscious processes. In healthy development, the child engages in play naturally to master reality. In abnormal development, that natural process can serve the therapeutic goal of helping dysfunctional children express their problems safely and move toward mastery.

RITUAL, MAGIC, AND SHAMANISM

Anthropology also serves as a source for drama therapy, particularly in its attention to ritual, magic, and shamanism as practiced in various cultures. To fully understand dramatic play, it is imperative to look at these anthropological practices. The dramatic action of a child playing with a doll has a ritual component. Ritual is a symbolic action repeated in a prescribed way to perpetuate the status quo, to affirm a common bond among members of a community, and to defend an individual or group against danger. Ritual is a conservative activity. In many ways it is more theatre than drama, as the subject takes on the role of player or celebrant and enacts a kind of predictable theatrical script through prescribed actions and words. The child who decapitates his doll, for example, might do it in a ritualistic fashion, repeating the same sequence of actions according to an internal scenario.

This image of the child at play with the doll suggests other kinds of ritual practices performed in certain non-Western cultures. A most obvious example would be the practice of voodoo, in which a doll represents an enemy, and prescribed violent actions toward the doll represent one's wish to hurt the enemy. Geza Róheim, in elucidating several instances of ritualized play or played ritual, offers examples from various cultures (1934): "A Vogul widow kisses and embraces a doll as a representative of her dead husband. The Chippewa make an image of a dead child and pretend that it is alive, the widow carries her husband's bones in a bundle and calls the bundle 'husband,' and the Chinese believe that grave puppets and straw 'souls' are living beings or may become so at any moment."

Ritual activity, thus, is dramatic, as it calls for the subject to create a representational world through symbolic means. Further, ritual activity has a magical, non-rational quality as, for example, a child plays out his fears through decapitating a doll, and a Vogul woman plays out her sadness over losing her husband by embracing a doll. Their actions do not affect the empirical world of cause and effect but rather the subjective world of feeling. In these instances, the doll becomes animated and transformed into a human being upon whom the subject can project his feelings. This act of projection is both a magical one and an imaginative, creative one.

The eidetic imagery theorist, Akhter Ahsen, writes that magic is an essential property of the creative process as well as the thought of children. For Ahsen, magic is about the intimate relationship between a wish and an act. He says (1982): "Thus, in a truly magical way we find that part is whole, contact is unification, imitation is reality, wish is action."

The child's wish for the power of his doctor, the Vogul wife's wish for the presence of her husband, the voodoo celebrant's wish for revenge upon his enemy become action through the ritual dramas of decapitation, lovemaking, and wounding. The magic of the drama is realized at the subjective level of feeling. The players achieve a certain satisfaction by controlling a reality which is literally beyond their control. For the child, pain is mastered and weakness is overcome. For the wife, separation and loneliness are assuaged. And for the voodoo celebrant, revenge is achieved.

With the passage of time, the practice of magic has become institutionalized. In contemporary Western cultures, that function is usually ascribed to the psychotherapist. The therapist is also known as the "headshrinker," a term implying a magical quality and an identification with a non-Western rite of war, the decapitation and shrinking of the heads of the enemy. Since its inception, therapy has included such practices as hypnotism and mysticism, again implying a link to the world of magic.

Traditional healing and divination have included the magical services of soothsayers, dream readers, astrologists, fortune-tellers, mystics, and shamans. Of this group, the most dramatic of magician/healers are the shamans.

Shamanic practices, though centuries old, are still quite prevalent in many non-Western cultures. The shaman embodies the functions of priest and therapist and works through magic to help the individual and the community achieve a sense of harmony and healthy functioning. The shaman's dramatic methods include role playing, chant, stylized movement, makeup, and costume in his healing rituals. He works at times with individuals who exhibit signs of mental illness. He also works with communities in staging ritual dramas that embody themes and supernatural characters representing the collective concerns of the group. The content of the dramas is often taken from myths. The form is highly ritualized. In staging the ritual dramas, the shaman will take on the role of supernatural characters, often allowing his body to be possessed by the spirit of a god.

Ritual dramas led by the shaman often function to help the celebrants release repressed emotion through catharsis. Not only are many of the rituals physically exhausting for the participants, they are also emotionally charged for the observers. An example is in the comic ritual dramas of Sri Lanka. Part of the drama allows the male observers, fearful of losing their virility and therefore becoming useless to the community, the opportunity to release their fears through laughter. They are presented with the powerful god, Sakra, who is portrayed as feeble and impotent. The men identify with the powerful one who has lost his sexual power. But as he is portrayed as a fool and subjected to a series of comic ridicules, they, too, ridicule him and thus release their own fears of impotence (R. and G. Obeyesekere, 1976).

Many non-Western cultures rely upon ritual dramas and shamanic practices to create a sense of harmony within the community, a sense of mental health within the individual, and a sense of communion between the spirit world and the mortal world. Unlike the professed scientific orientation of Western psychotherapists, the shaman's focus is unabashedly magical. His journeys to the spirit world of the gods and the psychic world of the mind are sometimes acts of faith, sometimes purely acts of creative performance, and almost always acts of the imagination.

Ritual, magic, and shamanism serve as excellent sources for drama therapy because they combine healing and performance and proceed through acts of imagination. When the ritual dramas are most effective and when the shamans are most powerful in embodying the supernatural, the celebrants are able to suspend their disbelief and participate in the drama. On a personal level, that might mean experiencing a greater sense of release and integration. On a community level, that might mean experiencing a greater sense of togetherness and hope—the crops will grow, the men will be potent, the women will conceive, and the community will prosper. On either level, the function of ritual, magic, and shamanism is therapeutic.

PSYCHODRAMA AND SOCIODRAMA

As a bridge from the religion and magic of shamanism to the behavioral science of psychotherapy, we turn again to psychodrama, a discipline developed by J. L. Moreno, whose life and work embodied a confluence of magic, science, and religion. Turning away from a scientific, medical model of treating symptoms and healing through medicine, Moreno, trained as a medical doctor, aimed toward a healing of the individual psyche, of the society, and of the planet.

At the heart of psychodrama is the notion that acting in everyday life parallels acting in the theatre. Long before Erving Goffman's sociological analysis, *The Presentation of Self in Everyday Life,* Moreno applied the dramatic metaphor to a profound analysis of human existence and developed a treatment strategy aimed toward a theatrical goal. The goal of the actor, according to Moreno (1946), is "to add a newness, vivacity, and dramatic quality to the faithful literal rendering of the playwright's script."

In psychodrama, that goal is to be accomplished through training in spontaneity, an essential property of the creative process and of play. Moreno contrasts spontaneity with stereotyped behavior and impulsive behavior. The stereotyped actor in everyday life is limited in his choices. He plays it safe, sticks to the rules, gives people what they expect, is predictable and conventional. The impulsive actor in everyday life acts independently of a social context. His behavior is often inappropriate to the situation and overly self-involved. He appears to be bound to emotions that need immediate discharge, regardless of the objective reality. Though apparently spontaneous and free, the behavior of the impulsive individual is based more upon need than choice.

The spontaneous individual, on the other hand, is the most liberated. He chooses to behave as he does. He is aware of the social context before him, but he is able to risk the possible disapproval of others in presenting an authentic role of himself. Spontaneous behavior has an existential quality, as it is based in a present, here-and-now time frame. It has a creative quality as it transforms the usual into the unique.

Further, spontaneous behavior is playful behavior, in that it is neither calculated nor goal-directed and is based in imaginative and intuitive functions.

A central concept of Moreno's theory of great relevance to drama therapy is role. For Moreno, role is the essential "unit of culture." Role precedes self. That is, self is not an inborn, genetic construct. It develops socially and emerges from the roles one takes on. Moreno identified four types of roles:

1. psychosomatic or physiological roles of the infant in relation to his mother, which includes the role of eater, sleeper, eliminator, and mover;
2. fantasy or psychodramatic roles of the developing individual in relation to magical and religious characters outside himself, including roles of gods, devils, and animals;
3. social roles based in actual relationships with others, including family, gender, and work-related roles; and
4. cultural roles determined by the demands of a particular environment, pointing to the way that an individual will play out his family, gender, and work roles.

For Moreno (1946), the function of role is "to enter the unconscious from the social world and bring shape and order to it."

Moreno did not emphasize the unconscious in his theory. Social and behavioral factors were of greater significance. However, because his theory was based so firmly on artistic, expressive experiencing, he did look at intuitive, non-observable processes. One of these, *tele*, represented the relationship between client and therapist and, more generally, between all human beings in a group. Moreno did not deny the importance of Freud's notion of transference, but he saw it as describing a negative and one-sided relationship between client and therapist. For Moreno, transference is a series of fantasies that a client projects onto the therapist. Tele, on the other hand, is a positive, interactive view of that relationship. It is the intuitive understanding that the therapist and client have for one another outside the context of fantasies and projections. Each sees the other as he is and thus affirms the separateness of the other and interdependency of the relationship. Tele implies a stable relationship between the client and therapist, a model of effective human communication.

In psychodrama, the *dramatis personae*, or cast of characters, are assumed present in the mind of the protagonist. The role of the director is to help give the characters an external form and move them through space in such a way as to encapsulate the protagonist's problem.

In sociodrama, the characters are representations of social types present within a given social context. Rather than focusing on personal dilemmas, the director, using the same principles as in psychodrama, examines the dimensions of a social issue. In working with conflicts between social types (i.e., men vs. women, blacks vs. whites, bosses vs. workers), the director attempts to uncover issues of sexism, racism, and exploitation inherent not only in the individual mind but also in society.

Consistent with his social aims, Moreno developed the science of sociometry which enabled him to examine the dynamics of any group. Through a series of directed questions aimed at viewing the power structure and interaction patterns of a group, he was able to diagram these patterns. The diagram, called a sociogram, became a representation of the group dynamics.

As sources of drama therapy, psychodrama and sociodrama are very rich. Moreno's work is the first significant Western attempt to view dramatic action as a formalized method of psychotherapy. Moreno went beyond the talk cure and the historical orientation of Freud into the realm of expressive action and spontaneity. Like the shamanic healers, he used his magical powers of intuition and creativity to fashion a representational dramatic reality within which a protagonist can expel his demons. But Moreno was also a scientist who formalized his theory of drama as therapy for the individual and for the society. Like Freud, Moreno developed a system for analyzing human behavior and treating mental illness. As a direct source of drama therapy, that system is based in the notion that normal everyday behavior is dramatic and that when the ability to play one's everyday roles spontaneously has been curtailed, then the proper means of restoring healthy functioning is through drama.

PSYCHOANALYSIS

The drama in Freud's system is not active. There are no actual characters confronting one another and no director moving them around a stage. The lighting effects and theatricality that Moreno was so fond of were anathema to Freud. With the exception of later developments in play therapy, the drama of psychoanalysis is an imaginative one, played out in the mind of the client.

Psychoanalysis presents a dramatic image of existence. The individual is at war with himself. The unconscious mind withholds information from the conscious mind. Threatening experiences and feelings are repressed, withdrawn from consciousness because they are too painful to look at. The repressed feelings, though, often take the form of neuroses:

abnormal behavior patterns that defend an individual against having to examine painful and confusing realities of his psychic life.

In the Freudian canon, there is further conflict among the three parts of the mind—the id, ego, and superego. The id, representing primal, spontaneous psychic experience, is the magical part of the mind that seeks immediate gratification and does not distinguish wish from reality.

The ego, on the other hand, is the part of the mind representing reason and responsive to the demands of external reality. It tempers the impulsivity of the id and seeks a delay in gratification until an appropriate moment. The ego leads the person to realistic action based on an assessment of an event in the world.

The superego, the latest construct to develop in mental life, is the voice of conscience, the moral principle that judges the actions of the ego and attempts to suppress the impulsivity of the id. Initially based in the sanctions of parents who teach the infant right and wrong, it later represents the moral and ethical codes of religion and society. The superego, though, internalizes and transforms the external morality, often to the detriment of the ego. It is a higher judge and often a harsher judge than the church or state, for the individual in the grips of his superego passes judgment upon himself. Such judgment often leads to the repression of anger, hurt, and passion, and to feelings of guilt.

In normal development, the id, ego, and superego are in a psychic balance, one checking the other against exerting too much control: the superego limiting the irrational, amoral subjectivity of the id; the ego safely channeling the id needs for play and magic into the outside world.

In abnormal development, an imbalance occurs and one part takes control. This can lead to highly impulsive behavior dominated by the id or highly moralistic, compulsive behavior dominated by the superego.

Freud's theory is a developmental one. The infant passes through three initial stages—the oral, anal, and genital—each representing the erotogenic part of the body central to the child's being at that stage. The fourth stage, that of latency, marks the transition between childhood and adolescence.

In illustrating the dimensions of the genital stage (from which the superego develops), Freud turns to theatre. He chooses the image of Sophocles's protagonist, Oedipus, to elucidate a central issue in child development. According to Freud, in the genital stage, the male child wishes to possess his mother fully and resents the presence of his father, who he sees as a competitor for his mother's love. Like the character

Oedipus, who unknowingly murders his father and marries his mother, the child cannot bring this wish to consciousness without dire consequences. Oedipus, tortured by the reality of his incestuous and murderous actions, literally blinds himself in punishment. The child, wishing for that which Oedipus achieved, blinds his consciousness of the wish through repression. His punishment, meted out by the superego, is guilt. In eventually resolving his Oedipus complex, that is, in seeing himself as an independent sexual being, the guilt will be assuaged. In remaining blind to the need for separation, the repression and ensuing guilt will remain constant.

In reference to the female child, Freud turns to a further theatrical image, that of Electra, claiming that the female child desires the father and harbors resentment toward the mother. Although his theory of female sexuality remains incomplete and at least implicitly sexist, he basically viewed the Oedipus and Electra complexes as identical.

At any point in the development of infantile sexuality, the oral, anal, or genital needs of the infant might be thwarted. If so, the later adolescent or adult might exhibit neurotic symptoms based in a fixation at an earlier stage and exemplified symbolically through his language, behavior, dreams, and fantasies. For Freud, however, the basic source of neurosis was in an unresolved Oedipus complex, in which the developing individual is unable to transfer his love of a parent onto another love object.

Four key psychoanalytical concepts are central to a theoretical understanding of drama therapy: transference, countertransference, projection, and identification, all of which are based in a symbolic role-taking process. From the Freudian point of view, these processes are primarily defensive, protecting the client from seeing crucial conflicts in his life. As we shall see, the drama therapist uses these processes to engage the client in a balanced form of therapeutic dramatization.

Freud has created a theory that incorporates much dramatic imagery. Psychoanalysis presents a dynamic image of man in conflict with himself, struggling to relate the internal to the external, and the need for instant gratification to the demands of reality. That struggle takes a dramatic form in the image of Oedipus, who blinds himself when he sees the forbidden, repressed truth of his existence.

The individual, further, re-creates his past through the universal phenomenon of transference, which, according to Freud, dominates the individual's relationship to his environment (Freud, 1925). Through transference, the client creates a representational world in the therapy session and dramatizes his past conflicts through casting the therapist in the role of a significant other. In analyzing the transference neurosis as well as the related defensive techniques of projection and identification, the therapist moves toward a resolution of the psychoanalytic drama.

DEVELOPMENTAL PSYCHOLOGY

Erik Erikson extended Freud's model of human development through the life cycle, incorporating social and cultural, as well as psychological, factors as determinates for growth. Although he based his developmental model on the oral, anal, genital, and latency stages described by Freud, Erikson identified four further stages accounting for the growth of the adolescent, the young adult, and the mature adult. For Erikson, each stage is marked by a psychic struggle between a positive self-affirming value and a negative, reactionary one. In reconciling the contraries at each stage, the individual develops a strengthened ego and proceeds to the next stage of development.

The first stage is marked by the conflict between basic trust and mistrust. It is the stage of infancy, equivalent to Freud's concept of the oral stage. The successful resolution of the infant's conflict at this stage leads to an attitude of hope and a trust of other people.

The second stage, equivalent to Freud's anal phase, is marked by the conflict, autonomy vs. shame and doubt. In normal development through this stage, the child acquires willful actions and a sense of self-confidence.

The third stage, initiative vs. guilt, is equivalent to Freud's genital, Oedipal stage. The child's resolution of this conflict leads to a sense of purpose and a faith in his own present actions and future development.

The fourth stage is that of latency which Erikson characterizes as industry vs. inferiority. Resolution at this stage leads the individual to a feeling of competence and mastery.

The fifth stage marks adolescence. At this point, Erikson views the psychic struggle as that of identity vs. role confusion. The successful resolution of the conflict leads the adolescent toward the development of a coherent sense of self in relation to other people.

In his early twenties, the young adult is seen as struggling between intimacy and isolation. The resolution at this stage is marked by the development of a capacity to love.

As the adult matures, his psychic struggle is characterized by generativity vs. stagnation. Out of that struggle the individual develops the ability to care for others.

Finally, the eighth stage, that of old age, is marked by the struggle of ego integrity vs. despair. For the individual who has struggled through feelings of despair, the reward is wisdom.

Like Freud, Erikson presents a model based in struggle between contrary elements of one's psyche. For Freud, the contraries are the demands of the unconscious, represented by the id, and the demands of reality, mediated by the ego. For Erikson, the contraries exist between the positive forces of self-liberation and the negative forces of oppression. At all stages, the conflicts are intensified by the demands of society, a force against which the individual must struggle in order to develop a positive identity and move toward achieving wisdom.

The notion of development as a struggle between contrary parts of oneself is basic to dramatic literature. The moment of awareness in the great tragic heroes (i.e., Oedipus, Antigone, Hamlet, Lear) comes about only as they experience their sense of power in relation to their sense of powerlessness. The notion of *hubris*, the tragic flaw of pride within the heart of the protagonist of a classic tragedy, is itself a reflection of the great psychic contraries between the individual as infinitely strong and wise, as endowed as if by magic with the ability to transform wish into action; and the individual as finite, as subject to the demands of the objective universe represented by the gods, other people, institutions, laws, and nature.

In exploring the contraries of human existence through role playing, the drama therapist also works with the notion of struggle—the individual against himself and against forces outside himself—finding dramatic forms in which to stage the great existential battles. The consequences of recognizing the contraries of existence in drama therapy are far less drastic and tragic than those that befell Oedipus, Antigone, and Lear. Insight in drama therapy might represent a symbolic death, an abandonment of an earlier stage of development. Erikson often turned to dramatic forms, utilizing dramatic play and world technique, the construction of scenes with miniature objects, as direct means of viewing the intrapsychic and interpersonal conflicts of his clients.

The image of man presented in developmental models is one oriented toward positive change, toward a process of growth through struggle. One of the most powerful developmental models which, like that of Freud, extends through pre-adolescence is that devised by Jean Piaget.

Unlike Freud's psychosexual model, Piaget's is a cognitive one. A significant source of drama therapy, it offers further understanding of the dramatic processes of imitation and play. Further, Piaget examines origins and dimensions of representation, a process fundamental to all dramatic activity.

For Piaget, the beginning of cognitive life is marked by sensory-motor intelligence, a period in which the infant is unable to represent experience by means of symbols. That is, for the infant from birth to approximately two years old, the world exists only in a subjective, egocentric form as an extension of his body. However, in this period, the infant constructs basic cognitive and affective structures that will lead to further development. One method of building these structures is through imitating the actions of a visible model (i.e., the hand movements of his mother). The function of the child's imitation is to enable him to accommodate himself to the external world, to behave as his mother has behaved.

At the second developmental stage, that of preconceptual intelligence, the beginnings of representational thought are evident. Starting at around two years old, the infant is able to make a distinction between self and world through symbolic means. The beginning of this process of symbolic representation is marked by a lessening of egocentricity, which Piaget calls "decentering." Through representation, the infant is able to evoke an object or event in his mind that is not present in reality. In doing so, he assimilates the external reality to the self. This higher level of representation is accomplished through play. For Piaget, intelligence is based upon the simultaneous interaction between assimilation through play and accommodation through imitation.

Symbolic play, as distinguished from play in general, is characterized by Piaget as not only assimilation of the world to the self but assimilation through a symbolic language created by the child. This language of the child, although transmitted to him ready-made from the adult social environment, is distinct from the grammatical language of adults. As expressed through play, the child's language has an internal, imaginative, dramatic quality. Through his language, the child represents or relives an experience, rather than simply recalling it. Piaget and Inhelder (1969) give the example of a child who, having seen a plucked duck on the kitchen table in the morning, plays the role of the duck in the evening by lying completely still on the couch and exclaiming, "I'm the dead duck!"

Following the stage of preconceptual thought, a transitional stage occurs from approximately four-and-one-half to seven years old. This is the stage of intuitive thought, marked by a further decentering not only of action but also of representation. This occurs because, with the formation of language and social relationships, the child's world becomes much more complex. The reality of the child now encompasses people who have points of view different from himself. In coordinating these with his own, he learns to take on different perspectives. In doing so, the child learns social skills that have cognitive as well as affective and moral components.

At the stage of concrete operations, from approximately seven to eleven years old, representation of the world is further developed through decentering. This stage is marked by the ability to reason in a chronological fashion and to classify objects in groups. Further, the child's earlier representations of the world as magical change into more rational notions of cause and effect.

At the level of concrete operations, a change in playing is noted. Children begin to prefer games with rules to symbolic play. This concern with the rules also reflects the development of morality, a conventional sense of right and wrong.

The final stage, that of formal operations, begins with pre-adolescence. It is the stage of ideals and the beginning of theoretical thinking, thought separated from concrete observation. On a social and affective level, the individual now develops a degree of autonomy that enables him to anticipate the future and choose a value system. His mental representations are characterized by the assimilation of viewpoints that differ from those in his immediate social environment.

As a source for drama therapy, Piaget's model is most rich in providing an understanding of the concept of representation and the processes of play and imitation. It further presents a useful means of diagnosing young clients and helping them proceed through symbolic, expressive means toward further stages of development.

Though based in cognition, Piaget's theory is an organismic one incorporating psychomotor, affective, and social factors. In combination with the models of Freud and Erikson, as well as those of more recent developmental theorists such as Selman (1971) and Kübler-Ross (1969), a developmental perspective emerges that responds to an essential developmental drama therapy goal. This goal is encapsulated by the drama therapist, David Johnson, as follows (1982a): "Whereas other paradigms suggest human dysfunction is due to something missing or out of balance, requiring things to be put right, the developmental perspective sees human disorder as a blockage or halt in development.... The overall goal of development ... is ... increasing the range of expression so that the person has access to, and the ability to move among *all* developmental levels."

SOCIOLOGICAL THEORY: SYMBOLIC INTERACTION

Drama/theatre has actually served as a source for sociological theory, most pointedly in its offering of the concept of role. Role initially referred to an object upon which the dialogue for a play was written. As used presently in theatre, a role is a character in a script played by an actor.

The best-known applications of role playing to sociology are Erving Goffman's seminal study of the natives of the British Shetland Islands and his later dramaturgical studies of institutional behavior. In characterizing the individual and social behaviors of his subjects, Goffman (1959) applied a dramatic metaphor, viewing their existence as a performance, a presentation of self in everyday life. Noting distinctions between behavior in role and out of role, Goffman proceeded to build a dramaturgical theory of social behavior based upon the notion of self as dramatic artifact. For Goffman, the self was determined by the roles one played in relation to given social circumstances.

Goffman's work in role theory has stimulated much research and writing in the social sciences. However, an earlier source has had an even broader influence on role theory: that of symbolic interactionism as exemplified in the work of George Herbert Mead. Mead's thought, though based upon a dramatic notion of representation through role taking, is more purely a cognitive theory, like Piaget's, that accounts for the development of the self.

A central question in Mead's work is: How does the self come into being? For Mead, as consciousness develops, a child becomes able to act toward himself as others have acted toward him. That is, he becomes "the object of his own actions" (Blumer, 1962). Once the child is able to make indications to himself through a symbolic process of thought similar to that described by Piaget as beginning in the pre-conceptual stage, then the self has begun its development through the dramatic process of role taking.

For Mead, role taking occurs within a social context. Initially, the child internalizes individual roles of significant people in his social environment, especially that of mother. By learning how mother acts in relation to child, he learns what child is supposed to do in relation to mother. Further, in mother's absence, the child acts toward himself as mother has acted toward him. Much of this action occurs through play. Mead characterizes the child at this early stage of play as an endless imitator, internalizing and playing out not only the mother role but roles of other significant people in his life.

A further development of the self occurs at the point when the child begins to play games with rules. He then internalizes a set of norms that govern his behavior as he acts toward himself according to the rules. He also begins to take on the role of the generalized other which is the social group—the parents, the school class, the team, the institution. Mead exemplifies this concept through the analogy of a baseball team. The shortstop knows the actions he must perform to the extent that he understands the actions required by all of the players on the field in relation to him. To play the role of shortstop, then, the individual must take on the generalized role of baseball team.

The self consists of two parts: the "I" and the "me." The "me" is the socially determined part of the self. It is conservative and controlling, a censor and check of impulsive behavior, similar to Freud's notion of the superego. The "I" is the more impulsive, independent part of the self. Although somewhat similar to Freud's notion of the id, the "I" is responsive to social circumstances.

The "I" and the "me" are interactive components of the self, representing the two poles of independence and creativity on the one hand, and social responsibility on the other.

In Mead's self theory, then, there is a notion of dialectic, not only between "I" and "me," but also between self as subject and self as object. This notion is equivalent to that of dramatic representation as a dialectic between imagination and reality, the subjective and objective realms.

Mead further refers to the concept of the double, applied by some non-Western cultures to a spirit force within the chest of individuals that can determine behavior and embody emotional states. He compares this to the imaginary companions that children invent to express feelings otherwise unexpressible.

These indications of dialectic help further our understanding of the dramatic basis of therapy. It is by journeying through the imaginary realm, the realm of the double, that the client in drama therapy can be brought to an understanding of the more objective realm of the everyday. More precisely, as the client is able to interrelate the imaginative and the actual, he will move toward more integrated, healthy functioning. This notion assumes that unhealthy functioning is an imbalance between the life of the imagination and that of the everyday, or, in Mead's terms, between the "I" and the "me." Through a process of role taking, that balance can be restored.

Symbolic interactionism is based in the idea that "human beings interpret or 'define' each others' actions. . . . Thus, human interaction is mediated by the use of symbols, by interpretation or by ascertaining the meaning of one another's action" (Blumer, 1962). Mead called the symbols "gestures." He characterized both animal and human interaction as a conversation of gestures. The gesture in human interaction has both a non-verbal movement component and a verbal sound one. The significant gesture or significant symbol is that which carries the same meaning to the self and to the other in a given interaction.

The notion of gesture and significant gesture has much relevance to drama therapy which aims to look at the movement and language of clients involved in dramatic interaction. Further, in examining the internal dramas of the individual client, the drama therapist can again refer to Mead's notion of thought as an intrapsychic conversation of gestures. In Mead's terms, the internal conversation of gestures occurs as the individual acts imaginatively and measures his actions against the sanctions of either significant others or the generalized other. Because of the ability to act imaginatively, the individual is able to consider different viewpoints and plan for the future. For Mead, then, the mind, like the social world, is a stage for symbolic interaction. The internalized voices of others become characters in an internal drama whose enactment will guide the future actions of the individual.

The idea of symbolic interaction and balance between the individual and the social world is exemplified in two other socially based models. The first is that of the looking-glass self, devised by Mead's contemporary, Charles Cooley (1922). Although Cooley's self theory was not as fully developed as Mead's, it was equally dramatic in its attention to role taking as the basis of self-awareness.

Cooley used the image of the looking glass to describe the role-taking process. Each significant other in one's social environment becomes a mirror that reflects back an image of oneself. Thus, through social interaction, the individual sees himself reflected in the other and thereby takes on the role of the other. Again, there is a balance between the individual and his social environment. He becomes a self only through incorporating the imagery of others and viewing himself as they have viewed him.

The second theory of social interaction, that of dialogue, was devised by the philosopher and cultural anthropologist, Martin Buber, another contemporary of Mead. Initially based in a theological understanding of the relationship between man and God, Buber extended his theory to encompass the interactions between human beings. In offering his model of human communication, Buber identifies the Greek etymology of dialogue as *dialogos:* a reasoning through. The individuals in dialogue develop their interaction through a mutual process of taking in the role of the other and playing out the role of self authentically. Through this process, a meeting takes place and the dialogue develops cooperatively. When there is imbalance, the dialogue, conceptualized by Buber as the "I-Thou" relationship, breaks down. At one extreme (the "I" pole), the individual exists in an egocentric state, having little ability to see or hear the other. At the other extreme (the "Thou" pole), the individual has made a full identification with a collective ideology (i.e., a religious or political philosophy) and simply utters the specified dogma, thus separating himself from the process of openly reasoning· through an issue with another.

Buber's model of human communication is similar to Mead's, in that it is based upon a balancing between the constructs of self and other. Both models view the growth of the self from a social and dramatic point of view. Not only are Buber's use of dialogue and Mead's use of role taking borrowed from the field of drama, but they also provide a source for drama therapy, a view of the processes of socialization and communication.

PERFORMANCE THEORY

Twentieth century performance theory, as related to the modes and purposes of theatre performance, provides a further source for drama therapy. Although most major theorists would agree that the ideal actor is one who has achieved a balance of physical, emotional, intellectual, and spiritual excellence, each has emphasized one aspect of the actor's being as essential to performance. Three theories that have profoundly influenced twentieth century theatre and that relate directly to a conceptual understanding of drama therapy are those developed by Constantin Stanislavski in Russia, Bertolt Brecht in Germany, and Antonin Artaud in France.

Constantin Stanislavski

Stanislavski's system, although developed over many years and subjected to changes of emphasis, has become known as a psychological, naturalistic system, based in an emotional approach to acting. This emotional emphasis appeared in Stanislavski's early work and was chronicled in his book, *An Actor Prepares.*

In his later work, Stanislavski focused more attention on developing the physical actions of actors and less on emotional issues. In our concern with drama therapy, we turn to Stanislavski's seminal work in training actors through the technique of emotion memory.

Stanislavski introduced a method of improvisation during rehearsal. Improvisation became the means to uncover not only the text of a play but also the subtext, the motivations, feelings, and behavior implied by the text. Although there is no evidence that Stanislavski was familiar with the work of Freud, he often used images of unconscious experience in his writing and aimed toward a sublimation of repressed energies into an artistic form. The following passage from *An Actor Prepares* illustrates this (1936): "Periods of subconsciousness are scattered through our lives. Our problem is to remove whatever interferes with them and to strengthen any elements that facilitate their functioning."

To get to the "subconscious," Stanislavski devised a technique based in affective memory, one that fostered an identification between actor and role, actor and viewer. Using this approach, an actor recalls a past experience in his own life which provokes an emotion similar to one associated with the required action of his character. In transferring the past emotion to the present and representing the emotion as if it were occurring for the first time, the actor creates a dialectical moment of living the present through the past, living the life of the other through the self.

For Stanislavski, then, the central problem of the actor is to balance the forces of past and present, self and other, so that he is able to present a dramatic fiction as if it were real life. If he is successful, the audience member will identify with the dilemma of his character.

Stanislavski's actors were taught to project their own feelings onto their characters in order to create an aesthetic and emotional naturalism. Though actors trained in the Stanislavski method and audiences viewing his productions often experienced therapeutic catharsis and/or insight, Stanislavski's primary objective was an aesthetic one. Though an aesthetic action occurs in drama therapy, the primary focus is on the therapeutic goal. Drama therapists often use naturalistic techniques of role-playing and psychodrama to uncover psychological issues. However, many drama therapy practices, including work with dolls and puppets, are based in less realistic and more distanced forms of enactment. Thus, we turn to a second theory of performance, one that rejected the psychological naturalism of Stanislavski—the epic theatre of Bertolt Brecht.

Bertolt Brecht

For Brecht, the theatre was sociologically based. The task of the actor was not to identify with and enter into the life of his character but to distance himself from his character and comment upon his character's behavior. For Brecht, the theatrical character was a social type, subject to certain social and political circumstances which determined his behavior. The Marxist orientation of Brecht was a long way from the more Freudian-based notion of Stanislavski, who saw the character as an individual, subject to internal motivation.

In his famous alienation theory, Brecht hypothesized that if the actor presents social issues rather than psychological concerns in a stylized and distanced fashion, taking pains to remind the viewer that he is in a theatre and not the real world, then the viewer will be able to think through the issues, see the injustices, and be provoked toward action in the world. The alienation effect is based upon a separation of thought and feeling. According to Brecht, the theatrical style of naturalism provoked conventional and ultimately conservative reactions from an audience. As the viewer is unable to separate natural events from theatrical events, his ability to think critically becomes impaired. Brecht sought to foster that critical ability through restoring the illusion of theatricality. Toward that end, he created aesthetic distance through musical, design, and documentary effects, and through presenting dialectical ideas in the text, the design, and the behavior of the actors (Willett, 1964).

Brecht's epic theatre was anti-catharsis. Like Brecht, the South American theorist, Augusto Boal, criticized Aristotle's idea of catharsis as reactionary. For Boal (1979), catharsis is "the purgation of all antisocial notions." Boal's revolutionary poetics, like Brecht's, called for a questioning and critique of the social and political order, rather than a purgation of doubt, pity, and fear.

Brecht saw his theatre as narrative rather than dramatic. He attempted to tell grand, epic stories of the struggles between the forces of darkness and light, featuring such characters as Galileo, Joan of Arc, Antigone, and Mac the Knife. The structure of many of his plays was novelistic. Each scene was presented as if it were a chapter in a book, introduced by a title which was projected on a screen or written on a placard. As a further means of distancing, Brecht would ask actors in rehearsal to refer to their characters as "he" or "she" rather than "I." To remove other subjective elements from the drama, Brecht often used masks, puppets, and oversized props, transforming the particular into the general, the individual into the type.

The great irony of the Brechtian aesthetic is that his great popularity as a playwright and poet rests on the failure of his philosophy of distancing and his call to political action. That is, audiences did identify with the dilemmas of Macheath and Polly, Galileo and Mother Courage. They cried when Mother Courage's daughter, Kattrin, was killed, and they laughed when the Chaplinesque figure, Arturo Ui, caricatured the movements and words of Adolph Hitler. The revolutionary Berliner Ensemble is now an established institution in East Germany that has more or less preserved the epic theatre models. The opening song from *The Threepenny Opera,* "The Moritat of Mac the Knife," has been recorded by endless popular singers and can be heard in elevators and supermarkets.

That notwithstanding, Brecht's epic theatre provides a significant model for drama therapy. In drama therapy, the client often needs to distance himself from his dilemma and to find a safe means of symbolizing it in visible terms. Thus, the drama therapist works toward distancing clients from feelings that are too threatening through the use of such projective devices as masks, puppets, and stylized props and dolls. Further, in playing a social type rather than a psychological character, and in telling stories rather than directly dramatizing experiences, the client is able to create distance from potentially overwhelming feelings. Generally speaking, the move from naturalistic techniques of psychodrama to more stylized projective techniques gives the client more space in which to present his issues safely.

Antonin Artaud

A third significant performance theory is that of Antonin Artaud, which based the theatre experience in the realm of magic and ceremony. Artaud viewed the theatre in cathartic terms but, ever the extremist, went far beyond Aristotle and Stanislavski in his understanding of catharsis. The purgation possible in theatre was not that of the feeling, but of the spirit, of the soul. Through the theatrical experience the "latent cruelty" of people could be purged, releasing a transformational spirit. Artaud compared the theatre to the plague, which he saw as destroying the conventional order to reveal the essential truth of existence (1958): "The action of the theatre, like that of the plague, is beneficial, for, impelling men to see themselves as they are, it causes the mask to fall, reveals the lie, the slackness, baseness, and hypocrisy of our world . . . and in revealing to collectivities of men . . . their dark power, their hidden force, it invites them to take, in the face of destiny, a superior and heroic attitude they would never have assumed without it."

Artaud's radical theories have led to modern, expressionistic forms of theatre based in improvisation and dependent upon extreme forms of nonverbal action and sound. Artaud's model, theatre of cruelty, has produced experiments with mythological, religious, and occult material.

The actor in theatre of cruelty takes on the role of a shaman; his performance becomes a ritual journey, a communion with the spirit world. As the viewer becomes involved, he takes on the role of celebrant who is not only dazzled by the intensely magical performance but participates through a purgation of his own spiritual hypocrisy. Many of the performances in the sixties and seventies that claimed to be theatre of cruelty were certainly more charged for the actor than for the audience. From the viewer's perspective, the action at times seemed self-indulgent and more distancing than Brechtian theatre. However, two effective and lasting theatre companies developed from Artaud's ideas: that of the Polish Laboratory Theatre founded by Jerzy Grotowski, and The Living Theatre founded by Judith Melina and Julian Beck. Both aimed toward a spiritual liberation of the actor, again viewing him as a kind of priest whose task is to reveal the truth of the human condition to and with the audience.

In combining the spiritual notions of Artaud with the political notions of Brecht, the Living Theatre sought to do no less than foster "the creation of psychic changes that penetrate the armor of the mind" (Beck, 1972). Even in the spiritual approach to theatre, Freud has a secure place.

In relation to psychotherapy, Artaud's ideas are closest to those approaches based in primal techniques. Primal therapy, developed by Arthur Janov (1970), is a treatment wherein a client relives and releases deep-seated childhood emotions through a powerful cathartic experience. Primal techniques, being radically underdistanced, are highly volatile and of dubious value. However, Artaud's attention to ritual, sound, movement, myth, and spontaneous improvisational experience has direct relevance for the practice of drama therapy. In circumventing the limitations of the script, the prepared speech, and the constraints of naturalistic acting, Artaud offers, if not a technique, then at least a series of powerful images pointing the way toward a more liberated intuitive life.

Each of the three theories of theatre performance provides a particular emphasis. In working with these theories, the drama therapist needs to discover a way to integrate the three modes in order to treat the total person before him. As we shall see later, a concept that fosters such an integration is that of distancing.

EDUCATIONAL DRAMA AND THEATRE

In an earlier book, the author portrayed drama therapy as a subset of the larger field of educational drama and theatre (Landy, 1982). Here, in positing drama therapy as a discipline in its own right, educational drama and theatre becomes one source for the related but separate field of drama therapy.

Considerable groundwork has been laid already to support this view. For some years, Richard Courtney has meticulously researched the social and behavioral sciences, philosophy, and the performing arts in order to uncover the theoretical dimensions of learning through drama. He discovered that drama is a central process in human existence, extending not only to learning but also to playing, working, thinking, and to healing. In fact, several years after the publication of his seminal *Play, Drama and Thought*, Courtney co-edited, with Gertrud Schattner, the first anthology of articles in the field, *Drama in Therapy*.

The British educational drama experts, Gavin Bolton and Dorothy Heathcote, view drama as a profound means of both experiencing and reflecting upon experience. Stressing the cognitive nature of drama as a means to think through an issue, they posit the dramatic as a central method of learning all subject matter content.

Both Bolton and Heathcote have worked extensively with emotionally disturbed and developmentally disabled populations in schools and institutions, although neither consider themselves to be drama therapists. Although their aims are educational, their thinking about drama and their applications of drama to the needs of special populations borders upon the field of drama therapy. They both work through extended dramatization or in-depth role-playing situations where the participant, whether disabled or not, is endowed with a particular role and challenged to act, think, and feel like that character. Bolton and Heathcote are unique in the field, as they not only create a complex, dramatic representation of reality but also a framework in which the participants can relate their dramatization to their everyday lives. Further, Bolton and Heathcote tend to focus upon social as well as individual issues.

In working through a more superficial technique—that of the creative dramatic exercise—educational drama provides a model for treating the short-term or the severely disabled client in drama therapy. Further, the use of simple drama exercises and games, such as mirroring, sensory awareness, and transformation of objects, applies to warm-up procedures helpful in beginning any drama therapy session.

Educational drama presents several models of human development through drama. Peter Slade (1954) refers to four stages. The first, from birth until five years old, marks the beginnings of drama as enacted through play. At this stage, the child tends to express himself in a circular configuration, acting all around his body. The second stage— that of dramatic play—occurs from five through seven years old. The child begins to make distinctions between his own space, that of another's, and that which is shared. His enactments tend to be more social and are characterized by free expression in an open space. The third stage, that of drama and play, occurs from seven through twelve. Slade calls this period "the dawn of seriousness," marked by the development of a moral sense of right and wrong and the formation of tight cliques of friends. Free improvisation in movement and speech further develop at this stage. The final stage of child drama, twelve through fifteen, is characterized by the breaking up of small group circles and the congregating at one end of the room. This new focus marks the readiness of the child to engage in theatre, directing his attention toward an audience.

Richard Courtney (1982) specifies six developmental stages, extending

Slade's model into adulthood. At stage one—birth to ten months old—
the infant engages in early identification with the mother. From ten
months to seven years, at stage two, impersonation through dramatic
play develops. From seven through twelve, the group drama stage, children tell each other stories in groups and dramatic play becomes
improvisational experiments with form. At stage four, from twelve to
fifteen, the small social group is predominant and improvisation often
leads to theatre, a formal showing. The stage of the older adolescent,
fifteen through eighteen is marked by a parallel growth of improvised
dramatic activity and theatre. Not all are concerned with "showing"
through theatre, but all will recapitulate earlier levels of dramatic
sensation, movement, and sound in order to maintain the ability to be
playful and spontaneous. The final stage of the adult marks a continued
socialization process through role playing. Some few will continue the
exploration of dramatic form through partaking in theatrical activity.

Generally speaking, the field of educational drama and theatre presents a model of dramatic experiencing that can be conceptualized along
a continuum. At one end is the early sensory-motor play of infants. This
is marked by the infant's experiments with sounds and movements
associated with his body and the ability to imitate a model, most notably
the mother. Then, through the development of the ability to think
symbolically and to distinguish self from other, the child is able to
engage in dramatic play which contains elements of identification and
role playing.

The next point on the continuum represents a separation between the
natural, self-directed dramatic play of children and an applied drama
directed by adults. At this point, a leader applies a dramatic exercise or
game to the recreation or education of a child. As the applied dramatic
activity becomes more complex, it develops into a more formal role
playing or improvisational situation. The improvised situation can also
develop spontaneously from the child with no guidance from a leader.
Many of the spontaneous dramas occur in imagination as the child
fantasizes about being a heroic, demonic, or romantic figure.

Improvisational action and fantasy provide a source for extended
dramatizations. Although primarily improvised, these dramas can be
highly structured according to a story line chosen by the participants or
given by the leader. The extended dramatization can also be based in a
published source, i.e., a myth, story, or newspaper article. With this

approach, the text is explored and expanded through the spontaneous speech and movements of the participants.

And finally, the most formal point in the continuum is that of theatre, where the text not only provides the ideas and the structure for the actions but also the words to be spoken and, in some cases, the actions to be performed.

The continuum would look as follows:

sensory-motor play ⟷ dramatic play ⟷ applied dramatic ⟷
                                                     exercise and game
improvisation and ⟷ extended dramatization ⟷ theatre
role-playing   performance

The arrows point in both directions, as the continuum is intended to be interactive rather than linear, with one level embodying aspects of others. For example, at the level of theatre, the actor might also engage in dramatic play and improvisation as a means of exploring the subtext and characterization.

This model relates well to drama therapy in its view of the ability to engage in representational dramatic processes as a measure of normal human development. From the drama therapist's point of view, abnormal behavior could be interpreted as a blockage at one point in the model. Starting at that point, the drama therapist could choose appropriate activities for helping the client move fluently among all points in the dramatic continuum.

Chapter Four

CONCEPTS IN DRAMA THERAPY—
THE BEGINNING OF A THEORETICAL MODEL

G iven the eight sources mentioned above, we can begin to construct a theoretical model of drama therapy, incorporating those concepts from the sources that are essentially dramatic. The following concepts will be discussed: self, role, other, role taking, imitation, identification, projection, transference, role playing, representation, distancing, catharsis, affective memory, spontaneity, and the unconscious.

To begin, let us look at the two most basic pieces of our model: self and role. To understand the relationship between self and role from a dramatic point of view, it is necessary to look at a third part, that of the other. In our model, self, role, and other are interdependent concepts. The self, one's essential uniqueness, relates to the other, a representative of the social world, through a role. Role is a mediator between self and other, between self and the social world.

SELF

The self is not visible. It only takes on a visible form through a role. As the social-psychologist, Theodore Sarbin (1954), writes: "The self is what a person 'is,' the role is what a person 'does.'"

Unlike the humanistic psychologist's notion of the self as whole and good, the self in the dramatic model is not at all fixed or separate from the context of role. Self changes as role changes. However, self is more than a mere recapitulation of behaviors in role. Further, it is greater than the sum of its roles. When a child internalizes the role of mother and plays out mother behaviors in the world, he has not become mother. Rather, he has become more of himself. The more one is able to take in and play out the roles of others, the more one develops a unique self.

As another example, an actor in the theatre, trained in the psychological method of early Stanislavski, internalizes a role to the extent that he takes on speech and movements patterns, thoughts and feelings of his model. In enacting or representing his character, he does not, in fact, become the character but rather a more proficient actor who has mastered the skills of characterization necessary for further acts of role playing.

The relationship between self and role is a variable one. People often have a tendency to identify too closely with a role or separate themselves too greatly from their role model. When the distance between self and role is balanced (when, for example, the child develops a positive sense of self through his interaction with mother, without merging too much with the mother role or remaining too much in the child role), a healthy developmental relationship is evident.

Self is one's uniqueness, distinguishing a person from all other people. But this understanding is paradoxically based upon relationships with others. As the role of of the other is taken in, it is transformed according to one's unique way of forming mental images. And, as no two theatrical actors ever portray the same role in the same way, even though each speaks the same words and performs the same basic actions, the everyday actor will likewise represent his unique version of child or mother. The "scripts" for these roles might be prescribed by social convention, but the specific interpretation of the script and the enactment of the role will change according to the unique characteristics of one's self.

As the self develops further through an extended process of role taking and role playing, it will further determine the quality of subsequent role taking and role playing. The developing child who has successfully internalized the mother role will be able to establish not only an effective relationship with his mother but also a range of relationships that reflect the intimacy of the mother-child bond, i.e., relationships with siblings, friends, and spouses.

When the mother role is not fully internalized and enacted, or when the dramatic process is based on a negative mother image, then subsequent relationships reflecting the mother-child one will be impaired.

The self, then, both determines the quality of the role and is determined by the roles one takes in and plays out.

ROLE

As mediator between self and other, self and social world, role embodies qualities of thought, feeling, and behavior taken on from another and represented in a way prescribed by social convention. In many ways, a role is a fixed entity, determined by one's actions (i.e., a worker works, a mother nurses a child, a businessperson takes care of business) and one's relationship to another (i.e., the role of the child exists in relationship to parents, the role of the teacher exists in relationship to students). However, the quality of the actions and the relationships is highly variable and dependent upon inner psychological factors as well as outer social and political factors. For example, the way a mother nurses a child (or whether she chooses to nurse the child at all) will depend upon the reciprocity of feelings between mother and child, as well as the mother's relationship to her family and society who perpetuate certain conditions of, and traditions for, child care.

Furthermore, actual role relationships are often projected outward and take on the symbolic quality of transference. For example, the role of child in relationship to parent might be replayed through other relationships so that, for example, an adult retains the role of the child while interacting with a spouse, teacher, friend, or therapist.

Role Taking

The self has the capacity to take on a myriad of roles. In a discussion of the process of learning language, James Moffett argues from a role-taking perspective. For Moffett (1968), liberation is a matter of hearing out the world, of incorporating the language and speech patterns of others. As the child does this, he develops the capacity to use language in a complex and unique way. The more rich and varied the linguistic environment of the child, the more potential he has to develop unique, creative speech skills.

Role taking is a complex dramatic process of internalizing aspects of the role model, the other. It begins at the point in human development where the infant is able to recognize a separation between self and other and, in Mead's terms, to act toward himself as the other has acted toward him; that is, to see himself as an object.

Imitation

The genesis of role taking is seen in the external process of imitation. Through this process the infant mimics the movements, sounds, and language of significant others. He plays with the external actions of his mother, for example, mirroring her movements and re-creating her sounds. In Piaget's terms, he accommodates himself to the role of mother, developing the cognitive schema necessary to see himself as a separate person. Although imitation begins as a mirroring of the behavior of others, a further development occurs when the child is able to imitate himself; that is, to take on the role, for example, of child eating lunch at a time when he would not ordinarily perform that task. Through this kind of playful self-imitation, the child further develops his ability to engage in role taking and thus to develop a healthy sense of self.

An individual, then, is able to take on two kinds of roles: those of himself, which are called psychodramatic roles, and those of others, which are called projected roles.

Imitation is not, strictly speaking, an internal process of role taking. It is, rather, an external action, a playful mimicry preparing the child for a developmentally more complex relationship with a significant other.

Identification

At a deeper level of role taking, the child identifies with the mother, taking on not only her external actions and sounds but also her feelings and values. Through identification, the child sees himself as being like his mother. Identification concerns the continual search for the answer to the question: "Who am I?" At each stage of development, the individual answers the question according to the role models he identifies with. When identified positively with her mother, the girl can assert her feminine identity. But when the objects of her identification become confused, unclear, or untrustworthy, the person experiences an identity crisis, a temporary blurring of the dimensions of the self.

In resolving the identity crisis, the person must be able to again find himself in significant others. This discovery or recovery of self occurs as he is able to incorporate the world view—the values, visions, and perceptions of trusted others—into his own mind.

Identification is an internal dramatic process. The child does not enact the role of mother. Rather he forms a mental image of himself as mother and recognizes his own abilities to act like mother and to act like son in relation to mother. The two roles of child and mother are separate but interdependent.

Projection

On the other side of identification is the dramatic concept of projection. The child involved in projection does not see himself as mother but, rather, sees mother as himself. Projection is a mental process of imagining that another feels as oneself feels or, more generally, is as one is. This process defends a person against the negative feelings he has toward another by transferring them onto the other. For example, he will change the reality of "I am mad at my mother," to "My mother is mad at me."

But projection also has a positive function. One projects aspects of oneself outward in order to play and to test reality from a safe distance. Doll play, puppet play, and mask play are all means of projecting aspects of the self onto another object. All dramatic activity, including early developmental forms of dramatic play, non-Western forms of ritual drama, and acting in the theatre, is inherently projective as the self enters into the body, the mind, the spirit of another.

Transference

The dramatic world view is not a simple one in which I am I and you are you. It goes beyond Buber's model of dialogue, where one meets another in his own uniqueness. For, in the dramatic model of role taking, things are not what they appear to be. Roles and realities are not fixed. You become me and I become you through the processes of identification and projection. Not only does the individual often see himself as a representation, but he also sees others as representations. That is, through the process of transference, one views, for example, a friend as a mother or a therapist as a father. Through transference, the individual transforms an actual role of another into a symbolic one. In effect, one re-creates reality according to one's subjective world view. Neutral external objects become charged with one's past experience, as, for example, a house in a neutral setting represents the house of one's childhood. One tends to relive the past through new associations with present objects and present others. The transference experience is the déjà vu experience. It is essentially dramatic in that it is representational, a transformation of past into present, of person into persona.

Transference, like projection, has a negative and positive function in drama therapy. At its most negative, transference defends a person from seeing the conflicts embedded in a past relationship. The transference

neurosis marks a point in the psychoanalytic relationship between therapist and client where unresolved past conflicts (i.e., a client's oedipal
struggles to free himself from his parents) are re-stimulated. The conflict
between son and mother is transferred onto the analytic situation, and
the client, in casting the therapist in the mother role, acts toward the
therapist as if he were the mother.

The experience of transference is essential in drama therapy as well as
psychoanalysis, for it gives form to unresolved feelings situated in the
past and sets the stage for their representation through spontaneous
enactment. At the most positive level, transference allows the therapist to
view a dramatization of a past moment in the life of a client. And, either
through his symbolic participation in the drama or through his establishment of clear boundaries between past and present, one reality and
another, the therapist moves the client toward a recognition of both sides
of the transference, of both poles of the representation.

Transference is a universal dramatic phenomenon. Without the ability
to transfer past to present, actuality to symbol, the individual would
exist in a drab, unidimensional world where play and drama are non-
existent and all things are as they seem. Transference can be seen as an
imaginative act of transforming individuals into archetypes. For the
creative thinker, the process of seeing individuals as gods and demons,
creators and destroyers is a positive exercise of the creative imagination.
The ability to see beyond the surface of people and objects and to think
metaphorically is an essential element in the creative process.

The healthy dramatic world view is marked by a balance of transference.
That is, the individual sees another both as he is and as he appears to be.
However, when transference becomes pathological and leads to neurotic
or psychotic distortions, a form of therapy is indicated that moves toward
the establishment of reality-based boundaries between past and present,
one person and another. Although it is desirable for the normal, creative
individual to transfer archetypal images and past experiences onto relatively neutral objects, it is undesirable to encourage the same from
disturbed individuals prone to prolonged, defensive flights from reality.

Role Playing

Identification, projection, and transference, as aspects of the role-
taking process, are based in mental, internal activities. The complimentary process of role playing is an external form of enactment. The actor

projects his thoughts, feelings, and behaviors onto another, then enacts them in the guise of the other, as if he were the other. Concurrently, the actor also identifies with the other, imitating his actions, taking in desired qualities of thought, feeling, and behavior, and allowing these assimilated qualities to guide his role-playing.

The reciprocity of taking in and playing out, of assimilating and accommodating, is essential in dramatic enactment. One without the other would imply an imbalance in the relationship between self and other, actor and role.

Role playing is a form of dramatic impersonation. The root word of impersonation is person. In the dramatic model, person is equivalent to self. Persona, on the other hand, is the mask, the social archetype, the role that hides the person. Through role playing, the person identifies with the persona; the face takes on the mask; the self takes on the role. Simultaneously, the person projects qualities of himself onto the persona. Then, in role, the actor presents his persona in physical action. Thus, role playing, though primarily an external process of enactment, implies a relationship between person and persona and between identification and projection. When any part of the two relationships is inhibited, an imbalance will occur which will lead to an incomplete representation.

REPRESENTATION

In normal human development, the dramatic concepts of self and other, self and role, identification and projection strive toward balance. There is a simultaneous flow of energy from world to mind and from mind to world. That is, as the world is represented in mental images, incorporated through role-taking, so it is represented in physical actions through role playing. Representation describes the dramatic process as twofold: as an internal process of transforming the world into mental images, and as an external process of enactment.

Given the transformational quality of dramatic representation, dependent so much upon the dialetics of self and other, person and persona, it is natural to assume that there will be many moments of imbalance. In normal functioning, these moments will be restored by the individual through a natural process of investing a greater or lesser degree of energy toward self or other, toward person or persona.

However, when the moments of imbalance become severe by nature of their duration or intensity, then intervention is necessary. During moments of protracted imbalance, the ability to play a single role or a range of roles completely is disrupted. In order to work toward a restoration of balance and thus to re-establish an individual's ability to competently mediate between self and world through the taking on and playing out of appropriate roles, the drama therapist needs to understand the crucial concept of distancing.

DISTANCING

Distancing is a key concept of drama therapy theory. Brecht's notion of distancing in the epic theatre focuses on overdistancing, a separation of thought from feeling, actor from role, viewer from expected response. There was to be no catharsis in Brecht's theatre, no re-stimulation and purgation of past emotional experience, and no restoration of equilibrium and acceptance of the status quo. For Brecht, the actor existed to stimulate thought in the viewer through portraying the familiar images of exploitation and greed as strange. To distance the familiar images, Brecht often set his plays in exotic locales.

India in *A Man's A Man*, China in *The Good Person of Setzuan*, and Chicago in *The Resistable Rise of Arturo Ui*, all resembled the streets of · Berlin, Frankfurt, and Munich. The familiar actions of the military, the mob, the dictator, and the privileged were caricatured and stylized to distance the viewer from an emotional identification and intellectual deadening. Brecht's aim was a liberation of vision through an emotional overdistancing.

For the purposes of drama therapy, Brecht's theory of distancing is incomplete, as healthy functioning requires a balance of feeling and thought. A fuller understanding of distancing is that of an interaction or intrapsychic phenomenon characterized by a range of closeness and separation. The range includes the overdistance of the Brechtian actor as well as the underdistance of the method actor who alters his physical and emotional reality to enter into the role of another. In everyday life, an overdistanced interaction might be characterized by two individuals who maintain a physical separation while talking, who are analytical and highly rational in their conversation, and who are careful neither to touch upon emotional matters nor to identify with one another. The overdistanced person is one who needs to establish rigid boundaries between himself and another. He will avoid identifications and all other psychic processes that intrude upon his separateness. However, in attempting to re-create the world in his own image, he will project his thoughts and feelings onto others, thus seeing the others as reflections of himself.

An underdistanced interaction would be the opposite, characterized by a physical as well as emotional closeness, a lack of discernible boundaries, a high degree of empathy, and a merging of selves. The underdistanced person thus identifies with another quite readily and sees himself reflected often in the behavior of others. In extreme situations, his propensity for identification can lead to a loss of boundaries between self and other.

On the intrapsychic level, the overdistanced person can be viewed as generally rigid, overcontrolled, disconnected, alienated. His role repertory is quite limited and he plays a single role with little flexibility. His behavior is controlled by a rigid persona that separates him not only from the outside world but also from himself.

The underdistanced person, on the other hand, can be seen generally as vulnerable, needy, with little sense of emotional control. His role repertory is too expansive and he plays a single role with few discernible limitations. Because he merges himself with so many people, his persona is infinitely malleable. Like the protagonist in Woody Allen's film, *Zelig*, he is an extended persona in search of a person.

At the center of the distancing paradigm is a balance between the two extremes of overdistance and underdistance. At this point, the individual is able to think and to feel, and to find a comfortable balance of physical, emotional, and intellectual distance. At this point of balance, there are clear boundaries between self and other, person and persona, one role and another role. The boundaries, however, are flexible, changing as the self or as the interaction changes.

To further understand balance of distance as it relates to drama therapy, let us look at the perspective developed by the social-psychologist, Thomas Scheff. Scheff's understanding of distancing is based both in the psychoanalytical and theatrical models. He reconceives the notion of catharsis as a state of being that occurs when the individual achieves a balance of distance.

For Scheff, the one extreme of overdistance is a state of repression. The overdistanced individual has blocked his ability to experience painful emotion. His primary mode of experiencing is a cognitive one. He remembers the past but detatches himself from present feelings associated with past experiences.

Scheff characterizes the other extreme, that of underdistance, as a return of repressed emotion. The underdistanced individual is overwhelmed by painful emotion and thus experiences a high degree of anxiety. His primary mode of experiencing is an affective one, and he relives the past rather than merely remembering it.

Affective Memory

The reliving of the past has become a hallmark of many actors trained in the technique of affective memory. In order to be able to live the moment on stage feelingly, to reenact an experience as if it were occurring for the first time, the actor must make present actual feelings associated with a past event, i.e., the death of a loved one or the birth of a child. In theory, the re-enactment of the emotion should be balanced between the reality of the actor's actual life and the fiction of the character's dramatized life. In the practice of affective memory, however, many actors do not achieve this balance and instead reach an underdistanced emotional level, often becoming overwhelmed by the re-enactment of negative feelings.

Aesthetic Distance

When the individual is at a point midway between the two extremes of overdistance and underdistance, he is at aesthetic distance, where catharsis can occur. At aesthetic distance, the individual achieves a balanced relationship to the past; that is, he both remembers and relives past experiences. In reaching this state of balance, he is able to experience a confluence of thought and feeling, to "see feelingly," like the blinded Gloucester in *King Lear.* Aesthetic distance is a point of liberation that responds to the question: If the reason one represses emotion is that it is too painful to look at, then how can one ever be able to bring that painful moment to consciousness? The answer is that at aesthetic distance one is able to simultaneously play the role of the actor, who relives the past, and the observer, who remembers the past. In other words, at aesthetic distance one retains a piece of the overdistanced, cognitive observer and a piece of the underdistanced, affective actor. When the two parts occur simultaneously, a psychic tension arises which is released through catharsis in laughing, crying, yawning, shaking, or blushing.

Catharsis

Catharsis in drama therapy does not need to be a large outburst of feeling, a gushing forth of tears or a paroxysm of laughter. It is often a modest reaction, a gentle moment of recognition. Catharsis implies the ability to recognize contradictions, to see how conflicting aspects of one's psychic life or social life, of one's thinking, speaking, or feeling can exist simultaneously. This occurs often in everyday life. As an example, one may look in the mirror and see an image of one's parent. The perception of me as mother might well cause some tension. The simultaneous recognition of the me that is like my mother and the me that is myself might lead to catharsis—a release of the tension through a shrug of the shoulders, a yawn, a smile. Catharsis, then, can be seen as the recognition of a psychological paradox.

Another example, reported in a drama therapy session, is of a man who, as a child, was undergoing a tonsillectomy. Fearful of the doctor and the ether used as an anesthetic, he was able to discharge his anxiety through a dream that occurred during the operation. He recalled that in the dream his mouth and throat became a "barrel of fun," a large, spinning barrel in a carnival funhouse. He was being chased by frightening puppet figures through the spinning barrel. Later, he realized that the puppets were characters he had seen on television. Although they were "bad guys," they became manageable representations of the doctor, as they were familiar and fictional. The image of the throat as the barrel of fun again distanced his fear of being violated by the doctor. After the operation, the man recalled feeling a sense of relief, a resolution of his fear of the doctor and of the operation.

Dreams, fantasies, and identifications with characters in plays, films, and literature often provide a natural means of balancing distance and discharging painful emotions. Everyday life presents endless moments of anxiety and potential conflict that lead to psychic imbalance. If a person's response to anxiety is to overdistance, then he will repress those emotions associated with a painful stimulus. If a person's response is to underdistance, then he might become overwhelmed by the anxiety. At aesthetic distance, he can experience the anxiety without becoming overwhelmed by it. He can "feel intelligently" (Witkin, 1974, see Chapter Twelve) and "see feelingly" and thus release the tension safely through catharsis.

Scheff (1981) has constructed a table, based on Harvey Jackins's theory of re-evaluation (1965), which describes the emotional reactions during the three states of underdistance, overdistance, and aesthetic distance for each of four primary emotions—grief, fear, embarrassment, and anger (See Table 1).

Table 1
Emotional States and Distance

Type of Distress	Underdistanced	Esthetic Distance	Overdistanced
Grief	Appears and feels sad with or without tears. Headaches, nasal congestion, swelling of eyes. Feelings of hopelessness	Sobbing with tears	Emotionlessness and/or distraction in situation of *loss*
Fear	Facial pallor, coldness in hands and feet, rapid and shallow breathing. Rapid heartbeat. Feelings of fright and immobility	Shaking with cold sweat	Emotionlessness and/or distraction in situation of *danger*
Embarrassment	Blushing, immobilization, lowering or covering of eyes and face	Spontaneous laughter	Emotionlessness and/or distraction in situation of *losing face*
Anger	Violence of movement or speech, repetitiveness	Hot sweat or spontaneous laughter	Emotionlessness and/or distraction in situation of *frustration*

The moment of catharsis is also a creative moment, rather like the discovery of a pun. Many take great delight in playing with language, in punning, because the mind and feelings serve one another reciprocally as a tension is created between two diverse meanings of the same word. That tension is resolved through laughter or a less overt expression of recognition. When Bottom in Shakespeare's *A Midsummer Night's Dream* is transformed into an ass, the audience is treated to a delightful variety of visual and linguistic puns. Shakespeare presents us with the image of the ass who is a fool, who looks like an ass (donkey), and whose name, Bottom, represents the part of the anatomy from whence the punning arises. The delights are, however, juxtaposed with potentially threatening images, in that Bottom's head, his top, becomes a "bottom" (an ass), and the divine Titania copulates with the beast (Bottom).

In coupling witty intelligence with an appeal to more instinctual, forbidden feelings, Shakespeare sets up a tension which can be released through catharsis on the part of the viewer. The viewer may laugh, smile, blush at Bottom's dilemma. In theory, however, the catharsis can occur only if the viewer has achieved aesthetic distance. In doing so, he would have to recognize something of his own repressed experience of being an ass or being seduced or thinking of himself in terms of anal imagery. But in allowing these feelings to reach consciousness, he would simultaneously distance himself from them, diffusing their overwhelming potential. The recognition that the theatre is a fiction and that Bottom is a character separate from himself provides a safe margin of distance for the viewer.

The concepts of distancing and catharsis become crucial in drama therapy when the natural means of distancing in everyday life break down. The client will often manifest his dysfunction or disability through an imbalance in his behavior, feeling, or thought. By improvisational means, the drama therapist will first help him represent that imbalance, then move toward establishing a balance of distance which takes a visible form in role playing and catharsis.

In general, the more the drama therapist chooses theatrically stylized devices for treatment (i.e., masks, puppets, and epic theatre techniques), the more he overdistances the client. In choosing more realistic devices, such as psychodrama and documentary techniques, the therapist will create less distance. This formula does not, of course, apply to all cases. For some, the mask is underdistancing and the enactment of the role of self is overdistancing. In either case, however, the therapeutic goals are the same: to move toward balance, toward aesthetic distance and the ensuing catharsis, and to strengthen one's ability to use role as mediator between self and social world.

Scheff mentions four choices that the therapist can make in balancing distance: the use of a present time frame vs. a past time frame; fictional events vs. reality-based events; a rapid reviewing of past events vs. a detailed recollection of the past; and the use of positive emotions vs. negative ones. A fifth item not mentioned by Scheff is the use of the psychodramatic role of self vs. the projected role of other.

In overdistancing, the therapist would focus upon a present time frame, fictional events, rapid review, positive emotions, and projected role playing. These choices would be especially appropriate for a beginning drama therapy group in which the members have yet to warm up to each other and an atmosphere of trust has yet to evolve. These choices would also be most appropriate for those clients who present themselves as underdistanced, i.e., hyperactive emotionally disturbed individuals. Although Scheff designates present time as overdistancing, this is often not the case in drama therapy groups. As we shall see later, one means of providing clients with greater distance is to help them focus upon the past, the "once upon a time" frame of the fairy tale. For many, current events are still too raw and threatening.

For those who present themselves as overdistanced (i.e., alienated, withdrawn individuals), an attention to a past time frame, reality-based events, detailed recollection of the past, negative emotions, and psychodramatic role playing might be indicated. However, even with an overdistanced population, one would not necessarily begin therapy with these choices, that is, by immediately focusing upon in-depth, negative, reality-based personal experiences. All groups need a period of settling-in and warming-up to develop trust and comfort. Further, many overdistanced clients will be encouraged to work through drama techniques based in a present time frame to help them get closer to a current feeling state.

Drama therapy groups will most certainly be heterogeneous as to overdistanced and underdistanced behaviors. Too, those who favor one mode will at times present themselves in another mode. The drama therapist, then, needs to develop flexibility in choosing techniques of distancing based upon three factors: the present needs of a client; the quality of distance inherent in the technique, whether a realistic psychodramatic technique or a more expressionistic projective one; and his therapeutic aims.

Generally speaking, diagnostic labels such as alienated, withdrawn, and autistic imply overdistanced behavior. Such labels as hyperactive and manic imply underdistanced behavior. The skilled drama therapist, though aware of the labels, must also be able to respond to the dramatic moments of role reversal, when the hyperactive assume controlled roles and the withdrawn assume active roles. In drama therapy, as in all forms of psychotherapy, labels often become ineffectual as signposts for treatment. In the role of mediator of distancing, the drama therapist looks for ways to lead the client through the spectrum of distancing by means of trying on new roles, extending old ones, and arriving at a point of balance, of liberation from impulsive acting out and compulsive withholding.

SPONTANEITY

Aesthetic distance, the point of liberation, marks the moment when the client is at his most spontaneous. It is the creative moment, the moment of infinite possibilities, the moment of play, the moment when the unconscious is accessible and ready to be symbolized through dramatic action.

Spontaneity is a midpoint between compulsive, inhibited styles of acting and impulsive, overinvolved styles. The compulsive, inhibited person is overdistanced and enacts a new task in rigid, prescribed ways. When given an improvised role to enact, he demonstrates a minimum of activity, performing his actions in repeated, conventional ways, separating self from role as much as possible. The impulsive, overinvolved person is underdistanced and enacts an improvised role with a maximum of activity and feeling, attempting to merge self with role. His behavior is often provocative due to its excessive quality.

The spontaneous person enacts an improvised role in such a way that self and role are distinct yet merged. That is, he is aware of playing a fictional role; yet, he enacts it with conviction and commitment. In everyday life, the child playing spontaneously with dolls is aware that the dolls are not people, yet interacts with them as if they were people.

Spontaneity, like catharsis, is based in the central paradox of dramatic experiencing. Two realities exist side by side: that of the real world and that of the dramatized/play world. When in the spontaneous state, the individual simultaneously exists in both realities. There is also an implication of existing simultaneously in two time frames: the past and the present. Although acting spontaneously means fully living in the present, fully focusing upon and experiencing the moment as it occurs, the spontaneous person is also basing his actions upon past experience.

The actor in theatre has rehearsed his lines and blocking. The Olympic gymnast has meticulously rehearsed his routines. The adolescent about to go out on an important date has rehearsed his behaviors and "social script." Yet, for the moment of performance to be spontaneous and thus excellent, the individual must behave as if he were performing his actions for the first time. He must act in a way consistent with his training, but he must also present a new, transformed image of himself.

Living in the spontaneous moment is risky, because one fears the unknown. It is safer to appear before an audience with a prepared speech than to improvise "off the top of one's head," risking imprecision or humiliation. It is safer to know what you want to say to a significant other than to meet him with no particular agenda. But the risks are tempered by the gain in self-esteem. By trusting what one does know and then letting that knowledge go, one learns to value a deeper sense of one's wisdom.

The British educational drama specialist, Brian Way (1967), emphasizes the importance of beginning drama at the point where the student is presently functioning, developmentally and pedagogically. Likewise, if the client in drama therapy is allowed to begin where he needs to begin, and if he is encouraged to trust that he has an intact past history that mitigates against beginning each task anew, then he is more likely to take the risk of letting go of the old and entering into the new, the unknown quality of the here and now.

THE UNCONSCIOUS

The drama therapist helps the client reach spontaneity through balancing the distance between person and persona, self and other. In the moment of spontaneity, at aesthetic distance, the unconscious is accessible. In this balanced state, the client is able to give form to repressed feelings without being overwhelmed by them. The unconscious is a vast storehouse of psychic phenomena—wishes, fantasies, complexes, and archetypes—not directly available to human awareness but capable of being released in the form of images and symbols. Through movement, sound, and/or language, the client gives shape to his unconscious imagery.

In drama therapy, both the Freudian and the Jungian notions of the unconscious are useful. Freud's view of the unconscious as a reservoir of infantile psychosexual feelings symbolized through language and behavior is useful in analyzing the dramatizations of clients in terms of their personal histories. In drama therapy, imagery associated with the Oedipus complex is especially pervasive. In working toward the successful resolution of that crucial dilemma, the drama therapist often turns to story material. In working with fairy tales, for example, he has accessible models of happy resolutions to fearful attachments children make with devouring witches, predatory wolves, evil stepmothers, and other embodiments of childhood fears regarding parental figures. Adapting the Freudian-based work of Bruno Bettleheim (1976) with fairy tales, the drama therapist can use the stories as means of exploring a child's desire and guilt and resulting fears of abandonment by and separation from his parents. Through the child's re-creation of the stories in terms of his own imagery, the therapist can help him discover means of mastering his personal fears.

From the Jungian perspective of the collective unconscious, the therapist would focus upon archetypal, universal images as well as personal ones. If the image of the devouring witch or wolf appears in a dream or an improvisation, it might not only be viewed as a fear of being consumed by one's biological parents but also related to universal myths and cross-cultural experiences. The unconscious from Jung's point of view is not necessarily a source of dark, disguised fears and desires but rather a morally neutral area that embodies the mythic substance of the human race.

In adapting Jung's perspective, the drama therapist might also work with literature but for an extended purpose: to look not only at the dark, personal implications of an image but also at the larger significance of, for example, the mother image or father image as that which procreates and punishes, which nurtures and stifles. Thus, the drama therapist would aim toward helping his client see that his unconscious imagery is not neurotic or perverse but, rather, connected to the normal interplay of opposites, of fantasy and reality, of love and hate—dialectical concepts that underlie a universal conception of human nature.

Because drama therapy, like other creative arts therapies, is so dependent upon symbolic processes (that is, the symbolic expression of feelings through an aesthetic form), the unconscious plays a key role in the therapeutic process. A major issue for the drama therapist, then, is how to help the client arrive at a spontaneous state and express his unconscious feelings through appropriate imagery. As we have seen above, this can be realized through moving the client toward aesthetic distance, a balance between the two realities of the actual and the fictional, the dramatic.

The notion of distancing and balance in the drama therapy model is similar to notions of balance in most of the theoretical models mentioned above. For many psychological theorists, healthy functioning is based upon certain psychic balances. In psychoanalysis, the healthy individual manifests a balance among id, ego, and superego, with the ego mediating between the id and the demands of the outside world. In Mead's theory of the healthy self, the *I* and *me* are in harmony, balancing the personal, impulsive needs with the demands of the social world. In Piaget's cognitive system, healthy functioning is determined by a balance of assimilation—a process of taking-in a piece of the world through play—and accommodation, a process of enactment through imitation.

When an imbalance occurs that cannot be resolved through everyday means and that impedes ordinary functioning, then a form of therapy is needed to restore psychic balance. Like many of the significant psychotherapeutic models, drama therapy proceeds to restore balance in the everyday context of one's life by working through the imaginary, symbolic level of reality. In drama therapy, balance is restored to the self by means of working through the role.

PART III
THE TECHNIQUES OF
DRAMA THERAPY

Chapter Five

STRUCTURING A SESSION

It is difficult to prescribe a single set of rules for structuring a drama therapy session, given a diversity of populations, time factors, institutional practices, and therapeutic goals. A drama therapy group for hyperactive children in a special school setting might meet for twenty-minute weekly sessions for the duration of a school year. With a group of clients in a short-term treatment program at a psychiatric hospital, a drama therapist might lead two fifty-minute groups for the duration of their stay. On the other hand, a drama therapy group in a nursing home or long-term facility might be ongoing, meeting once or twice a week for an indefinite number of weeks and/or months. As more drama therapists enter private practice, they establish their own parameters of treatment, whether short-term, in dealing with a particular crisis situation, or long-term, in exploring a deep-seated issue affecting many aspects of the client's existence.

In planning a session, then, the drama therapist needs to consider several factors. First, he needs to understand the nature of the client population. Generally speaking, those populations that most lack inner controls and balance require the most structure on the part of the therapist. Thus, the extreme poles of overdistance (i.e., the severely depressed) and underdistance (i.e., the hyperactive) call for a more structured approach in order to help the client arrive at a state of balance. As an individual approaches aesthetic distance, the structure can be freer, allowing the client to choose among techniques and forms, as needed.

Second, the drama therapist needs to consider his own natural style of leadership. Some will naturally follow the non-directive approach of Carl Rogers and/or the approach of many play therapists, making few interventions during a session. Others will take on the more active model of the theatre or psychodrama director, setting up scenes carefully and purposefully, helping clients enter into their roles, and assuming a role themselves, in order to direct the action from within the drama. The

111

drama therapist's leadership style should be flexible, especially in work-ing with a diversity of populations whose needs conflict with his accus-tomed style.

A third factor the drama therapist should consider in structuring a session concerns institutional practices. The major practical question faced by any beginning drama therapist is how much time, space, and support his employer will provide. A newly trained drama therapist might begin a job eager to do in-depth therapy but discover that the drama group is scheduled for twenty minutes a week with a different client population at each session, or that he is required to direct a production of *Oklahoma* within three weeks time, including the teaching of the musical and dance parts. Institutional demands can weigh heavily upon many newly employed drama therapists. Before they can effect any change, drama therapists need to familiarize themselves with the given institutional practices. Once settled in and knowledgeable, the drama therapist can work toward effecting change not only in the lives of his clients but also in the life of the institution.

In structuring a session, the drama therapist also needs to know the viability of his techniques in the context of work with a particular population in a particular setting. One would not generally attempt to direct a production of a scripted play with a chronic population who cannot remember lines and blocking due to medication or level of cognitive functioning. Further, one would not use a games or play approach with those elders, for example, who are fearful of being treated as children.

Finally, in structuring a session, the drama therapist should consider his therapeutic goals, again in the context of a particular population and place. Although a single therapeutic goal—the development of an ability to play a diversity of roles and/or a single role more spontaneously—can apply generally to all populations, the drama therapist needs to consider specific goals determined by the realities of the group and the institution. For example, one cannot aim toward in-depth therapy with a group of short-term patients who might only attend one or two forty-five-minute sessions. Likewise, if one leads an ongoing group that meets twice a week for a year within a setting that works toward in-depth psychotherapeutic treatment, one would want to choose techniques that transcend simple creative drama exercises.

It is debatable whether any given technique is inherently superficial or in-depth. The theatre games approach, developed by Viola Spolin and others, can remain at a superficial level as practiced by some but achieve a rather profound level of exploration in the hands of others.

Once the drama therapist has considered the factors of the client population, his own particular therapeutic style, the demands of the therapeutic setting, the viability of his techniques, and the therapeutic goals, he is ready to structure his session. Although there will be a diversity of approaches, most sessions adhere to a three-part structure that includes a warm-up, action, and closure.

WARM-UP

The warm-up in drama therapy can be compared to the warm-up that a performer or an athlete goes through in preparation for a performance: the dancer carefully stretches his muscles; the singer carefully exercises his voice; and the actor sometimes engages in meditation, as well as vocal and muscular warm-ups.

Warm-up is preparation. Following the paradigm of distancing, it is not only a gearing-up from a more distanced to a less distanced state; it can also be a calming down from a state of excitability. At the beginning of any therapy group, some clients are likely to be anxious. For those who express their anxiety by withdrawing, the warm-up might function to decrease the distance and thus bring them closer to the creative state of balance. For those who express their anxiety through manic behavior, the warm-up might serve as a means of increasing the distance and providing the emotional safety in which to work.

In drama therapy, as in the performing arts in general, the warm-up is a means of engaging the imagination. This notion is comparable to several theories that attempt to explain the creative process. For example, in his "Preface to the Lyrical Ballads," William Wordsworth conceived the origin of creating poetry as "emotion recollected in tranquility." For Wordsworth, the poet contemplates the past until a present emotion is produced. That emotion is based in but is not the same as the past experience. The present transformed emotion becomes the raw material of poetry. Wordsworth's theory is one of warming up the emotions. Through recollecting the past in a tranquil, meditative setting, the poet achieves a creative state and is ready to discover an appropriate form in which to express his feeling.

Stanislavski, as we have seen, had a similar theory of the creative process. Like Wordsworth's notion of poesis, Stanislavski's notion of acting through emotion memory is a process for activating the feelings and the imagination. It can be seen as an essential factor in both a creative process of making art and of psychological healing.

The warm-up can take many forms and apply to several parts of an individual's functioning. Often, the warm-up will be a physical one, aimed toward loosening up the muscles and generally reducing the tension level in the body. The sources of physical warm-up are to be found in dance, yoga, creative drama, and acting exercises. Many drama therapists will include deep breathing and relaxation exercises not only to warm up the body but also to bring the mind to a creative state. Specific warm-up exercises can be found in the writings of Stanislavski (1949) in actor training, Viola Spolin (1963) in theatre games, and Brian Way (1967) in educational drama, among others. They all stress the particular importance of relaxation of muscles, concentration of attention, and activation of observation skills through sensory awareness.

Sometimes the warm-up will be based in mental imagery rather than movement. The drama therapist might begin a session by asking the clients to close their eyes and to imagine a particular scene, such as the house in which they grew up. Through a series of projections in imagery, the therapist warms up the client's imagination. Imagery can be generated by verbal directions from the therapist or through sensory means. An example of the latter is the use of sounds created by the therapist to generate imagery within the client.

In many instances, the warm-up will be verbal. Such is often the case in psychodrama sessions in which each member of the group verbalizes a feeling or narrates a recent event from his life.

A good warm-up exercise can apply, with appropriate modifications, to almost all populations. As an example, let us look at a basic physical exercise: the isolation of body parts. Clients are instructed to move different parts of the body, one at a time, in order to experience the articulation and integration among the fingers, hands, arms, shoulders, etc. Given an able-bodied, non-delusional population, this exercise should cause no particular problem. But with severely disturbed individuals whose body images are confused, such an exercise would be difficult. The therapist, then, might focus upon a limited section of the body (i.e., the fingers, hands, and wrists), helping the individual succeed at that level. For a population of severely orthopedically disabled individuals, incapable of articulating body parts, the exercise would also be problematic. However, the therapist might instruct them to work through mental imagery, visualizing the body parts and moving them in imagination.

The viable warm-up, then, should be challenging but not too anxiety-arousing. It should provide a balance between overdistance and under-distance so that the withdrawn person has a chance to warm up to the activity at his own pace and the manic person has a chance to let go of some of his impulsive tendencies and "cool down" before entering the action part of the dramatization. The warm-up activity often contains the germ of the idea to be enacted in the action part. Further, it should engage as many aspects of the client's functioning as possible—the body, imagination, feelings, senses, thoughts, intuition.

The warm-up is a prelude to action, a means of preparing the client to engage in a creative process of self-exploration. It applies to the therapist as well as the client. The degree of distance experienced by the therapist will most certainly affect the group atmosphere. The therapist who is balanced and who himself has reached a creative state will be most prepared to satisfy some of his own creative needs as he helps others through therapeutic dramatization.

ACTION

The action part of the drama therapy session refers to the actual dramatization that will occur once the clients are warmed up to their feelings. In some ways, the distinction between warm-up and action is artificial as one stage often flows directly into the next. Let us look, however, at several differences.

For one, the action concerns a deeper level of enactment than that which occurs in the warm-up. The action often focuses upon a single client (referred to in psychodrama as the protagonist) and involves the group as auxiliaries in helping him explore his issue. Further, the action provides a dramatic form through which the protagonist can move, speak, think, and feel as he enacts his dilemma. That form can be either psychodramatic or projective.

In terms of the structure of dramatic literature, the warm-up is the exposition, the details of a play that inform the audience as to time, place, and characters; and the action is the dramatic unraveling of the intricacies of the protagonist's dilemma, the progression of events that often leads to catharsis and recognition.

As in a theatrical play, the action stage in drama therapy builds through a series of tensions and rhythms. The therapeutic session is unlike the play, however, in that the action is rarely linear and preconceived but, rather, improvisational and spontaneous. This flow is determined by both the protagonist, who is often the leader of his own dramatization, and the therapist, who often assumes a follower role, helping the protagonist to stay within the boundaries of his dramatic form. The therapist will often determine the specific dramatic form for enactment (i.e., that of storytelling), although he will encourage the client to tell the story in his own particular way.

Much of drama is based upon conflict; that is, character A, the protagonist, wants something, and character, or circumstance B, stands in his way. Classical drama often concerns not only an external conflict between opposing forces but also an internal tension between different parts of the protagonist. The most complex of classical dramatic protagonists (i.e., Oedipus, Antigone, Hamlet, Lear) are characters at war with themselves. Both models of classical drama (that of external conflict and that of internal tension) serve as substance for dramatic enactment in a therapy situation.

During the action stage, the client is given or chooses a form in which to express both his interpersonal conflict and his intrapsychic tension. Others in the group can represent opposing sides of the conflicts or tensions. Like a playwright, the client can fashion his own script. The therapist aids the client by assuming a director's role and guiding the dramatization in ways that best represent the client's conflict and tension.

The theatrical training of the drama therapist comes most into play during the action stage. For the therapist, the action presents a problem that is at once psychotherapeutic and theatrical. The therapist needs to ask himself not only "What form will best contain the client's outer conflicts and inner tensions?" but also "What form will best provoke the intuitive, imaginative, spontaneous parts of the client to enable him, like the protagonist in a play, to take a dark, risky voyage toward self-discovery?"

Many drama therapists, directing the action stage, work toward a moment of catharsis. When it does occur, catharsis is not confined to the action part of the drama but can also take place during the warm-up or closure. In its original Aristotelian conception, catharsis was a property of the audience rather than the actor. In a drama therapy situation, catharsis is germane to both the client, who releases emotion when properly distanced in relation to his role, and to those group members who identify with the experience of the client.

In classical tragedy, the audience expected at least one major dramatic moment of emotional power. And the playwrights, from Sophocles to Shakespeare to Arthur Miller, delivered these moments without fail. Many tears were shed as Oedipus appeared before all Thebes, eyeless; as Lear raged on the moor and gently examined his dead daughter, Cordelia, for a sign of life; as Willy Loman, recognizing the desperation of loving his son, drove into the night to his death. In drama therapy, the moments of catharsis and recognition are no less powerful, but they are not necessarily large tearful moments. A father's recognition of his love for his child might occur in the process of an improvisation enacted around the story line of *King Lear* or *Death of a Salesman*. Or, as he is playing with masks that represent his children, he might become aware of his inability to validate the life chosen by his son or daughter, a life that has become very painful due to his disapproval. These moments of recognition, if properly balanced, might indeed be tearful. But they do not evoke the kind of despair that drives Willy Loman to suicide. They are moments of insight, of rearranging an old configuration of images so that new visions are accessible.

The moments of catharsis and recognition, when they occur, are often part of the action stage. They may occur after an extended period of time working through a recurring theme in a person's life or within the time frame of a single session as a significant issue is explored dramatically. Following catharsis, the therapist generally moves into the third stage of the drama therapy session, which is that of closure. Even when there is no catharsis evident during the action stage, the therapist will move toward closure at a point near the end of a session or when the clients have concluded a particular dramatization.

CLOSURE

For many, closure is the most difficult part of the drama therapy session. A popular myth about drama therapy or psychodrama is that the powerful therapist is skilled at opening clients up and causing them to bare their souls but has neither the inclination nor the skill to safely close the session. When the session is over, the myth goes, the therapist walks away leaving potential Willy Lomans and Hamlets at the edge of their graves. The myth is not a spurious one. A potential client or student of drama therapy knows what happened to Willy Loman when he saw the truth. He knows, too, of the power and at times grandiose personalities of theatre directors and therapists who have espoused the cathartic, primal force of drama.

But within the myth of the destructive healer, the demonic guide, is a lesson for present and future drama therapists. That lesson is: beware the abuse of your power. A concomitant one is: take a hard look at the implications of your techniques or, like Pandora, you might dislodge more sorrow than a client can handle.

In the myth of Pandora, the one blessing that emerges after all the ills have been unleashed on the world is hope. If during the action an inordinate degree of sorrow and despair has been unleashed, the drama therapist will use the closure not only as a period of reflection, pointing to what has just happened, but also as a period of hope, pointing to the work yet to be done, the journey toward healthy functioning.

Closure, unlike the conclusion to a classical drama, is not necessarily about the resolution of a client's problem. It is, rather, a calming down, a transitional point between the action and the moment that the client will leave the session and re-enter the everyday world. It is a time for allowing the client to let go of the role he had assumed in the action, to drop the dramatized mask, and to take on a more reflective or proactive persona. During closure, the client is "off stage." But he is still in role—that of the off-stage actor who has just finished his performance and needs to form an opinion about it. The mark of the good therapeutic performance is the degree to which the client has been able to act spontaneously and to work toward a balance of distancing between everyday role and fictional role. During closure, the client looks at his resistance to reaching spontaneity and balance. But he also looks at the successful moments of spontaneity and balance, drawing inferences and insight from them.

Closure is not only purely cognitive and verbal. With a group of verbal, analytical clients, a discussion and highly verbal reflection might be most desirable. But with a less verbal and analytical group, or with a group that tends to use language primarily as a defense, closure might take a different form. For example, the client may be asked to find an image expressing his present feelings through movement or visualization. Many therapists close a drama therapy session with a group ritual experience, in which all form a circle and offer both a present feeling through words and/or movement and a hope for the future.

Closure is important not only for the individual client but also for the group. Individuals who have made strong identifications with or projections upon the client might well need to close their similar issues. Further, if a particular session threatens the integrity of the group, then the closure should move toward a reassurance to all that the group will remain intact and continue to provide a safe environment within which each individual can explore his issues.

As the individual and the group need a sense of closure, so does the therapist. He, too, needs to feel a sense of balance, an ability to re-enter the everyday world of his life without becoming preoccupied with what he did or did not do to advance the life of the group. In order to find his own sense of balance, he might participate in the final group ritual, sharing with the others his present feelings and hopes for the future. Or he might play a more summarizing or analytical role, when appropriate, offering some reflections upon the action and some prescriptive thoughts concerning alternative means of moving toward spontaneity and balance.

Closure, then, serves three functions corresponding to past, present, and future. As pointing to the past, it is a moment of reviewing or reflecting upon what has just occurred in a session. Further, it functions to ground the client in the "here and now" of the present, affirming his present feelings and allowing him to assert a sense of self.

Finally, closure points to the future, the moment when the client will leave the session and enter his everyday environment. In expressing a fear or hope during closure, the client and the therapist, alike, prepare to make the sometimes difficult transition from the charged, focused reality of the therapy session to the more diffuse reality of the everyday.

One danger of closure is succumbing to the pressure of client and therapist, alike, for closure to be resolution, completion, a closing up. Some clients will need to feel that they have solved all their problems in one or two sessions. Some therapists will need to feel that they can solve deep-seated problems in several sessions and thus will work toward resolution and completion. But like the flawed playwright who exposes layer upon layer of conflict among members of a family, then, unsure of how to resolve his characters' dilemmas, simply imposes an arbitrary, inauthentic conclusion; the drama therapist seeking an easy "happy ending" will likewise prove ineffective.

The problem of closure is similar for the drama therapist and the playwright of psychological family drama: given the depths of feeling that have been exposed in the drama, how can one conclude a play/session without demeaning the characters through imposing an inauthentic resolution? The answer lies in a paradox. In many ways, closure is an opening up, another part of the journey toward authentic existence that points toward the future, incorporates the past, and validates the present level of feeling. Closure is about affirming the subjective truth of each individual and the more objective existence of the group. When one makes the transition from therapy group to family group, from institutional life to everyday life, one needs to be opened up rather than closed down. Ideally, the opening will be a balanced one, neither too withdrawn and cautious nor too frantic and eager.

Chapter Six

PSYCHODRAMATIC TECHNIQUES

THE WARM-UP

The structure of warm-up, action, and closure has marked the practice of psychodrama since its inception in the early 1900s. As psychodrama primarily involves a protagonist playing the role of himself in relation to significant others in his life, the warm-up experience will prepare him to engage a part of himself that needs further exploration.

Warm-up techniques in psychodrama and drama therapy are often identical, both drawing from verbal, movement, and imagery sources. A specific aim of the psychodramatic warm-up, however, is to trigger a response in an individual to a particular exercise. When he exhibits a certain degree of feeling, he is ready to assume the protagonist role and move into the action phase of the drama.

Psychodramatic warm-ups can be purely verbal as each member of the group talks about the experiences of his week or about his present level of feeling. A more projective verbal warm-up is one in which individual A addresses the group in the role of the person sitting beside him, individual B. Following his enactment, B assumes the role of A and also addresses the group. This simple role reversal often is provocative as one becomes aware of his view of another and another's view of him.

A less distanced verbal warm-up is called the "behind-the-back" technique. In this exercise, one individual is asked to remove himself from the group by turning his back on the others. The group is instructed to talk about him as if he were physically absent. This exercise provides feedback to an individual as to his status and stature within the group. It further allows group members to freely express their feelings toward the individual. The behind-the-back technique could easily lead to the central action in a psychodramatic session as the absent member in the role of protagonist explores his relationship to the therapy group or other significant group.

A less threatening warm-up involves focusing upon one aspect of an individual, often an external characteristic such as a piece of clothing. An example is an exercise which begins as the group members sit in a circle and display their shoes. All focus their attention upon the shoes, and, one at a time, each person speaks of the shoes from a distanced, third-person perspective, beginning with: "These shoes are...." The individual is instructed to speak of externals—texture, color, shape, etc. He is to end by describing his own shoes.

As a second part of the exercise, each participant adds associations and projects feelings onto each pair of shoes. Finally, each group member is asked to think of a person represented by each pair of shoes. The psychodrama director may or may not choose to participate in this exercise. If he is interested in exploring issues of transference, he might well decide to include his shoes.

During a recent demonstration, the director chose to wear a pair of cowboy boots which took on rather powerful projections from the group. After the initial warm-up, he took off his boots and asked the group members to do the same. Then he asked the group members, one at a time, to act out a drama, non-verbally, using only the shoes. He instructed each protagonist to choose the pair of shoes he felt closest to, and enact a scene in relation to the director's shoes. Thus, the warm-up led quickly into the action.

Non-verbal warm-ups are also used quite frequently in psychodrama. In work with a group of alcoholics, psychodramatist Peter Pitzele searched for an image to dramatize the individual's dependency on alcohol. As a warm-up, he asked participants to work in teams. Each person was to lean on his partner, and the partner was instructed to support him. Then the partners reversed roles. Thus, each person was warmed up to the feelings of being both dependent and depended upon. That non-verbal experience led into the action, a psychodramatic enactment of a protagonist's issues of dependency.

Another example of a non-verbal warm-up was used in a joint drama therapy/psychodrama group exploring issues of collaboration. Each person was asked to conceive of one hand as oneself and the other hand as a significant other. Through the hand play, each was to symbolically enact that relationship.

According to Adam Blatner (1973), the psychodramatic warm-up is geared primarily to the development of spontaneity within all of the participants. Blatner describes the necessary conditions for spontaneity as follows:

1. a sense of trust and safety;
2. norms which allow for the inclusion of non-rational and intuitive dimensions;
3. some feelings of tentative distance, which is one element of "playfulness"; and
4. a movement toward risk-taking and exploration into novelty.

THE PROTAGONIST

During or immediately after the warm-up, the director will choose a protagonist. The choice will be based upon several factors: he will be warmed up to his feelings; he will have reached a state of spontaneity; he may have identified an issue that encapsulates larger group issues; and there will be a workable sense of tele between the director and protagonist.

After the protagonist has been identified, the director will help him focus upon specific issues in his life that need further exploration. Part of the focusing process involves the identification of several dramatic elements that foster specificity (i.e., the setting, characters, time, and action). From the hand play exercise mentioned above, a protagonist was chosen who worked on an unresolved relationship with a former professor. She set her scene in the professor's office five years past and described the two characters in some detail. The action involved a discussion of her leaving her country to study in America, an idea initiated by the professor.

Following the establishment of a clear dramatic focus, the protagonist will begin to identify others who will assume complimentary roles in the psychodrama, the auxiliary egos.

THE AUXILIARY EGO

There are several types of auxiliary ego. The one most central to the psychodrama is that of the significant other. The significant other often plays an antagonist role in relation to the protagonist. He can represent an actual figure in the protagonist's life, most often a sibling, parent, spouse, or intimate friend.

The auxiliary ego can also be a generalized other, a representative of a social group. If the protagonist is working on his relationship to women, men, blacks, whites, rich, poor, he might choose an auxiliary who represents the collective rather than an individual.

At times, the protagonist will focus his psychodrama upon an archetypal or mythological figure, wishing to explore his relationship to the devil or God, or to the "Cinderella" part of himself. Thus, the auxiliary ego becomes more abstract. Further, the auxiliary can become an inanimate object, an image generated in a dream or an important part of one's memory. A security blanket, a bed in the room of one's childhood, or a smooth stone on the beach can all become animated as the protagonist plays out his wishes, hopes, and fears in relation to these auxiliary egos.

The auxiliary ego can also represent parts or roles of the protagonist's self, i.e., the angry or judgmental part. Further, the auxiliary ego can take the form of the double, representing the alter ego or inner voice of the protagonist.

The auxiliary ego serves several purposes. The main one is to provide a means of dramatizing the protagonist's dilemma. As an auxiliary, he takes on a secondary role in the psychodrama. He challenges the protagonist, sometimes provocatively, helping him focus upon his issue, stay with his feelings, and reach a point of either catharsis or recognition.

Further, the auxiliary ego is a means of balancing distance. Through his choice of abstract or concrete action, past or present orientation, the auxiliary helps create or diminish distance within the protagonist or between himself and the protagonist. In assuming the archetypal role of the devil, for example, the auxiliary can choose dance-like, stylized movements, stereotyped gestures and words, and a rather humorous demeanor. This choice might be appropriate for an underdistanced protagonist who feels too close to the demonic side of himself and needs to approach his demons cautiously. On the other hand, given a protagonist who is too overdistanced from his demons, a more realistic, emotional, here-and-now orientation might be indicated. There exists an infinite variety of ways to play the devil or any other character/object in a protagonist's social atom, a phrase coined by Moreno to represent all significant characters or objects within the totality of a person's life. Thus, the director can draw out different degrees of distance from the auxiliary to further help the protagonist reach a point of balance.

The director often asks the protagonist to choose auxiliaries from the group. The choice is based upon identifying qualities of group members that are like those of the auxiliary role. At times, however, a director will work with trained auxiliaries, those sensitive both to the psychodramatic process and to the technical and emotional demands of acting. The advantage of working with a trained auxiliary is that he often warms up quickly to the role and is trained to immediately focus in on the protagonist's problem. Further, the trained actor is often adept at portraying both stylized and realistic characters. The disadvantage is that actor training can promote artificial or superficial role playing and thus lead to a less than authentic enactment. In moving toward a quick presentation of character, the trained auxiliary might bypass some of the more subtle psychological actions essential to the protagonist's search.

As well as challenging the protagonist and helping him to arrive at a point of balance, the auxiliary plays a supporting role. As symbolically part of the protagonist's social atom, he needs to balance his often provocative actions with gestures of support, geared toward reinforcing the strengths of the protagonist and the nurturing functions of the group.

There are moments in psychodrama in which the auxiliary ego does not actually appear. One example is when the protagonist works with an empty chair, a technique popularized by Fritz Perls in Gestalt therapy. In using the empty-chair technique, the protagonist plays to an imaginary other whom he visualizes in the chair. Some protagonists need this extra dimension of distance in order to work with a significant other. Further, the chair can be physically manipulated—kicked, tossed around, and moved easily from place to place, according to the protagonist's emotional needs.

At times, a director will provide a protagonist with two or more empty chairs, each representing a distinct part of the protagonist. For example, the director might ask a protagonist to visualize the selfish part of himself as sitting in chair A and the generous part of himself as sitting in chair B. He might warm the protagonist up to both parts by having him give a monologue in each role and by having the group ask him questions which he must answer in one chair or another. Following the warm-up, the protagonist might then engage in a dialogue, spontaneously assuming both roles as he moves from chair to chair.

A further dimension of this technique is the monodrama where the protagonist is asked to play all the roles in the psychodrama, including the auxiliary ego, double and, at times, the director. The monodrama is often confusing and frustrating and thus should be used sparingly and only with those who are well able to distinguish roles.

During the closure of a psychodrama, there are times when an auxiliary ego reports that he had trouble staying in role. In exploring this further, the director often discovers that the auxiliary identified too closely with the dilemma of the protagonist and thus lost his own sense of character. When the director becomes aware of this, there are several approaches he can take. One, he can ask the auxiliary and protagonist to reverse roles. In that way, the auxiliary has sufficient distance in which to separate out his issues from those of the protagonist.

If, however, one's identification is deep seated, then a temporary role reversal might not be sufficient. The director might then need to choose whether to replace the auxiliary or to move into a new session with the auxiliary as protagonist.

The director can also use the technique of the double. By providing the auxiliary with a double, the director establishes a means to keep him within the bounds of his role. The double can alter statements and actions that digress from those bounds. Again, this technique is only effective to the point of amending moderate digressions. When the auxiliary is deeply identified with the protagonist, a more radical remedy is needed.

The techniques of role reversal and doubling apply equally to the protagonist and auxiliary. Let us now look at further functions of each technique.

ROLE REVERSAL

A maxim employed by many psychodrama directors is: When in trouble, reverse roles. Because of the complexities of the role-playing structure of psychodrama, there will be many moments of confusion for protagonist, auxiliary, and director, alike. During those moments, an imbalance of distancing will occur and one will either merge too closely with a role, withdraw too far from a role, or mistake one role for another. The role reversal serves to remedy all three imbalances.

The role reversal provides breathing space through a shift in perspective. The protagonist who is too closely identified with his role, and thus too much the actor, achieves distance as he takes on the role of the other and becomes an observer of himself. The protagonist too far removed from his role, too much the observer, can become more of the actor as he takes on the less threatening auxiliary role. And the protagonist, who is confused as to who he is in relation to one or more auxiliaries, is able to make clearer distinctions through the role reversal, which dramatizes the differences between the different characters.

Further functions of role reversal from the point of view of the protagonist include: demonstrating for the auxiliary how to play his role more convincingly; altering the nature of the auxiliary's role from a real to a fictional character or vice-versa; and generally modifying the emotional tone of the enactment. Let us look at an example of role reversal. The psychodrama concerns a man who is warmed up to a childhood memory of feeling hurt after acting in a play, without receiving any approval from his mother. In the session, Jim Sacks, the director, asks the man, Mr. A, to compose an imagined letter to his mother, played by an auxiliary (Landy, 1982):

> *Mr. A:* Dear Mother, I remember where you sat that Sunday. In spite of the fact that everybody else was there, how much I just needed your approval, how much I just needed you to tell me that you were proud. You never did that. I did so many things just to get you to say that it was good. So many times I still need you to say that ... especially since you are the only parent. . . .

> *Sacks:* I'd like to ask you to reverse roles with your mother. Assume that your mother has actually received that letter. What is it you might have liked her to say to you?

> *Mr. A* (as mother): I do appreciate you. I can't express it in the way you probably needed it. But I was very proud of you. And I've been very proud of you many, many times. I wish I could tell you how, but I can't do that. I love you.

> *Sacks:* Reverse back again. In similar words, maybe you [auxiliary] can give him the experience he would have liked by taking the role of his ideal mother.

> *Ideal Mother* (played by auxiliary ego): You know, son, it was so moving. You did such a beautiful job. I acknowledged that to everyone else. . . . I'm sorry I wasn't able to acknowledge it to you also. It's just communication was so difficult, and I hope you forgive me for not being able to put that in words. I had to lead my own life the only way that I could at the time. I hope you continue to do well, even though I haven't always been there for you.

> *Mr. A:* A lot of the things I do now I do because I need you to approve.

> *Ideal Mother:* You're free to do the things you want to do. Whatever you want to do, even if you don't do it well, is fine. It's good and it's enough. . . .

> *Sacks* (to Mr. A): I'm not sure of the feeling inside of you or the extent of the capacity for forgiveness at this point. I wonder if in some nonverbal way you could express what feeling would be in you after hearing your mother speak in this way.

> *Mr. A* (to mother): I'd just like you to hold me and tell me I'm good enough. (They embrace.)

In this example, the protagonist used the role reversal to dramatize for the auxiliary how he wanted her to play the role of his mother. The director picked up on Mr. A's needs and instructed the auxiliary to assume the role of the Ideal Mother when the roles were reinstated. Following the role reversal, Mr. A's drama deepened considerably, leading to a moment of catharsis. The emotional depth was a direct consequence of Mr. A's ability, while in the role of the mother, to say: "I wish I could tell you how [proud I've been of you], but I can't do that. I love you."

Further, in Mr. A's psychodrama, Ms. B, the auxiliary, reported a strong identification with Mr. A. Through the role reversal, she was able to separate her need for approval from her parents from that of Mr. A.

During a psychodrama, audience members may experience a strong identification with the protagonist. In the closure, the director might ask an audience member to take on the role of the protagonist for a dual purpose: to allow him to express his feelings through the role of the protagonist, and to allow the protagonist to see that his issue is a universal one and that he is not alone with his feelings of rejection.

From the point of view of the director, role reversal can be a most useful technique in dealing with issues of authority in the group. It often happens that a member of a psychodrama group will play out his needs for approval and control through challenging the authority of the director. This might manifest itself in questioning the director's competence, refusing to participate, or portraying inappropriate auxiliary roles when chosen by the director. In such cases, the director might ask the person to reverse roles with him. The director might then mirror his antagonistic behaviors to help him see the dimensions of his actions. Following the role reversal and ensuing action, the session can be closed by a discussion of one's relationship to authority figures.

At times, the director, too, might behave in ways that have a disturbing effect upon the group. Should he recognize this problem and be secure enough to examine it within the group, he might ask another to reverse roles with him. From this distanced viewpoint, he might well be able to look at ways he is seen by others in the group.

Role reversal, then, is a means of helping any member of a psychodrama group—protagonist, auxiliary, audience, or director—to see another's point of view. Through the role-reversal, one's own limited perspective becomes more properly distanced and thus expanded. From that more balanced place, one can re-enter one's given role of self with more spontaneity and insight.

THE DOUBLE

The double is the most direct extension of the protagonist. As representing the inner, unexpressed thoughts and feelings of the protagonist, the double is a very powerful psychodramatic figure. Like role reversal, doubling is a method of balancing distance. For the overly cautious person, the double can provide a deeper connection to feelings and pave the way toward more risk taking. For the overly impulsive, imprudent person, the double can provide a safe means of diffusing potentially overwhelming feelings.

Most often, a protagonist will choose his own double, one whom he feels can both challenge him to a deeper level of exploration and provide a safety net in the event that he becomes overwhelmed by feelings. Sometimes, the director will double for a protagonist, either at the protagonist's request or more spontaneously, when he intuits that he can bring the protagonist to a more focused point in his psychodrama.

Other auxiliary egos might also be assigned doubles by the director. At times, the director will assign multiple doubles to either a protagonist or auxiliary in order to further support or challenge the person in role, or to give voice to the collective feelings of the group. The use of the multiple double as a voice of the community echoes the function of the chorus in classical Greek drama and some experimental forms of contemporary drama.

The primary function of the double is to help the protagonist (or auxiliary) focus on his feelings and express them directly through words and movements. As the inner voice of the protagonist, the double has the freedom to speak at will. The protagonist must translate the double's words and actions into his own, redirecting them back into the drama. If the protagonist disagrees with the double, he alters rather than ignores the double's message.

In classical psychodrama, the double mirrors the body posture and movements of the protagonist, providing him non-verbal feedback as to the attitudes he is communicating through his body. The double often sits or stands to one side and slightly behind the protagonist, so that he is unobtrusive yet visible enough to provide a source of feedback.

There are many ways to double. Blatner (1973) mentions seventeen that range from dramatizing an individual's feelings to dramatizing those of an audience. Let us look at several examples typifying various kinds of doubling.

In the case of Mr. A, above, several opportunities for doubling are evident. Mr. A might, for example, have trouble expressing his anger toward his mother. His attempt at emotional expression: "Mother, why didn't you applaud for me after the show?" might be altered by the double to "Mother, I am furious at you!" In dramatizing the protagonist's anger, the double transforms the question into a statement and focuses in on the primary emotion implicit in the protagonist's question. If Mr. A had expressed his anger with a meek gesture, the double could also extend that gesture through his own more aggressive action directed toward the auxiliary.

Should Mr. A feel overwhelmed by a sudden outburst, the double could support him through such an expression as: "It's all right for me to be mad at you. You [mother] really deserve it, you know."

The double might also help the protagonist reach a degree of balance through assuming an opposing point of view. Thus, if Mr. A says: "Please forgive me, Mother, for being such a bad actor," the double might counter with: "Acting on stage has nothing to do with it. It's you, Mother, who acted mean toward me."

Further, the double can assume an ironic or humorous role, gently mocking either the tendency of the protagonist to take himself too seriously or the absurdity of an auxiliary's position. Mr. A might be unable to respond spontaneously to such a statement from his mother as: "But, darling, I was always there for you. You just didn't hear my applause because of my poor arthritic hands." The double can come to his aid by countering with: "Your poor hands weren't so weak when you slapped me for disturbing you!"

Although the double needs to be wary of interpreting a protagonist's issues, he might help him focus upon transferences and/or generalizations that might be evident in his psychodrama. This kind of doubling can be best served by the director. In underscoring Mr. A's tendency to generalize, the therapist as double might say: "I don't know; every time I'm in a performance situation, I always feel like nobody will like me, especially women."

Doubling requires a great sensitivity to a protagonist's dilemma as well as a properly distanced stance that is neither too identified with nor too removed from the protagonist's point of view. As an auxiliary ego, the double is there to help the primary ego, the protagonist. He will be most helpful to the extent that he, too, participates authentically, becoming a mirror reflecting those images that the protagonist needs to look at.

CLOSURE

The action part of a successful psychodrama often ends with a moment of either catharsis or recognition on the part of the protagonist. In the case of Mr. A, the action part ended with a tearful embrace and an understanding of the son's need to let go of his mother's judgment. At times, the psychodrama session will not proceed as smoothly and neatly as that of Mr. A. The protagonist's resistances might be too strong; the auxiliaries might be unable to get to the heart of the issue; the director might make misinterpretations or be resistant himself. Even if there is no satisfactory conclusion within the action part of the psychodrama, the group can use the closure period to examine their reactions to the process, their feelings of incompletion, and/or their issues with the director.

One main purpose of the closure is to help the protagonist integrate the issues he has just dramatized and prepare to move from the reality of the psychodrama to that of the everyday world outside. In working toward these aims, the director encourages the protagonist to review his drama and express his present feelings. Should the protagonist need more distance, the director can turn to the group to provide support through feedback and through a sharing of their own life experiences restimulated by the protagonist.

Sharing is a major part of the closure process. Its value is not only to the protagonist but also to those group members who have made an identification with the protagonist. In the sharing, they will also have a chance to express their feelings and move toward a more balanced state.

During the sharing period of Mr. A's psychodrama, the group discussed some feelings about their own experiences that had been touched off by Mr. A's enactment. An example is as follows (Landy, 1982):

> *Mr. C:* I identified very closely with your need. The only difference was the women in my early life did give me a lot of approval, maybe too much, and I didn't get enough from the men. And I always kind of wondered why the men didn't, and I wanted more approval from them. I kind of blamed some of the men in my life for not giving me that kind of approval. It's only now that I've just begun to learn that the men did give me the approval. They

just weren't demonstrative about it. They did it in other ways. The lesson I learned is in working it out with my own children, making sure they are aware when I do approve.

In many forms of dramatic education and therapy, closing is an opening of further possibilities and visions. An authentic psychodrama, deeply felt by the protagonist and strongly supported by the auxiliaries, will no doubt touch the lives of many viewers, whether present in the room as audience or more distanced, perhaps watching the session on television. For Moreno, psychodrama breeds further psychodramas; as more and more viewers become protagonists, entire communities will become transformed into more humane, positive, spontaneous environments.

AUTOBIOGRAPHICAL PERFORMANCE PIECES

The essence of the psychodramatic experience is direct work with autobiographical material. The protagonist plays himself. His mask is that of a part or several parts of himself. Drama therapy work in creating autobiographical performance pieces is similar, in that the client plays the role or roles of himself, unmediated by a character in a script. The differences, however, are striking.

The therapist's role in the autobiographical performance piece is first to set specific ground rules. The following are examples: Each member of the group is to focus upon a limited experience in his life—a turning point, a crisis, a celebration. After recalling the experience and the associated feelings, the client determines the setting, action, props, and means of characterization necessary to create an appropriate dramatic form. Thus, he is to think like a stage designer, director, and actor. The piece is to be a one-person performance. There will be no actual, live auxiliaries, although the client is encouraged to use objects and such projective devices as puppets, masks, dolls, and tape recordings to represent significant others in his drama.

The client constructs his set and his script on his own, with no help from the director. He is given several weeks to think through the emotional and aesthetic issues of his piece and to engage in a creative process of translating those thoughts into actions. He does not necessarily need to write out a formal script and memorize lines but, rather, to create a basic scenario of actions and technical requirements.

Other ground rules of the therapist can include the setting of time, space, and technical limitations. The length of a piece can be 15–20

minutes. The performance should take place in a room with some flexibility as to seating and movement. Such equipment as slide projectors,
tape recorders, and record players should be available. It is important to
discourage a larger-scale technical design, as the focus of the piece can
then easily shift from the person to the technology. In some cases,
however, when the theme of a piece is technology, a more sophisticated
technical design can be implemented.

During the actual presentation, the therapist becomes a member of the
group, a non-judgmental onlooker. With rare exceptions, he will remain
separate from the action. The client will be responsible for all aspects of
his performance, including setting up, arranging for technical support,
and striking the set.

Following each piece or a series of pieces, the director can lead a
closure session to examine the question: How does the creative process
lead toward the exploration of particular emotional issues?

Performance pieces, like psychodramas, are very powerful when the
client is able to find a balance of distance between self and other, and self
and role. One woman's piece was created around a painful divorce
experience. In thinking through her issue, she recalled a time in her
childhood when she was given a bride doll by her grandfather. She
dramatized that moment and several others in her childhood and adolescence when the voices of adults all seemed to be pushing her toward a
marriage with "Mr. Right." Then, in an imitation of her bride doll, she
became the bride, reading her actual wedding invitation to the group
and donning her doll-like wedding dress to marry a doctor—her family's
idea of a perfect groom. Finally, she narrated the unhappy ending of her
fairy tale: incompatibility, abortion, separation.

Upon reflection, the woman recognized how the voices of her past
interfered with her authentic search for herself as a woman. She recognized her need to assert her identity apart from the dolls and dresses and
fairy tales imposed upon her by her family and culture. In the form of
the autobiographical performance piece, her unresolved feelings were
expressed directly. Since she was properly distanced, she was able to
recognize these feelings as based in a history and as pointing to a future
where their control might well be minimized.

Although psychodramatic in nature, as the client portrays the unmediated role of self, the autobiographical piece also incorporates aspects
of dramatic projective techniques, so crucial to the experience of

drama therapy. As such, it is a bridge between the disciplines of psychodrama and drama therapy which are, after all, intimately interrelated.

Chapter Seven

PROJECTIVE TECHNIQUES

In drama therapy, the concept of distancing leads most directly into practice through the use of projective techniques. Projective techniques are inherently more stylized and distanced than psychodramatic ones, as aspects of the person are projected onto a persona and a graphic distinction is made between self and non-self. In the following chapter, we will examine several projective techniques that are at the heart of the drama therapy experience.

PHOTOGRAPHY

.A photograph, though still, is a dynamic representation of a specific time, place, and action. It contains a vast potential for drama which occurs through one's projection onto it. As a realistic object, a photograph embodies characters and settings in a literal way. But through the processes of identification, transference, and projection, the client engages a dramatic method that can transform the mode of the real into that of the ideal, fearful, or fanciful.

One group exercise involves two photographs of the client—one in a past setting (implying greater distance), the other in a present setting (implying less distance). As a warm-up, each client verbalizes three things he likes and three things he dislikes about himself as he appears in each photo. Then, one person is chosen to work. The therapist instructs him to choose one photograph and set up a still life sculpture representing it with members of the group and objects in the room. As part of the sculpture, the client casts another in the role of himself. He then takes a distanced position, assuming the role of director. In that role, he instructs the group to move and interact according to his feelings. The therapist remains on the sidelines throughout much of this process, encouraging the client to engage in a balanced exploration of the issues implicit in the photograph. Finally, the therapist tells the client to freeze the action when he feels ready and to address the character representing himself in

monologue, telling him three things that he likes and three things that
he dislikes about him.

Working from a more distanced position, the therapist might ask the
client to simply focus on the photograph, allow mental images to form,
then tell a story within a "once upon a time" frame, transforming the self
into a fictional character.

Taking a less distanced, more psychodramatic point of view, the therapist can ask the client to assume the role of himself at the time and place
of the photograph and play out his issues in relation to auxiliaries
representing significant others in the photograph or off-camera.

The family photo album can be a rich source of material for drama
therapy sessions. This approach is especially valuable in working with
groups of elders who are able to review their lives and move toward
dramatization based in the old photographs.

VIDEO

In drama therapy, video technology provides a means of instant
feedback, self-perception, and self-analysis. As a naturalistic projection
of the self, it is a direct confrontational device that allows a person not
only to see an image of himself in present time but also to speak to and
analyze that image.

At the most basic level, a drama therapy session can be videotaped and
played back to the clients. Their self-perceptions and feelings can be the
basis for further discussion and/or enactment.

A more creative use of video, though, would involve direct interaction
between the client and video technology, in which the camera and
monitor are themselves objects to be reckoned with. One experience
begins as a client sits alone in front of a camera for five minutes. He is
instructed to just be there with the camera. Following that time, he
watches the playback of his first sitting. During this second phase, he
speaks directly to his image on the monitor, addressing it in second
person, as "you." He specifies what he sees in the image, including
external appearance and internal feeling states and thoughts. This enactment is also recorded on videotape.

A third sitting involves watching a playback of the second phase.
Following the playback, the client is asked to record his impressions in a
journal, noting his feelings as he watched himself address his image and
naming the roles of self enacted and observed.

This particular experience can be varied. For example, in exploring a relationship between two clients, both can sit together through the three phases of the exercise, noting qualities of their interaction. One powerful example of this was a video experience created by the artist, Joan Logue, who sat in front of a camera with her mother for approximately ten minutes. In that time, a highly charged, nonverbal drama occurred. Initially, the mother was rather nervous and took on a rigid, smiling expression that became a fixed mask. The daughter took on a distanced expression that also became fixed, a mask that denied affect. After some minutes, the mother's mask began to crack. The rigid smile melted and tears began to flow. A great sadness was expressed and the daughter took her hand, all the while trying to maintain her own mask. But then she, too, cried, letting go of her invulnerability. Finally, the catharsis ended. The mother attempted to resume her smiling mask, but with difficulty. Toward the end of the tape, she succeeded. The daughter found her former mask again, but she seemed somewhat changed, less distant. There was more sadness than before in both sitters.

This experience was not one in therapy. It was an aesthetic experience in video art, displayed in a prominent New York City art gallery, The Kitchen. However, it was clearly therapeutic in nature and could serve as a model for further therapeutic sittings.

The experience of video can also be used over time with an individual client who is asked to respond to his live image. When used over time, the therapist and client are able to view the changing relationships between self and image, and changing perceptions of self. The drama therapist, Renée Emunah, has used this technique effectively within an extended drama therapy group process. She asked one particular woman, who had great difficulty seeing herself realistically and positively, to engage in a series of talkbacks to her projected image. Over a period of several months, her ability to see herself and discover a glimmer of hopefulness changed radically. From a rigid, removed persona, her image became more flexible, more recognizable as that of herself.

Video can further be used in exploring issues of transference. In working with a camera and a microphone, for example, the client might be asked: "Who is the camera for you? Who is the microphone for you? Give it a name." As a removed, judgmental, or intuitive eye, the camera can take on many projections. The microphone as ear can also be highly charged. For one client, the microphone became "the best listener I've ever had." For another, the camera became a machine gun, an object of destruction.

In applying the distance paradigm, this work can be brought to balance through altering the distance between client and video equipment. In addressing the camera as "it," the client allows more distance; in addressing the camera as "you," the client works closer to his projection or transference; and in taking on the role of the camera and speaking as "I," the client works with identification, the least distanced form of self-confrontation.

As a projective technique, video is often one element in a drama therapy session that combines naturally with storytelling, puppetry, mask work, and extended dramatization. As a source of immediate feedback, it is an excellent means to help the client see the dimensions of and distinctions between the roles he plays.

OBJECTS, DOLLS, AND PUPPETS

Photography and video, as used in therapy (see Fryrear and Fleshman, 1981; Krauss and Fryrear, 1983), present realistic projections of the self and thus are inherently underdistanced. In working with dolls, puppets, and objects, the mode of reality changes substantially. A doll, a blanket, or a hand puppet might not at all resemble the child playing with it. Yet, through an act of the imagination, the child projects aspects of himself onto the object. Further, the child can transfer aspects of significant others or fantasy figures onto the object, so that the doll becomes mother, the puppet becomes "the bad guy," and the blanket becomes a friend. The child might also make an identification with these devices, especially if one is charged with a particular affective or moral quality. For example, a child at play with a police doll might begin to see himself as the keeper of the peace in his family.

Of the three devices, the object is the most abstract and distanced. A ball, a bat, a glove, a blanket, a shoe, and a tambourine are all inanimate objects. But, like the thought of the adult based in a shamanic world view, the thought of the child is magical. For the child there is life in objects. A blanket is a feeling thing in its warmth, safety, softness, and pleasure. The child does not see these properties as being part of himself or part of his real or fantasy mother. Given this kind of thinking, the use of the objects in a therapy situation can be helpful in discovering how the child sees himself and what he needs from significant others.

In the standard creative exercise, transformation of objects (a rope, for example) is passed around the circle and each child, through his physical manipulation, transforms it into something else (i.e., a snake, a scarf, a hat). The purpose of the exercise is to stimulate imaginative thinking. In drama therapy, work with objects is not usually so directive. Rather than transforming the objects, children are simply asked to play. A variety of objects are present in the room, including those that tend to be aggressively or negatively charged (i.e., a bat made out of soft material like Styrofoam™ or rubber), those that tend to be more positively charged (i.e., certain musical instruments and soft, furry objects), and those that tend to be more neutral in nature (i.e., gloves and odd-shaped pieces of wood or plastic).

The drama therapist might also ask the client, child or adult to bring objects with him to therapy that he likes or dislikes or that might serve as props in a particular story. In a "show and tell" format the therapist might say: "Tell me about that object" or "Show me what you can do with that object." If the client begins to project a particular power onto the object, then the therapist might ask him to tell a story or enact a scene from the point of view of the object.

Whether working through a non-directive play situation, a "show and tell" structure, or a storytelling session, the therapist uses the object as a means to externalize and focus feelings. The object becomes a symbol, an anchor for the unconscious. In animating an object, the client partakes in a therapeutic rite through the projection of his fears, fantasies, wishes, and hopes onto a thing that is not himself, his mother, or his demons, but that magically contains properties of the same. In recognizing the properties of the charged object outside himself through playing them out, the client begins to recognize the properties inside himself that have led to disturbed feelings or behaviors.

Dolls and puppets serve a similar projective function. Unlike objects, however, they often exist in a human or animal form and thus are less inherently distanced. Yet, not all projective techniques work the same for all clients. The lion doll that is aggressive and threatening for some might be exciting and liberating for others. The soft, furry bear puppet that most children approach without any anxiety might be frightening to one particular child.

In a play therapy situation, dolls and puppets are very common. Again, the therapist will often provide the client with a range of dolls and puppets. For the young child, animal puppets are often present, including more docile ones constructed of soft materials, more aggressive ones with extended mouths and claws, and neutral ones. For the older child, dolls and puppets that project a range of conventional moral types can also be used. Examples would include "good" figures, such keepers of law and order as police, firefighters, and superheroes. "Bad" figures might include robbers and devils, and more neutral figures might include characters in particular working roles. The choice of characters should be balanced as to gender and race. Also, the figures should represent a range of realistic and stylized types, so that, for example, the good figures are not all realistic and the bad figures all abstract.

In a well-stocked play therapy situation, the therapist would also provide puppets and dolls that are representative of family roles, i.e., mother, father, son, daughter, grandparent. These can be rather realistic in nature or more abstract as seen, for example, in a family of animal dolls.

The advantage of using puppets as opposed to dolls is that the former have more movable parts and can be directly animated by the hand of the puppeteer. For those with severely limited hand-eye coordination skills, the doll is indicated. The doll does not have to be moved at all but can simply become animated through the voice, focus of attention, and/or gesture of the client.

Like cartoon characters, puppets and dolls can sustain all kinds of disasters without physical consequences. They can be beaten, kicked, dropped from heights, thrown across the room and still survive. As such, they are safe containers of aggression on the part of the client. Further, they are safe containers for tender, affectionate feelings. A doll can be cuddled, a puppet can be kissed and can kiss and touch back, again without consequences. For most clients, the distancing factor of puppets and dolls allows unexpressed or partially expressed feelings to be fully enacted.

Reference was made earlier to needle play in a hospital setting. At St. Lukes-Roosevelt Hospital Center in New York, two drama therapists, Maria Scaros and Loretta Gallo-Lopez, have worked extensively with young chronic cancer patients, using dolls and puppets to help the children express their fears of doctors, intrusive instruments, illness, and death. The therapist first encourages the children to choose a puppet or doll, made out of soft stuffed fabric, and then play with it, using the medical instruments provided, i.e., syringes, stethescopes, and intravenous tubes. As the children play, sometimes quite aggressively, the therapist helps them assume the role of doctor by doubling them. She also doubles for the dolls and puppets, thus expressing the fears and desires of the children. As one three-year-old boy repeatedly injected his doll with a needle, the therapist cried: "Stop, please. You're hurting me. I want to go home!"

Through the needle play, the children are endowed with the power of the doctor, projecting their weaker roles upon the puppets. As the therapist gives voice to the puppets, the children are able to recognize some of their fears and continue to play them out. The fact that the pain is absorbed by a puppet and the one inflicting the pain is "playing" provides the proper distance needed for balance.

Dolls and puppets are also used with much success with adult clients. In such cases, the figures can be constructed by the clients themselves, rather than determined by the therapist. An example concerns a representation of the family structure. Individuals in a group are asked to build several puppets representing mother, father, siblings, and self. Each puppet is to be constructed with materials, colors, and textures appropriate to the particular family member. The client is also to carefully consider the form of the puppet, whether hand puppet, stick puppet, or marionette, whether small enough to fit on one finger, or large enough to be propped on a broomstick. The client who claims that he is not artistic can be given some basic objects (i.e., a box, a sock, a stick with a piece of cardboard pasted on), which he identifies as a particular family member and decorates accordingly.

Once the puppets are constructed, they can be introduced to the group. Introductions can serve as a warm-up. Each group member begins by talking about the puppet as an object, as an "it," then working his way into assuming the role of the puppet through animation.

Following the warm-up, each client is instructed to construct a model of the house in which he grew up using available objects in the room. Once the house is constructed, each is to place the puppets in the appropriate rooms of the house.

At this point the therapist focuses upon one client at a time, asking him to play out a family drama with the puppets. He can either do this nonverbally or add sounds and words as appropriate. Following the enactment, the issues that arose can be discussed in the group or a further projection can occur through storytelling. If overdistance is needed, the story can be told by the client out of role in a "once upon a time" fictional frame. If underdistance is needed, the story can be told by the client in the role of a particular family member in a present-time, realistic style.

Not only are puppets useful in therapeutic dramatization, but they can also serve diagnostic purposes. The drama therapist, Eleanor Irwin, and her colleagues have devised a diagnostic technique, called the puppetry interview, wherein the child enacts a story through a puppet, in dialogue with the drama therapist (Irwin and Shapiro, 1975; Irwin and Rubin, 1976). In analyzing both the content and the form of the story, the therapist is able to make certain diagnostic judgments which can inform the future direction of the treatment.

MASKS

Because they are worn on the face, masks are inherently less distancing than puppets, dolls, and objects. As the face is covered, the body becomes visible in a new way. Often a frozen, rigid body becomes more flexible, more likely to move once the face is masked.

The mask has a powerful, transformational quality in drama therapy that is directly related to its anthropological and theatrical sources. Many cultures, Western and non-Western alike, use the mask for ceremonial purposes, as a means of communing with the spirit world, influencing the future, playing, and releasing feeling. In her book, *The Mask in Modern Drama*, Susan Smith (1984) delineates four functions of the mask in theatre: the expression of the satiric and grotesque, representing the foolishness and beastiality of mankind; the embodiment of the heroic, representing the nobility and godlike quality of mankind; the expression of dreams, representing the psychological, often fragmented projections of mankind; and the embodiment of social roles, representing everyday role playing. All four functions can apply to drama therapy.

As in the case with puppets, the drama therapist can display a range of masks that represent negative, positive, and neutral characters. After observing the client playing freely with masks, the therapist can move into a storytelling session or discussion.

A more powerful use of masks, though, involves those constructed by the clients. In the context of an ongoing group, the therapist might ask the client to build masks representing two sides of a dilemma or several parts of a person. For example, let us look at the case of a woman deciding whether or not she should become engaged to a particular man.

Through mask work, she constructs three images of the man—a satiric, exaggerated face, an heroic, elevated face, and a more balanced, naturalistic image. She chooses three people from the group to wear these masks. As they play out their roles improvisationally, she explores her relationship to the several parts of her potential spouse. Further, through role reversal she herself assumes the satiric, heroic, and naturalistic roles, thus seeing the man's point of view more clearly and exploring the parts of herself that she might have projected onto the man.

A further example concerns the expression of an individual's identity within a group. The only deaf woman within a particular drama therapy group felt very isolated from the others and had difficulty expressing this feeling until she was asked to construct a mask representing a hidden part of herself. Her mask extended over the ears. She had painted eyes upon the ears, because she hears with her eyes. A painted hand and mouth surrounded the openings of the actual eyes. Another hand image covered the mouth, as she speaks with her hands. Through presenting her mask to the group simply as an object, she became visible. Through communicating her world and her separateness from the world of others, she was able to work toward a greater sense of connection with the group.

In staying with Susan Smith's theatrical mask model, the therapist might also use masks to explore dreams. The often irrational, surreal quality of dreams lends itself well to the abstract quality of masks. In identifying central objects and characters in a dream, a client can then begin to construct masks representing them. The mask-making process can, itself, be quite simple. The therapist might have available paper bags or paper plates which can be decorated with crayons, magic markers, and paints. Further, he can provide various fabrics to be glued or stapled onto the mask.

In working with dream imagery, the client can either direct others whom he has cast in masked roles or assume a masked role himself within an improvisational drama directed by the therapist. In exploring the dream, the therapist works toward clarifying a central image or central concern of the client. As a stylized projection of a feeling state, the mask often is a clear representation.

The fourth function of the mask in Smith's model is that of the expression of the social role. Consistent with Mead's notion of role taking, this function leads well into drama therapy practice. If we come to know who we are through incorporating the roles of significant others, then we might be able to better explore issues of self through working with representations of others.

In one exercise, examining family dynamics, each client is instructed to build four masks representing mother, father, sibling, and self. Each mask is to be constructed on the client's face; that is, each mask is to have the same basic structure: a realistic imprint of the client.

The easiest way to build such a mask is with gauze impregnated with plaster of paris. The gauze can be cut into small strips moistened with water, and then layered on the face, which has been first prepared by applying a thin coat of petroleum jelly. One layer should be applied at a time, leaving space for breathing through the nostrils and/or the mouth. After that layer has been allowed to dry (a process that can be accelerated with a hair dryer), a second layer is applied to give the mask solidity.

Following construction of the four masks, the client is asked to decorate each individually. The decorations with paint, fabric, or objects will reflect the client's feeling toward the roles of mother, father, sibling, and self. Those who have never known a parent or sibling are nonetheless asked to build those masks as representations of an ideal or real other who embodies parental or sibling qualities.

During the warm-up part of the exercise, each client speaks about the process of making the masks. This often proves quite powerful in itself, as clients report their feelings of creating images of their families. Some have spoken of the magical quality of the mask-making, comparing themselves to shamans and witch doctors. Others have seen themselves in a Pygmalion or godlike role, reconstructing the family in their own image. Many have reported the feelings of mystery, wonder, and fear as self transforms into parent, brother, sister.

Following the warm-up, each person is asked to construct the house where he grew up, using available objects. Then, the masks are placed in appropriate spaces within the house. At this point a protagonist is chosen by the therapist. He is instructed to take each mask, one at a time, put it on, and enact that character through movement. Then, he chooses four members of the group to play each of the roles. He warms each one up to his role through creating a series of movements in character, which each one mirrors.

Once warmed up, the family group is sculpted in a still-life tableau by the client. Then, he begins to direct them verbally, asking them to move and interact as he chooses.

Finally, the therapist calls "freeze" and asks the client: "Which character do you most identify with now?" The client takes on that role by holding the mask in front of him. In role, he directs a statement of feeling toward each masked character. Then, out of role, he directs one final statement of feeling to the others. The experience ends as the client sets up a final tableau, sculpting the family members in relationship to one another.

The closing discussion involves a look at the projections of self onto the family masks. The group examines ways that one gets to know himself through knowing not only the realistic roles of other family members but also their idealized, heroic qualities and their demeaned, satiric qualities.

Mask work in drama therapy is a literal representation of the notion of the double, the split between individual and archetype, body and spirit, the hidden and the revealed. The mask transforms a person to a persona. Though the persona is a type, an idea, it also embodies images charged with feeling. The mask as persona is dialectical, embodying individual and society, dream and reality, myth and autobiography. As such, it is a device of distancing that aids the person in moving toward balance, toward an exploration of the self through the role.

MAKEUP

Makeup is an alternative form of masking. It tends to be less distanced than mask work, as it is applied directly onto the face and cannot be separated from the face intact. Like the mask, makeup has its roots in shamanistic, magical practices.

Many clients in drama therapy will be quite familiar with makeup either through their daily use of it or through their experiences with theatre. For them, makeup work might not prove as strange and foreign as work with masks or puppets.

Considerable therapeutic work with makeup has been done by Nancy Breitenbach in France. She has worked extensively with children, some with severe emotional problems. Through her research and practice, she built a developmental sequence (1984) delineating stages at which children construct "facial compositions." Her sequence begins with the pre-two-year-old child who has not yet learned to differentiate self from parent. It proceeds to the most advanced adolescent stage, that of "decorporeity," where the makeup assumes the quality of pure design and tends to be asymmetrical and fluid. Rather than being a literal image of the face, the make-up becomes a more abstract symbol in its own right.

In drama therapy, makeup, like mask work, is a projective device that conceals in order to reveal parts of the self not yet fully expressed in everyday life. Like Breitenbach, the drama therapist can take a non-directive approach, providing the face paints, rouges, pencils, and creams, and allowing the client to play freely upon his face. The therapist might also take a more active approach, instructing the client to locate a particular image on his face and to give it form through the application of makeup.

In taking the latter approach, the therapist warms up his clients by asking them to cleanse their faces. For those wearing makeup already, the warm-up involves the literal removal of a mask. For those not wearing makeup, the warm-up has a ritual quality of preparing the face for the drama.

Then the therapist gives the following instructions: "Look at your face in the mirror. Try to see as many parts of your face as possible. Let your thoughts go. See if an image comes to mind, possibly of a person, either a real person or a type of person, such as a funny clown or an old woman. Or maybe the image will be of a feeling of happiness, sadness, togetherness, loneliness. Once that image appears, begin to make yourself up as that image. If you have chosen a feeling, try to make yourself up as a person who is feeling that way."

Following the application of the makeup, the therapist instructs the clients to begin to move in role. When appropriate, he might ask the group to leave the room and walk outside. Following their movement and/or walk in character, a series of non-verbal improvisations are set up, keeping within the abstract nature of the experience. The purpose of the improvisations is to examine a variety of character relationships.

To conclude the experience, a series of Polaroid photographs can be taken and passed around the group. Then the clients remove their makeup, restoring their faces to normal.

Like the projection of a part of the self onto an object, doll, puppet, or mask, the experience of makeup allows the client to examine a role of the self from a properly distanced perspective. Through the experience of makeup, the role is given a tangible form which can be taken on, played out, and taken off. During the closing discussion, the therapist will aim toward helping the client clarify and recognize the dimensions of the role.

Makeup is often used in conjunction with other techniques, most notably storytelling. In making oneself up as a character in a story, one is able to explore his identification with some distance and in some depth. In the following discussion of storytelling, we will look at such a process.

STORYTELLING

Characters in a story can become objects of identification for a client. When telling, dramatizing, or listening to a story, the client who is properly distanced in relation to a character will be able to release emotion and recognize certain aspects of his life that are like those of the character.

In working with storytelling or story dramatization, the narrative point of view is extremely important. A third-person narrative is the most inherently distanced. For example, one client began to tell a story from the point of view of a murderer but soon had to stop, as he became overflooded with emotion. The therapist asked him to switch from first person to third person, so that "I" didn't do the killing but, rather, "he" did it. Within that more distanced frame, he was able to complete the story and later look at his own homicidal fantasies. Conversely, the therapist might move toward a first-person point of view with the client who has distanced himself too much from his story.

Time is also an important factor in manipulating distance in a story. The classical time frame, "once upon a time," provides more distance, while a here-and-now orientation of a story removes distance.

Drama therapists will often choose stories to tell to a drama therapy group. When choosing the story, certain factors should be considered. For one, the story should be relatively simple in form in terms of plot and character definition. Subplots and character complexity will often confuse some clients and potentially lead to difficulty in finding an identification and/or object of projection. Many myths and fables are quite focused as to plot and character. Those tales that tend to be more complexly structured can easily be simplified in the retelling by the therapist. The journey of Odysseus from Troy to Ithaca, for example, can be related simply, framed in the struggle of Odysseus to return to his family and focusing upon a single adventure that impedes his voyage, i.e., the temptation of the Sirens. That is not to say that the thematic or psychological complexity of a story should be reduced to platitudes. It is the therapist's job to simplify and focus without trivializing the deeper issues contained in a story.

The drama therapist needs to carefully choose a story that embodies a theme of therapeutic relevance to the group. *The Odyssey* would be quite relevant for those unable to return to a domestic life after experiencing a highly stimulating, adventurous life abroad, i.e., the Vietnam veteran. Give a mixed group of men and women, or a group of women, the Odysseus figure might become a woman, with the sirens transformed into men. Or another story might be chosen with a female protagonist, i.e., Medea, Pandora, Antigone, Electra.

An old Greek story, part of the oral tradition, has been used with groups working with Oedipal issues of separation from family. In the story, a mother and daughter live together in a small house outside of town. They love each other very dearly and are inseparable. Because of their love, the girl does not seek out any further friendships. One day, however, she meets a friend on the way to market. They begin to spend much time together and soon they, too, become inseparable. But the friend is jealous and becomes angry each time the girl talks about her mother. Finally, the friend tells the girl: "You must choose between your love for your mother and your love for me. If you love me better, then you must kill your mother, cut out her heart and bring it to me for proof. If you refuse, then you will never see me again." The girl becomes deeply confused. Finally, she decides upon a plan of action. She comes home late one night while the mother is sound asleep, kills her, and cuts out her heart. She takes the heart and puts it in a sack, then journies back to town to show it to the friend. On the way, she trips on a stone. The heart rolls out of the sack, looks up at the girl and says: "Did you hurt yourself, my child?"

"The Story of the Heart" is economical in terms of plot and character. It is highly dramatic and well focused as to theme: parent-child struggle for connectedness and separation. Further, the entire universe of the story is charged. The sack in which the girl carries the heart and the stone upon which she trips can easily become dramatized through a projection on the part of the client. There are neither too many objects and characters in the story, nor too few. Each image—that of the endlessly loving mother, the jealous friend, the conflicted child, the immortal, immovable stone, the containing sack, and the bleeding heart—symbolizes a psychological attitude, a state of being, a part of the self that can be looked at dramatically. Not all stories told in a drama therapy group need to be dramatized. But, because each image in this story is so vivid, primal, and sensual, the story lends itself well to dramatization.

"The Story of the Heart" is a powerful one that might well underdistance members of a group. In order to create balance, work with this story can be done in conjunction with makeup, as the clients create personae to help them into character.

A drama therapy session focused upon the issues in the story begins with a cleansing of the face, as mentioned above. As the faces are cleansed, the therapist tells the group "The Story of the Heart." Following the story, he asks individuals which characters they have identified with. Once that is determined, each client begins to make himself up in the role of that character. The therapist encourages the group to freely experiment with the makeup, creating whatever forms seem appropriate.

As a next step, the therapist asks the group to move in role, finding the characters in their bodies. As before, the clients can be encouraged to move outside the room and into the everyday world in character. Upon their return, the therapist asks each to give a brief monologue in role. At that point, he can decide upon the protagonist for the session.

In one session, the therapist focused upon a young woman who chose the role of the girl but applied almost no makeup to her face. This was in stark contrast to the others in the group who had painted rather expressionistic shapes and colors on their faces. She was put in a scene with another, in the role of mother, and asked to interact with her non-verbally. The therapist informed her that she didn't have to be totally true to the story but could make modifications as needed. In her actions, the woman appeared quite resistant. She worked herself up to the point of returning home for the purpose of matricide but could not bring herself to the action of killing. The therapist interceded: "You don't have to find a violent action at all. All you need to do is to touch the mother and she will be dead. Even the slightest touch will kill her."

As the woman remained resistant, the therapist set up another scene: a confrontation with the friend. With the help of a double, she was able to tell her friend that she cared for her deeply and knew that she had to free herself from her mother, but simply could not and would not kill her under any circumstance. At that point, the therapist asked the woman to drop her role and to retell the story, in third person, altering whatever part of the story she desired. In retelling the story, the woman changed the ending radically. Instead of having the girl kill the mother, she had the girl kill herself.

In closing this experience, the group first removed their makeup, again cleansing their faces and symbolically leaving their characters behind. During the closing discussion, which carried over into the next session, the group looked at issues between parents and children. Although the woman who played the girl did not at that time have the distance necessary to see the implications of her symbolic suicide, she was able to begin a process that led to a clear recognition of her problem: separation from her actual mother.

Another use of storytelling, in which the therapist assumes a more active role, is the mutual storytelling technique, involving the improvisational creation of a story by a client. Through his questioning and direct participation in the storytelling, the therapist alters the client's story, guiding him toward a satisfactory therapeutic resolution (Gardner, 1971). If, for example, the woman above had invented "The Story of the Heart" spontaneously, ending with a suicide, the therapist might lead her toward an alternative ending—a discovery of a non-destructive way to separate from the mother.

Storytelling is a means of focusing in drama therapy. As a projection and/or identification, it provides a way to balance the distance between the worlds of reality and fantasy. It is a familiar form to most clients—children and adults alike. As an embodiment of archetypal imagery, it becomes a bridge between the heroes and demons of mythology and literature, and those lurking within the unconscious mind.

THEATRE

The use of literature in drama therapy, embodying scripted characters with whom the client can identify, takes its most obvious form in theatre performance. As in the case of storytelling, theatre performance implies two forms: one based in improvisation and one based in a formal script.

In the improvisational approach, the clients spontaneously create the dialogue and action of their characters. This approach tends to be the least distanced of the two, as the role and the self are often closely identified.

Theatre based in improvisation is not necessarily theatre that is presented improvisationally. The improvisational approach is most often used during rehearsal as a means of defining the characters and actions. Through the improvisational process, a script is developed which will eventually be performed to an audience. An example of an improvisational rehearsal process leading to performance is in the work of the New York based group, Common Threads. The members of the company met in a drama therapy group. Their collective work developed following their experience in creating autobiographical performance pieces based upon significant life events. As several individuals chose to continue this type of work, a group formed to extend the experience in the process of drama therapy to the product of theatre performance. Their improvisational pieces eventually became scripted. Their common themes evolved into a theatrical production designed and developed collaboratively.

Common Threads began performing to audiences they deemed "safe," that is, those sensitive to the notion of theatre as therapeutically based. Such audiences included students and professionals in the fields of mental health and drama therapy, as well as special groups of social service clients. The fact that their performance was explicitly autobiographical brought the audiences into the common ground of shared experience through identification.

Common Threads has since performed to a more general audience in a university theatre. Though still employing the improvisational form of creation, they added further theatrical devices, i.e., an outside director and multimedia technology to conform to audience expectations and to provide themselves with further aesthetic distance.

There are dangers inherent in the transformation of improvisationally based theatre, created in a drama therapy setting, into more conventional performance for general audiences. For one, the actor/client is often too exposed, too unmasked. While this reality can be appropriate when performing for a "safe" audience, it can become problematic when the group modifies its work to please a general audience. When the actor/client confuses performance as a properly distanced search for healthy expression with the more underdistanced need for immediate approval, and if the actor as self, rather than the actor as character, is asking for that approval, then the therapeutic value of the experience becomes minimized.

Improvisationally based theatre as therapy and more commercial performances based in similar improvisational processes are incompatible. Should the drama therapist confuse the two, he would most certainly compromise the integrity and safety of his group. Common Threads was able to make a safe transition from drama therapy group work to the presentation of autobiographical performance pieces. Their development was gradual and thoughtful. When they finally moved toward a more theatrically based performance, they chose a theatre director sensitive to the drama therapy process. Further, they retained a process of group exploration, meeting regularly to discuss conflicts and periodically inviting a drama therapist to help them work through interpersonal issues.

The second form of theatre performance, that based on the use of a formal script, is considerably more distanced than that based in autobiographical material, created improvisationally. The scripted approach has been used with some frequency. Such plays as *Marat/Sade* (Brookes, 1975) and *Our Town* (Rose, 1982) were produced successfully by psychiatric patients within hospital settings. One group, The Open Gate Theatre, maintained a performance space within Bellevue Psychiatric Hospital for three years, producing *Dracula*, among other plays, with a cast of former psychiatric patients.

The choice of such plays as *Marat/Sade* and *Dracula* are relevant to work with psychiatric patients, as they both concern mentally ill characters, i.e., the inmates of Charenton and the Renfield character in *Dracula*. In that both plays are highly stylized and theatrical, a distancing factor is provided by the script.

In working with such plays, the drama therapist needs to have considerable skill as a director of theatre. For the experience to be fruitful, many hard questions must be addressed. First, what are the values in producing difficult plays that require a knowledge of specific styles of acting—in the case of *Marat/Sade*, that of epic theatre performance, and in the case of *Dracula*, that of melodrama? Will this experience primarily be therapeutic or aesthetic? Or do the therapeutics come through the aesthetics? Further, for whom will the actors perform? Will they perform to audiences of peers, professionals, and/or general audiences? If they perform to general audiences, what will be the purpose—to entertain? to educate? to prove that psychiatric patients can perform complex material well?

Another series of questions involves casting choices and the level of identification between actor and role. How will the roles be cast? Should there be auditions, assigning the leading roles to the most talented actors, or should the roles be cast according to psychological needs and potential therapeutic benefits? Should Renfield, an overtly manic mentally ill character, be played by a client who is closely identified with the role, very withdrawn and distant from the role, or more balanced in relation to the role? Who should decide these issues—clients, therapist, client in consultation with therapist?

The final series of questions focuses upon the act of performance itself. What are the therapeutic values of theatre performance? Does the distancing paradigm hold when moving from process to product, from improvisationally based projection of self to scripted identification with a character? Does the act of performing in a therapeutic theatre become confused in the minds of drama therapist, client, and audience with the act of performing in the commercial theatre? How can these confusions be recognized and resolved?

There are, of course, no easy answers to these questions. But they need to be addressed by drama therapists and clients alike before embarking upon an experience in scripted theatre. There have been several articles written about the positive therapeutic effects of theatre performance (Brookes, 1975; Johnson and Munich, 1975; Johnson, 1980; Rose, 1982; Johnson and Emunah, 1983). Most of the writers agree that in order to facilitate the development of positive self-concept and social interaction through the theatre experience, the drama therapist must develop support groups both during and following the performance experience and must not lose sight of the therapeutic needs of the performers through focusing on the entertainment needs of the audience.

As a projective technique, theatre provides a distancing factor in the space between self and role, performer and audience. Both improvisationally based and more formal scripted theatre performance can be highly beneficial to the client. Current research, however, indicates that improvisationally based performance holds more potential therapeutic value (Johnson and Emunah, 1983).

Given a script based upon the lives of the actors and developed through an open process of improvisation; a drama therapist/director sensitive to the therapeutic needs of the clients and skilled as to the aesthetic demands of theatre; a group willing to examine their lives through the projection of self upon role; a group process that provides time for reflection and discussion of problems that arise in relation to performance; and an audience aware of the therapeutic process preceeding the performance and not expecting a slick Broadway production—the elements essential to excellence in therapeutic theatre will be intact.

SOCIODRAMA

Sociodrama concerns the projection of the self upon a social, collective role. Like the actor in a highly stylized play who is asked to assume the role of Mrs. Malaprop or Mr. Mauler or Everyman, the client playing a sociodramatic role takes on a universal, collective persona, implying a less naturalistic, more exaggerated style of enactment. The social role tends to be larger than life and thus more distanced from the self than that of the individual role.

In classical sociodrama, as developed by Moreno, however, the social role would at times provide an intense personal projection on the part of the protagonist. In particularly sensitive sociodramas (i.e., Arabs vs. Israelis), protagonists have been known to immediately underdistance, merging fully with the role and becoming overwhelmed with feeling.

Since Moreno developed the concept of sociodrama, many modifications of the form have evolved. One example is in the work of Linda and Michael Gregoric, originally at the University of Connecticut at Storrs, who combined video and role playing as a means of exploring social issues within particular institutional settings (Gregoric and Gregoric, 1981). Through their program, Media and Arts for Social Services, the Gregorics have worked within prisons, schools, and social service agencies to develop scripts that represent the immediate social realities of an environment. Sometimes the script would be written down, rehearsed, and performed by the participants who included actors, clients, and social service personnel. Most often, the script would be improvised on the spot. As the script is enacted, the experience is videotaped. The videotape product is used not only as a means of direct feedback and self-confrontation for the participants but also as a means of educating social service personnel as to the problematic issues of prison life, parole, and the like.

A recent videotape shows Linda Gregoric and Carson Ferri-Grant working with a group of child molesters and sex offenders in a prison setting, attempting through role playing and video feedback to break through their resistance to examining intimate relationships. Research conducted by Ferri-Grant (1984) has validated the positive effects of sociodrama on the sex offender.

Within a drama therapy setting, sociodrama can be used as a means of exploring a particular social issue germane to the life of the group. As an example, let us look at a group that focused upon the issue of race. The therapist warmed up the group by asking each person to write the name of one race—black, brown, red, yellow, or white—upon a large piece of paper and then attach that paper to their clothing as a sign. The group was arbitrarily divided into dyads. Each person was instructed to begin to move freely in his social role, extending his movements into caricature and stereotyped behavior. Further, all were asked to interact with their partners, initiating and responding to movements when appropriate.

As individuals became more spontaneous in their exaggeration, an atmosphere of play pervaded the room. Yet, many were uncomfortable with their caricatures and much embarrassment and overdistance was evident. Others were able to discharge their discomfort through laughter. The playful exaggeration helped those for whom race was a particularly charged issue.

Following the initial play, the therapist asked each dyad to reverse roles. Then, all were asked to choose the role/race they felt closest to and write a five-minute piece on the back of their sign, from the point of view of a specific boy or girl, man or woman of a specific race. In the piece, the writer was to specify: Who am I (age, name, socioeconomic status, etc.)? Where am I? What am I doing there? The experience was one of free writing, expression limited only by the five-minute time period but unlimited as to content and form.

Following the writing, the therapist divided the group into A, one-half of each dyad, and B, the other half. Group A formed an inner circle, with Group B on the perimeter. Individuals in Group A were asked to speak either in monologue, addressed to another listener, or soliloquy, an expression of interior thought addressed to no particular listener. Basing their speeches upon their free-writing, they were to assume the role of that character in voice, body posture, affect, and thought, and to enact that character so that the group would know of his life as a black, brown, red, yellow, or white person within a particular environment. People in Group B were asked to observe the enactments of their partners, as they would later provide feedback.

Following Group A's enactment, Group B engaged in a similar process of storytelling and expressive action. During the enactments, distance was removed as individuals assumed the realities of their characters, some identifying quite closely with their roles. Many of the presentations took on a seriousness and profundity as, for example, a man in the role of a black soldier recounted his experiences in Vietnam and a woman in the role of a Vietnamese girl told of her struggles to immigrate from Southeast Asia to the United States. Others remained more distant, using humor or cliche as a means to separate more from their roles.

During the enactments, the therapist did not intervene at all. There were several moments of catharsis through laughter and crying. The group remained attentive and supportive. During closure, the dyads re-formed and each provided his partner with feedback as to the other's presentation of issues involving race. A central focus of the closing discussion was upon identification, from the point of view of the actor and observer.

In concluding the sociodramatic experience, the entire group discussed issues of race that were stimulated by the enactments. As a summary statement, the therapist offered the observation that difficult social issues often become more focused and more immediately understood through the guise of a personal role. In working with a combination of social and personal projections, exaggerated and realistic styles, the group was able to view a complex issue with some insight. As a projective technique, sociodrama provides the mask of Everyman, which, when worn by an individual, provides a properly distanced means of looking at the universal condition through the particular case.

DREAMS

A dream is an intrapsychic projection, a series of images of the self projected onto internal objects, people, animals. The psychic screen upon which all these images are projected is the mind. Three conceptions of dream, those of Freud, Jung, and Perls, are all important for an understanding of dreamwork in drama therapy. For Freud (1965), the dream is a manifestation of unconscious repressed wishes and fantasies that take on symbolic forms. The dream, though a representation of one's present experience, refers to the past, to unresolved infantile conflicts. Through the psychoanalytic verbal process of free association, one comes to understand one's dream imagery.

For Jung (1968), the dream embodies archetypes of the collective unconscious. Through an analysis of these archetypes, one comes to know the central issues in his own life in relation to a universal conception of culture and transpersonal experience. In working with the dream, Jung focused upon the immediate context of the dreamer's life, viewing the imagery, first, through the short lens of the present, then through the longer one of the universal and timeless. Unlike Freud, Jung did not only work through verbal means to uncover the dream imagery. Using the method of active imagination, he would often have patients express their imagery through drawing and movement.

Perls goes further than Freud and Jung in conceiving the dream as a dramatic representation of the roles of self. For Perls (1969), the dream is a manifestation of present experiencing, the here-and-now. It neither refers to the past nor to a collective notion of human experience. In working with the dream, Perls shuns all analysis, moving instead into the technique of dramatization. The client in Gestalt therapy acts out his dream in order to reclaim the separate, split-off parts. For Perls, every object in the dream is a part of the self that can be reintegrated through a process of enactment.

Taking the notions of Freud, Jung, and Perls together, we can conceive of the dreamworld as an altered state of consciousness that contains repressed elements from an individual's past, archetypes from the collective past of mankind, and split-off parts of the self reflecting one's present state of being. Further, we can see the dream as pointing to the future, to the hopes, wishes, and fantasies of the dreamer. Adding a more theatrical notion, the dreamworld can be seen as a stage containing sets, props, costumes, colors, and characters. The characters and objects in the dream perform in any and all styles, combining elements of farce, tragedy, and melodrama at will, and disregarding the classical unities of time, place and action.

In working with the dream, the drama therapist can begin by asking the client to reconstruct his dreamworld as if it were a theatrical setting. This can be done with available objects representing shapes, settings, and characters in the dream. One woman, for example, worked on the top of a table with objects from her purse. In setting up her dreamworld, she used a round piece of foam rubber to represent a pond. She put keys of various size within the pond as fish. A compact with an open mirror became her son. An area on the far side of the table represented a larger body of water.

After her dream set was completed, the therapist asked her which object she felt most connected to. She indicated the largest key/fish in the foam rubber pond. She was then instructed to play upon her set, taking on the point of view of the large fish who could speak or remain silent, as she chose.

The woman first extricated the large fish from the small pond, exclaiming: "There's not enough room for me here anymore." She then engaged in a scene with her son who mirrored her feeling. The mirroring was quite literal, as he was represented by her compact mirror. He spoke, too, of needing more space and feeling cramped in his tiny room in their tiny apartment.

Finally, the large fish approached the larger body of water. She played there cautiously for a while, then slowed down, which appeared to the therapist as a sign of overdistancing. He intervened by moving the big fish to the very edge of the table, at a precarious point of balance. The client hesitated. Then she went down to the floor below the table, taking the big fish with her. She referred to this space as the ocean and began to play much more freely.

The therapist then asked: "Is there any other character you want down there with you?" She took the smallest key/fish from the pond on top of the table and proceeded to move it near the edge. But it slipped from her fingers and fell to the ground. She became disturbed and began to put it back on the table. The therapist asked her to let it stay on the ground and to continue to speak about the incident from the point of view of the small fish. Through this monologue, the woman became aware of the small, fearful part of herself that could only enter the larger world of experience and risk through being thrust into it, as if by accident. As she recognized this, she experienced catharsis through crying.

With the big fish and the little fish together in the big ocean, she felt balanced, having recognized a painful progression—first feeling like a big fish in a small pond, then feeling like a small fish in a big pond, and presently feeling both big and small, strong and weak, within the largest and most challenging arena yet.

Within this dramatization, elements of past, present, and future flowed together. During the closure, the client spoke of her past life in a small town and her need to escape. She further spoke about her fears of moving to a large, urban area, the adjustments she had to make for herself, and the struggles of her son that, in fact, did mirror her own. And finally, she spoke of her hopes for the future, the ability to integrate the frightened small fish with the more courageous big fish.

Dreamwork in drama therapy can also involve more group participation. If the woman had had difficulty engaging in her drama, the therapist would have asked her to work with others in the group as auxiliaries. As before, she could begin by building the sets with available objects. Then she would cast the dream, choosing appropriate group members to play the roles of fish, son, small pond, intermediate body of water, large ocean, and cliff. Through a psychodramatic process, her dreamworld could be explored in action.

At the end of Shakespeare's *A Midsummer Night's Dream*, Puck, the playful fool, enters and, outside of the play structure, apologizes to the audience for any offense that the play might have caused them. He refers to himself and the other characters in the play as "shadows," to the scenes as "visions," and to the theme as "idle" and dreamlike. The play is very much a dream of the lovers, the fairy, Titania, the clown, Bottom, the playwright, Shakespeare, and finally, the audience. And what an elegant dream! As in much of Shakespeare's work, the distance between shadow and substance, idleness and profundity, dream and reality is not very great at all. It is the idle dream, the foolishness, the mask of reality that contains the deepest truths of the human condition. And it is through wearing that mask himself that the actor/client can approach those truths.

The dream is, in effect, another mask that separates self from role and takes on myriad projections of the self. For the client willing to look behind the mask and enter into the extraordinary world of projections, there exists the potential for integration in seeing reality anew, in recognizing experience past and present, and in moving toward a greater confluence of roles in the future. In working at this poetic level, the client is hardly an idle dreamer. And at this poetic level, no apologies are necessary.

EXTENDED DRAMATIZATION

Extended dramatization is a depth drama therapy approach that incorporates many of the projective techniques already discussed. It requires the structure of a consistent group, working together over an extended period of time. The extended dramatization makes use of three levels of projection: one, the self is projected onto a fictional character; two, images of the family are projected onto a fictional family; and three, images of community life are projected onto a fictional community. Working through their fictional roles at the individual, family, and community levels, the group members proceed to uncover their actual intrapsychic, family, and community issues. Let us look at the structure of one such group to see how the technique works.

The group was conducted in an urban university setting and consisted, initially, of twelve members: two men and ten women. The ages of the members ranged from mid-twenties to early fifties. The setting was equipped with video cameras, monitors, and microphones. The experience was set within a time frame of 30 hours over a period of three weeks.

As an initial warm-up, the therapist asked each member to focus in on the camera and to complete the sentence: "To me, the camera is like a ... " Then, he asked each to create a movement in relation to the camera, based in the image previously chosen. In freezing the movement of each person, the therapist asked: "Who are you?" Through a series of questions and answers, each person took on a fictionalized persona with a name, age, gender, and set of behaviors, feelings, and thoughts. Each was asked to speak a monologue in role to further help establish character.

Then the therapist arbitrarily divided the group into three subgroups of four each, representing three families. Each family met separately to decide upon the relationships among the four and a name for the family. In closing the session, each family group identified itself by name. The families became Williamson, Shaw, and Rotapaley. Finally, individuals out of role spoke of their feelings regarding the initial process.

On the second day of the group, the two men dropped out, leaving the group with ten women. As both men were part of the Rotapaley family, that subgroup was left with two members, one of whom had chosen the role of a man. The family decided not to dwell upon the loss of the men and the therapist proceeded with a warm-up. All were asked to address the camera directly (in role), this time removing some distance and speaking to it in the second person as "you." Many entered into a closer relationship with the camera—challenging it, flirting with it, scolding it, all actions somewhat distanced by their role playing.

Next, the therapist asked the group members out of role to visualize three places—one where they would like to be, a second which they would find frightening, and a third which is a composite of the previous two. All were asked to sketch the three places in their notebooks. Following the sketching, each family met to discuss common characteristics of their drawings. Then, the entire community discussed commonalities of their drawings. Repeated images of water, light, and airiness emerged, juxtaposed with images of darkness, industry, and a presence of the military.

As a community, the group was asked to decide upon a name. Ideas were offered and debated until the group finally elected the name, Tempest Alley. Each family was then instructed to build, with available objects, a part of Tempest Alley, based upon recurring imagery in their drawings.

Following the construction of the community, the therapist led the group through a condensed day in Tempest Alley, beginning at 7:00 A.M. and ending at bedtime. The experience was geared toward helping the group establish a connection to the environment, a relationship to their families and to others in the community, and a sense of their own characters through the activities of a day.

Following "A Day in Tempest Alley," the therapist closed the session again with a process of de-roling, letting go of the fictional characters and expressing feelings around the dramatized issues in relation to actual roles, families, and communities. The therapist also asked each person to prepare a family history, a written piece on how their family came to Tempest Alley.

The next session began with a presentation of these stories, fictional projections of either one's actual or idealized family history. Following each story, the storyteller sculpted her family group by setting up a group portrait, placing each person in a representative posture and relationship to the others. She also included herself in the sculpture. Each sculpted group portrait was recorded on videotape.

Then, to help establish the integrity of individual families, as well as to explore tensions between families, each family group was asked to gossip about the others as the subjects of the gossip listened. There were many criticisms expressed at this time; however, one theme strongly emerged: the need for a common ground of understanding, for further clarification and sharing.

During the closure of the session, a sense of imbalance was expressed. One woman mentioned having a "splitting" headache. At that point, the therapist asked her to construct the headache with foam rubber objects available. The imagery created was quite haphazard. She named her construction, "Turmoil." She played with the split-off pieces of Turmoil, letting out some of the tension held within her body. When she stopped, a more coherent pattern was evident. The therapist then asked her to dissemble Turmoil. In doing so, she rearranged the foam in a symmetrical, balanced fashion. A balance of distance was restored not only for her but also for others in the group who had identified with her imbalance, her inner turmoil.

Psychodramatic and sociodramatic techniques were used in conjunction with the video equipment to help pinpoint an issue or uncover the mystery of a role. During a psychodramatic experience, for example, the therapist focused upon Jane, a woman having trouble recognizing the dimensions of her chosen role of Joe, an angry Vietnam veteran. At one point in the sociodrama, Joe exclaimed: "I wish the Russians would invade this island." The therapist took on the role of camera and said: "Do you know who I am, Joe?" Joe responded quite unexpectedly: "You're an academic." Then, both switched roles, Jane/Joe becoming the camera, the academic, and the therapist becoming Joe. As she assumed the camera role, Jane was literally given the live camera and asked to focus upon the therapist in the role of Joe. Experiencing difficulty, she said: "I'm tired of having to focus."

In exploring her issue further, Jane began to recognize the characters of Joe and the Academic. For the first time in the extended dramatization, Jane said: "Joe is exactly like my ex-husband. I've hated the character all along." She also realized that the Academic was a part of herself that she liked very much at that point but had trouble focusing upon. The therapist closed the psychodramatic enactment by asking Joe to give a soliloquy, expressing her inner feelings. Coming to a point of balance, Jane said: "Maybe there's room in the world for two kinds of people." Later she concluded: "I think it's two parts of myself."

The therapist moved to a more graphic representation of the several roles of the self, introducing the projective techniques of masks and puppetry. The work began as each person was asked to construct a mask representing a hidden part of her Tempest Alley character.

Each introduced her mask to the group, first by speaking about it, then by wearing it and moving in role. The character, Jerome, a very old, slow-moving, wise, spiritual man, became a mischievous little boy through the mask. The aggressive, controlled Joe became sad and depressed in mask.

The therapist then asked each person to name her mask, place it in an appropriate position in her space, and write a letter, orally, to the mask character. Patti's role was Chris Rotapaley, an affable, strong older brother, very much responsible for taking care of his younger sister. Patti's mask character was very different. She named him Sad Sack, the needy, lost part of her character. During the letter writing she began: "I don't want you hanging around our house, Sad Sack." But then she ended: "But it's not all that bad, Sad Sack; it's really not. If you have to be anything in my house, you can be a dog."

At that point, the therapist asked Patti to assume the role of Sad Sack, the dog, by wearing the mask and imitating the movements of a dog. In role, she was able to get to her Tempest Alley sister, Melissa, to pet her and to care for her. The session ended with Patti expressing that it felt good to reverse roles, to take on a needy role for once and receive some attention from her sister.

For the following session, the therapist asked the group to build a puppet that represented a part of the Tempest Alley character that had been only minimally expressed but needed to be more fully seen by others in the family. As before, the warm-up began with each person out of role introducing the puppet in third person. As each warmed up, she then took on the puppet role, speaking in first person to the camera or microphone. Rhonda/Jerome, who had initially expressed much discomfort concerning the video equipment, used her role of Taki, a tiny, curious, naive baby, to address the microphone: "I'm pleased I can say hello to 'Michael' now which before was very awesome for me."

Although the puppets generally helped the group to overdistance and approach those people and objects which were previously unapproachable, it had the opposite effect for Kathy. Her puppet, Yearny, representing the part of her Tempest Alley character that felt lost and yearned for security and calm, exclaimed: "People always go away. I wish people wouldn't always go away." Through a balanced identification with her puppet, Kathy was able to release her own sense of sadness.

The warm-up was followed by a dinner table scene, focusing upon one family at a time. All were instructed to use both puppets and Tempest Alley characters at will to express feelings to the family and, more generally, to reveal the family dynamics to the Tempest Alley community. During the scene, each character was to find a motivated reason to leave the table; and in her absence, the others were to talk about her.

Following the scene, all were asked to choose a family member with whom they experienced some unfinished business and to write her a letter, in the role of the puppet character. Kathy's sadness, expressed during the warm-up, carried over to the dinner table scene. In Sue's puppet role as a snotty, distant little sister, she wrote to Kathy (Marcy): "Dear Marcy, I know you're going through a difficult time now. Try to keep yourself under control." When it was Kathy's turn to write a letter, she passed, feeling underdistanced and unsupported in the drama.

The therapist then asked the group to let go of their Tempest Alley roles and to write letters to appropriate receivers out of role. Sue amended her letter to read: "Dear Kathy, despite what Dorothy (Sue's puppet character) thinks, you don't really have to keep things under control." As others also supported Kathy out of role, she was able to respond by thanking them in a letter addressed to the entire family.

When the therapist questioned Sue as to why she was able to be more supportive of Kathy out of role, she replied: "I could only speak according to the limitations of my puppet role." When questioned further as to the possibilities of transcending the role, Sue replied: "It wouldn't have been right. I needed to be a good girl. I didn't feel I was supposed to."

In closing, the group discussed the limitations and possibilities of roles both in Tempest Alley and in everyday life. The therapist underlined his stated goals in drama therapy: to increase one's repertory of roles and one's ability to play a single role competently, spontaneously, and flexibly.

·In closing the Tempest Alley experience, the group focused upon issues of saying good-bye. Following a brief warm-up discussion, each person began to work herself into her Tempest Alley role through movement in front of the camera. Once she found the character in her body, she froze the movement. Then, her frozen image was played back on the monitor. She was asked to focus in on the still image and, out of role, to say good-bye to the character. She was further encouraged to retain that part of the character that she didn't want to leave behind. Then she put on the mask and found the mask role through her movement, as before. The image of the mask character was also played back and frozen, and she said good-bye to that part of herself. Likewise, the puppet character was recorded, played back and bid good-bye. Further, clients were encouraged to say good-bye to the video equipment, as desired.

Following that sequence, the client, as self, was asked to focus upon her live image in the video monitor and to say hello to herself in three different ways. The experience concluded as the client articulated three wishes—one for herself, one for her actual family, and the third for her actual community.

In saying good-bye to her three characters, Barbara first focused upon her Tempest Alley character and said: "You've been helpful, but you're tired now and I hope you'll be gracious enough to make room for other parts." To her mask, she said: "Sabrina, you need to be less excessive. Good-bye to tinsel and flash, but not forever." The mask had been placed on a technician holding a boom microphone. The therapist asked Barbara: "What is Sabrina holding?" Barbara responded: "A scepter. She's a goddess."

Then Barbara spoke to her puppet character: "You're the poor part of me. But in the screen, you look like a princess. Whatever's in me that felt poor will be richer for having found you out."

The closing ritual to the thirty-hour extended dramatization occurred as the therapist asked the group to assume Tempest Alley roles one last time and say good-bye to each other non-verbally in role. Then, he asked them to let go of their characters and to say hello to each other in words and action.

The extended dramatization offers an excellent confluence of projective techniques. The above example included several successful therapeutic moments. But for many, the experience is arduous. There is much resistance, and the distancing techniques do not work equally well for all. However, within an atmosphere of trust and given sufficient time and training on the part of the therapist, the extended dramatization can be a powerful yet gentle means of working through projection and moving toward integration.

THE WORLD TECHNIQUE

The world technique, like the extended dramatization, involves a dramatic representation of self, family, and community. Unlike the extended dramatization though, the world technique proceeds through small objects which represent one's inner vision of the world. As one projects his image of self, family, and community onto the objects, manipulating them through free play, he enacts a drama in the presence of a therapist.

The world technique was first developed by the British child psychoanalyst, Margaret Lowenfeld (1939). She based her work generally in psychoanalytic theory and more specifically in the play therapy notions of Anna Freud and Melanie Klein. Related work in sand play was developed by Jungian analysts, most notably Dora Kalff (1981) in Switzerland. The basis of the world technique is in the sensory and intuitive experience of both children and adults, although most of Lowenfeld's work was with children.

Lowenfeld's clients constructed their worlds in a sand tray. She provided them with small objects of several classifications. The first included people, divided into three types—ordinary, military, and special types of circus figures, mythological figures, and cross-cultural figures. Ordinary people were men, women, and children in occupational and family roles. Lowenfeld specified that there should be variation as to the body positions of the figures, some standing, some sitting.

Other classifications included houses and buildings, trees and fences; animals, both wild and tame; transportation, including cars, trains, and boats; street signs and equipment; and more non-descript objects such as sticks, stones, and irregularly shaped objects.

As the children constructed their worlds and played with the objects, the therapist would record their activity in several ways: taking notes, making drawings, and taking photographs. According to Lowenfeld, the very act of constructing and recording was therapeutic, bringing about a sense of control and a lessening of pathology for some children. Unlike many of her American colleagues who translated her technique into diagnostic tests (Michael and Buehler, 1945, Bolgar and Fischer, 1947), Lowenfeld conceived of her work as an in-depth means of exploring the intuitive thought and sensation of children. To that end, she worked through many projections of worlds with a single client, proceeding carefully and thoroughly until a total picture of the child's inner world emerged.

Working from a similar point of view, Erik Homburger Erikson extended the world technique into therapy for adults as well as children. Erikson's early research centered in world constructions with college students at the Harvard Psychological Clinic in the 1930s. Like Lowenfeld, he used small toys and asked his subjects, all Harvard undergraduates, to construct a dramatic scene for a film script. In observing and analyzing the play of his subjects, Erikson discovered a profound connection between their inner life and their play constructions (Homburger, 1937).

Erikson collaborated in his research with Henry A. Murray, whose work in psychology also extended into the world of drama. Not only did Murray explore the unconscious of subjects through projective play, he also explored the psyche of several literary characters who were charged with the symbolism of drama and myth. His study of the characters in Melville's *Moby Dick* (Murray, 1951) is a monumental exploration of the psychological interplay of the demonic, id forces, represented by Captain Ahab, and the moralistic, superego forces represented by Moby Dick. He worked further with Hawthorne's symbolic story, "The Minister's Black Veil," concerning a parish priest who one day appears in church masked in a black veil, which he continues to wear until his death. In his research Murray (1938) asked his subjects to revise the tale and explain the meaning of the veil.

In drama therapy, the client can work through world techniques in several ways. He can work through the free play of the Lowenfeld technique, using the given objects to construct his representational world. He can also use given objects or objects of his own choice to construct the world of his dream. In dreamwork, the objects might even be specifically constructed by the client in order to explore a specific dream.

As a further innovation, the drama therapist might build upon Murray's psychological investigations into literature and focus the play world upon that of a literary text. In working with *Moby Dick*, "The Minister's Black Veil," or classics such as *The Odyssey* and *Antigone*, the therapist might first ask the client to read the text, then construct the world of the text with given objects. Finally, the client can revise the story in the sand tray according to his inner identifications, projections, and transferences. Or, the therapist might first provide text-related objects (i.e., those of whaling) for the client to play with without making any explicit reference to a text. After the client's play with the objects, the therapist might then introduce the text, using it as a means of uncovering further levels of understanding.

In concluding his psychoanalytically based paper, "Configurations in Play," Erikson notes that the use of the miniature world provides dramatic means for the client to resolve a traumatic episode in his childhood. Through playing out, for example, his fears of permanent alienation from his family, the client, like Odysseus, can engage in his magical odyssey over and over again, until he has resolved his separation anxiety. Says Erikson (Homburger, 1937):

> Dramatic and traumatic events have one psychological element in common. Both are events which transgress the boundaries of the human ego, the first in widening it beyond individuation, the second in nearly extinguishing it. In other words, in a truly dramatic moment the individual is confronted with a choice which may make him the heroic or tragic master of human fate in its eternal aspects; he is allowed one chance to overcome the bondage of gravity and repetition. The traumatic moment destroys individuation, chance and choice, and makes the individual the helpless victim of repetition compulsion.

Through the projected play of the world technique, the client dramatizes his inner life, recognizing problematic issues of self, family, and community, and moving toward more spontaneous, integrated functioning.

PART IV
THE POPULATIONS AND SETTINGS
FOR DRAMA THERAPY

Chapter Eight

SCHOOL SETTINGS

One common setting for drama therapy practice is in the school, primarily the special education facility. Given the proliferation of special classrooms and schools for various disabled populations since the passage of the Education for All Handicapped Children Act in 1975, new methods of education needed to be implemented. Although the most common approaches have been based upon behavior modification models, the creative arts therapies have also made a significant contribution to the education of the disabled.

Although drama therapy in special education is a relatively recent phenomenon, its kindred form, play therapy, has been applied to the education of emotionally disturbed and other disabled students since the early work of Lowenfeld, Klein, and Axline (1947). Given the psychodramatic and projective techniques mentioned above, many of which are integral to play therapy practice, let us look at several special populations and schools where they are or can be applied.

THE EDUCATION OF THE DEAF THROUGH DRAMA THERAPY

It is rare that a disabled person fits neatly within a single diagnostic label. A deaf person is one who cannot hear, but some deaf individuals can hear sounds with the assistance of a hearing aid. Some can speak; others cannot. Not all deaf people sign, and all who sign do not communicate with the same sign language. Deafness is a condition subsumed with the larger category of hearing impairment. Although deafness is rare, hearing impairment is widespread. Hearing impairment may be mild, affecting partial hearing in one ear, or severe, implying a total hearing loss (Schein, 1982). Further, a deaf or hearing impaired child might also manifest a secondary disability. Due to his problems of adjusting to a hearing world, he might well develop emotional problems. If he is raised in a harsh environment, there might be social and behavioral problems impinging upon his development, as well.

St. Joseph's School for the Deaf, which is situated within a depressed urban area, the South Bronx, is dedicated to the educational philosophy of total communication. Students are taught to use both oral and sign language and to develop all possible means of communication. The teachers are a mix of hearing and non-hearing. All are urged to both speak and sign when communicating with their students.

Vicki Havens, a trained drama therapist, is deaf herself and highly sensitive to the needs of deaf individuals. She works with both individuals and small groups to foster communication skills, appropriate social behaviors, and emotional expression. Many of her students manifest multiple disabilities. Havens draws upon a range of projective techniques, including world technique, puppets, masks, and dolls.

Len, a nine-year-old Puerto Rican boy, meets with Havens once a week for fifty minutes. He comes from a poor family of Spanish speaking, hearing parents. He wears a hearing aid and thick glasses, as he is partially blind as well as deaf. Len has a history of severe emotional problems, including poor impulse control, withdrawal from social contact, perseveration, and ritual-like behavior. Wherever he goes, he carries a large globe of the world. Each night, Len sleeps with a smaller globe. To help develop communication skills, Havens proceeds through the medium of play.

In one recent session, Len entered the playroom with his globe and placed it on a table. Havens took up a hand puppet made from a glove that she had designed for use with deaf children. The fingers of the glove are used to sign; thus, the puppet can "talk."

Len became angry at the hand puppet and took it away from Havens. He was not yet warmed up to communicating. He then took a water pistol from the shelf and shot at her, communicating his anger.

Throughout the playroom are common play objects and projective devices, including guns and planes, miniature furniture and people. But there are other objects suitable for deaf children, such as a bell and a large drum, open on the bottom, whose sounds can be felt if not heard by the deaf child.

After being shot by Len, Havens tried to establish contact by ringing the bell. Len, however, did not respond. He wanted to "take off," so he found a small airplane. Havens followed after with a larger plane. Encouraging movement, she flew her plane around the room, providing a mirror for Len. But he remained aloof, absorbed in his personal play. Len finally landed and hid his plane under a block table. Havens attempted to approach him with a small boy figure. He was not ready for people contact and took off again, landing the plane on his globe. He spun it wildly as the plane made contact with the surface, creating a loud noise that he could feel through his fingers. Havens took up the drum and began beating it. Len was attracted to the rhythms and took the drum from her, wearing it over his head like a hat. She beat on the drum and he seemed to enjoy the stimulation. Finally, he took the drum off his head and brought it to the globe. He then spun the globe and beat the drum simultaneously. Havens asked if he could hear the sounds. He responded by spinning the globe wildly. Havens mirrored him by beating the drum.

The therapist's main objective in this session was to bring Len into contact with her and with people and animal objects. In weaning him away from the globe and the drum, she took out two pieces of foam rubber in the shape of bats, each with a plastic handle on one end. Len took one and hit Havens's bat mildly. He also hit other objects in the room before he was ready to engage with Havens in a mock duel. But his attention flagged and he again went to the drum and beat it strongly. Leaving the drum, but retaining the drumstick, he crossed to the closet where hats are kept. He took one of a McDonald's counterman and gave Havens a captain's hat. Wearing the hat, he began to engage in ritualistic actions, rubbing the bat on objects of furniture and stroking the drumstick across the bat as if he were a butcher sharpening a knife. He then focused upon the emblematic McDonald's arches, tracing their forms with the drumstick. He ended abruptly and put the hats away.

Next, he set up a new scene, placing the two bats side by side and rolling the drumstick repeatedly across the smooth surface. Havens then introduced a boy figure saying: "The boy wants to be your friend." Len rejected the figure, knocking him out of the scene. Havens introduced a soft animal figure, but that, too, was rejected. Finally, she touched Len with the boy figure, walking it up his arm. He did not reject her advances. She then reintroduced the boy figure within the play scene. Len allowed it to stay but rolled it with the drumstick, then hit it and tossed it from the scene.

Taking up a parrot puppet with an extended beak, Havens assumed the role of the boy and said: "You hurt me. I'm crying." Len became interested in this and expressed some mild aggression toward the parrot. In attempting to get Len to communicate further, Havens crossed to the blackboard and began to draw. Len joined her and drew four circles in a row, each with a dot in the center. A line with an arrow went through the circles and pointed to a stick figure, followed by three more circles and an arrow pointing downward.

After the drawing, Len put the bats away. Havens then announced that the session was over. Len was not ready to go, and he took up a position on a balance board. He was unbalanced, tipsy. Havens allowed him time to find his balance, literally and figuratively, then led him from the room.

Although the above description is only of one session, it reveals much about Len's inner life and provided the therapist several clues in planning further work with him.

For one, Len carries around an enormous burden wherever he goes. Like Atlas, he must support his own world. His internal world is so fragile and undefined that he must symbolize it in a tangible, bounded form. Further, his perseveration on images of globes, arches, and circles, plus his obsessive rolling and spinning actions, suggest an inability to separate from the mother figure, symbolized by a drawing of four breasts pointing to a boy and leading him to fall off a three-wheeled platform. Len's private world is not only cut off by emotional barriers but also through two primary senses: hearing and sight.

In working through the projective objects, the therapist aims to, first, open up the channels of communication so that there is a free flow of sensation between Len's outer and inner worlds. The use of the drum, bell, and signing hand puppet provide means of moving from outside to inside and back. Through her work with the small human figures and animal puppets, the therapist further attempts to help Len accept living beings into his world who, like him, are capable of feeling and sensing. Through taking on the roles of these figures and expressing feelings, she provides a model for Len.

Over time, the therapist aims toward helping Len reconstruct an inner world that is not only made of globes but of male symbols as well, identifying Len as a boy, separate from his mother, capable of expressing some of his feelings and letting go of his Herculean burden. In keeping with the distancing model, Len needs to play out his own emotional, sensory, and cultural imbalances until he can find a balance of distance and re-enter his everyday environment with a greater sense of security.

Although Len is an extreme example, many deaf children, adolescents, and adults experience emotional problems as a result of their hearing impairments. Like Vicki Havens, the drama therapist within a special school setting can work on a one-to-one basis through play therapy and related projective techniques to help the individual explore his communication and emotional issues, which often are inseparable. Being sensitive to the needs of the deaf student, the therapist can modify conventional puppets, masks, and objects, as in the use of the glove puppet and the open-bottomed drum. The drama therapist can also work through a group process, using a range of dramatic techniques to uncover the interpersonal dynamics and move toward increased capacity for total communication.

Although many schools for the deaf that offer drama focus solely upon theatre performance, play and projective techniques often go further in affecting the inner lives of students and helping them externalize a richer, more total use of language and feeling.

THE EDUCATION OF THE
EMOTIONALLY DISTURBED THROUGH DRAMA THERAPY

Like deafness and hearing impairment, emotional disturbance is a broad diagnostic category incorporating a range of disability from mild to severe. Almost all individuals manifest some degree of emotional disturbance some of the time. These individuals might be able to function quite normally within the bounds of a particular work place, school, or family. But within the person, a host of conflicts and tensions might be present. When these conflicts intrude upon one's feeling of well-being, leading to an over or underdistanced state that affects one's ability to play a role spontaneously and competently within one's social world, then a more active degree of emotional disturbance is present.

For most, emotional disturbances are brief in duration, based in a particularly stressful situation, i.e., the death of a loved one, severe illness, or divorce. Other forms of emotional disturbance are more deeply rooted and based in unresolved life issues.

The mildly disturbed person is often not treated through special education or therapy. The learning disabilities in his disturbance often dissipate as a stressful life issue is resolved through the passage of time, discussion with trusted intimates, or the development of successful defenses. The more acutely disturbed person (i.e., the hyperactive or depressed child) who manifests not only a disturbed behavior pattern but also a protracted duration of the symptom, requires special education and/or therapy. The most severely disturbed individuals, those labelled schizophrenic or autistic, are sometimes educated in schools and at other times subject primarily to clinical treatment through drug therapy and/or psychotherapy.

The special education classroom is most often heterogeneous as to types of emotionally disturbed students. A common characteristic of the students, however, will be the inability to learn through conventional methods. As the favored educational label of these students tends to be learning disabled, focusing upon the learning problem rather than the underlying psychological issue, the teacher using drama therapy techniques will be expected to focus upon cognitive processes (i.e., reading, writing, and mathematical skills). For those students whose learning disabilities are organic, based upon a brain dysfunction or chemical imbalance, and who do not manifest disturbed behavioral patterns, the purely cognitive approach would indeed be the most fruitful. But for those students who manifest disturbed behaviors and whose disabilities are not so clearly organic (that is, those whose backgrounds involve such psychogenic factors as abuse by parents and broken homes), the focus on cognitive learning should also be balanced with emotional, sensory, and social learning.

Applying the drama therapy model, emotional disturbance can be seen as an imbalance in distancing. At one extreme, the overdistanced individual is withdrawn and highly defended, living in an isolated, protected world. The catatonic schizophrenic adult and the autistic child are the most radical examples. At the other extreme, the underdistanced individual is hyperactive and impulsive, living on the edge of overwhelming fear and rage. A radical example is the group described by Redl and Wineman (1951) as "children who hate"—hostile, angry individuals who live in a world dominated by violent fantasies and magical thinking.

In educating the emotionally disturbed person in the classroom through drama therapy, the teacher/therapist aims toward a balance of distance and a flexibility in role playing. These aims can be realized through work with literary texts, student-generated texts, and, more generally, psychodramatic and projective techniques. Let us look at the application of several drama therapy techniques to the education of emotionally disturbed individuals.

Paul is a sixteen-year-old boy, hyperactive and obsessive-compulsive. Throughout childhood and adolescence, he has obsessed upon mechanical objects, often imitating their movements. He identifies strongly with literary and television characters who move fast and are highly active. Although Paul has never traveled in an airplane, he fantasizes heavily about the moment of takeoff, speculating that he might die from the excitement. Whenever possible, he runs rather than walks and seeks approval from adults for his speediness.

Paul has been in a special school for the emotionally disturbed throughout his adolescence. Academically able, he studies a standard curriculum including science, math, history, and English. In that his English teacher is also a drama therapist, Paul often works through the medium of drama. The teacher frequently combines drama with writing. Paul is a prolific writer and tends to express his obsession with movement and flights through his poems and compositions. Over time, the teacher worked through the characters Paul had invented or identified with in literary texts, i.e., Huck Finn and Holden Caulfield in *Catcher in the Rye*. The teacher's aim was to help Paul express his obsession through a projection onto a character, then to begin to extend the behavior of the character into other domains.

The teacher worked with Paul for a year through role playing, world technique, and writing. For several months, Paul held on tight to his obsessive world view, reducing each session to a representation of running and flying. Gradually, his world pictures, representations of literary texts, and personal writings became less mechanical and he began to see the limitations he imposed upon himself. In his role playing with his teacher, he began to reach out to another and became less wound-up and impulsive.

At a crucial point in the therapeutic process, Paul's writing changed. He recognized that Salinger's character, Holden Caulfield, was one who "holds onto people and experiences in order to have things to remember." In a composition, Paul wrote that the name, Caulfield, meant "calling through the field," and that "Holden expressed his want to make people understand him by trying to feel sorry for them, perhaps calling for them through the field of rye where he caught the children who he thought were losing their identity or disappearing—one of Holden's chief fears." Indeed, Paul recognized that this was one of his own chief fears. He, too, was disappearing, so he needed to hold on and to call out to people, obliquely, through his field of motion.

Paul's drama therapy ended with the school year. If there was more time, he might have engaged in further projective techniques, until he could comfortably expand the singular obsessive role, then move into new roles, modeled upon other more distanced literary characters. From the overdistanced projective techniques, the therapist then might have moved into less distanced ones, such as video work, to help Paul find a complex, human image of himself. The next logical step might have been to introduce Paul within a drama therapy group, helping him to examine not only his personal roles but also his social ones.

Joan, like Paul, was an adolescent in a special school for the emotionally disturbed. She had a history of hospitalizations for severe depression and suicidal tendencies. Like Paul, she was quite intelligent and expressed herself well in writing. However, her speech tended to be flat and affectless. She disguised her femininity through dressing in shapeless clothes covering as much of her body as possible and wearing her unshaped hair so that little of her face was exposed. She signed her papers with the pseudonym of Suomy Nona, anonymous spelled backwards. In many ways, Joan wanted to disappear.

In working within a drama therapy group each week, Joan presented herself as frightened and withdrawn, incapable of self-directed action. In the early sessions, Joan would participate minimally, taking care not to expose too much of her body, thoughts, or feelings. The drama therapist allowed Joan to maintain her safe distance for several sessions, encouraging her to participate at her own level in the improvisational scenes, physical warm-ups, and sensory awareness exercises.

Several weeks into the group, Joan showed a poem to the drama therapist. For the first time, she shared a piece of her inner life with him. Although the poem was abstract and oblique, it did offer a glimpse into the hidden world of a very frightened person. The therapist responded positively and Joan continued to share her poetry with him. The relationship established through Joan's poetry carried over into the drama sessions. The therapist recognized that Joan was too frightened to enact an improvisational role that might be construed as real. She needed a sufficiently distanced projection in order to participate, but, at that time, the group was working with roles close to themselves.

When the group began to work on a script, Beckett's *Waiting for Godot*, Joan began to participate more. She identified strongly with the two clowns, Estragon and Vladimir, who she saw as two lost souls, shapeless and hobo-like, waiting for a sign of hope that is always deferred. In playing the role of Vladimir, the more rational and verbal of the two, Joan was able to think through a significant issue of her existence: trying to make sense of a non-sensical world. In the costume of the hobo-clown,

Joan re-created her everyday costume. And through the makeup, movements, and gestures of Vladimir, Joan was able to recognize some of her
own characteristics. Even the tautological arguments of Vladimir led
Joan to a point of identification and recognition. Like Vladimir, she
thought that in life "your only hope left is to disappear" (Beckett, 1954).

Over time, Joan came to recognize the connection between Vladimir's
thoughts and her own. Through her identification with the tragic-comic
Beckett figure, Joan was able to look at her own state of despair, her need
to disappear and sleep, to engage in apparently meaningless habits and
confusions. Joan was further able to look at the contradictions between
life and death, hope and hopelessness, that she so needed to resolve. In
doing so, she began to recognize that they can exist together in a dialectical relationship.

In her writing, too, a change began to occur. The former images of
death and suicide took on new meaning. Death of the self meant the
possibilities of new life. The most dramatic breakthrough was in a poem
written after the *Waiting for Godot* experience about a butterfly emerging
from a cocoon. She concluded the poem:

> Eager to bring
> LIFE
> as she pollinates
> each bud.
> HOW SAD THOUGH,
> to leave
> her soft body
> and
> innocence behind
> in a cocoon.

Joan, too, was growing, moving out of a cocoon, a safe, protected,
asexual world of self-imposed exile. Ironically, a significant move from
that world was sparked by an identification with the sexless derelicts in
Beckett's absurd, bleak landscape of the mind. But, like the San Quentin
prisoners identifying with the characters and themes in Herbert Blau's
production of *Waiting for Godot*, Joan discovered a world view that mirrored
her own. Within Beckett's world she saw a small glimmer of hope, a
vision of passing the time through action, humor, ritual, and finally
through companionship with another—Gogo and Didi are tied to one
another as are Pozzo and Lucky. As difficult and absurd as these relationships seemed, there was still enough hope to go on.

The drama therapy group worked on *Waiting for Godot* for two months and finally presented it to audiences of fellow students, teachers, and friends. Joan appeared on opening day in her baggy costume with her scraggly hair obscuring her face and body. By the fourth and last performance, Joan's face was exposed and her body was animated. She finally wanted to be heard and seen.

Within a special school setting, the issues arising from drama work with projective or psychodramatic techniques can be rechanneled into academic work. That is, an issue that arises in a role-playing session can be the basis for an English composition or an investigation into the history of a family or an epoch.

With younger children, the recommended method of drama therapy is that of play and world technique. The link between drama/play therapy and academics is not always an obvious one. But without the ability to express one's vision of the world, to let out the repressed feelings and sensations, academic experiences will remain academic, and cognition will remain split off from affect and movement. In moving toward balance, the drama therapist helps the student express his subjective world, recognize it, and reconceptualize it. With balance intact, all forms of learning—affective, psychomotor, social, aesthetic, and cognitive—are possible.

THE EDUCATION OF THE
MENTALLY RETARDED THROUGH DRAMA

According to the current *Diagnostic and Statistical Manual of Mental Disorders* (*DSM-III*, 1983), mental retardation is based upon three factors: low intellectual functioning, determined by an IQ of 70 or below; impairment in adaptive behavior, based in developmental comparisons; and onset before the age of eighteen. Although the cause of mental retardation in many cases is unknown, 25 percent of the cases appear to be due to biological abnormalities, a common example being Down's syndrome. The 75 percent majority may be due to psychosocial factors, singly or in combination with biological factors.

Many special classes and clinics treating mental retardation have taken on the more general and less stigmatized label of developmentally disabled, which, along with mental retardation, includes a host of other diagnostic categories such as learning disabilities and neurological impairments. For the purposes of clarity, we will focus attention upon the singular diagnostic category, mental retardation, which in itself is highly variable and often interwoven with related emotional, motoric, and behavioral disabilities.

Mental retardation can be seen in terms of four subtypes: mild, with IQ levels of 50–70; moderate, with IQ levels of 35–49; severe, with IQ levels of 20–34; and profound, with IQ levels below 20. The term, *educable mental retardation*, refers to the mild group (the largest category) and implies that individuals are capable of learning academic skills through at least the sixth grade level. Further, they are capable of developing many social and vocational skills necessary to care for themselves as adults. This is the most prevalent group in special education classes and thus the most likely to be exposed to drama therapy.

The moderate group, known as trainable mentally retarded, is also likely to be treated within the special classroom. The emphasis in working with this group is in developing social and self-help skills. Individuals can be expected to develop minimal academic skills, equivalent to approximately second grade level, and can be trained to work at unskilled or semi-skilled occupations.

Severe and profoundly retarded individuals are generally unable to develop significant academic or occupational skills and need much support in developing language, hygiene, and social skills.

IQ scores and medical labels are often misleading, as many low functioning mentally retarded individuals are unable to respond conventionally to conventional testing methods. The stigma of mental retardation often predisposes teachers and social workers to expect little from their students/clients. But, in working through the creative arts, new possibilities can be seen if the teacher/therapist is open to the people before him.

In applying drama therapy techniques to the special education classroom, the teacher must first be well aware of the diagnostic realities of the group. However, the teacher should also be mindful of those moments of creative expression suggesting that the individual can go further than was expected into extending an old role or discovering a new one.

Eileen Yagoda works at the New York League for Early Learning where she teaches two-, three-, and four-year-old mentally retarded students social and personal skills through drama, music, and movement. Given the limited language skills of her students, Yagoda generally begins her sessions with a song, involving the repetition of a chorus, to foster a sense of group cohesiveness. The song might be in the form of a name game, wherein each child is encouraged to sing his own name and to repeat, in chorus, those of the other group members. Another song involves naming clothing each person is wearing, and a third focuses upon various body parts, naming them within the rhythms of the song.

The learning of names, clothing, and body parts is accomplished through a dramatic game structure. Even the most distanced students, with minimal attention spans, can be drawn into the play through a connection to the music played on guitar and rhythm instruments. Yagoda sings for the nonverbal students, encouraging them to participate in the rhythm and movement of the activity.

In teaching the concept of directions, Yagoda uses an elastic circle of colorful scarves. Each person in the circle holds the material and together they enact the concepts—up, down, left, right—through their connected movements. Yagoda initiates the movements and the others join in playfully, calling out the word which corresponds to the gesture.

In working with adolescents, one useful method is puppetry. Puppetry is especially valuable for those whose disability has led to over-distanced behavior and limited language skills. Puppeteer Lea Wallace has used puppetry extensively in teaching speech skills to educable mentally retarded individuals. In using a dog puppet with a large mouth and movable tongue, she demonstrates for her students appropriate methods of forming sounds and words. The students tend to mirror the puppet's movements readily, as the puppet is a safely distanced, uncritical object.

Further, Wallace encourages her students to improvise stories through puppet roles, manipulating the puppets and speaking at the same time. For many, hand-eye coordination is a significant learning problem. Work with hand puppets provides a safe means of developing coordination skills. Again, the pressure is off the individual to perform the motoric task successfully; it is the puppet who must glide through the air like a bird, run the marathon, or jump over the mountain range.

Speech and cognitive skills are further developed as the students invent dialogue for their puppets. For those whose thought is very concrete, the stories might be based upon an episode in their lives, in the news, or in a movie. For those able to work more imaginatively, the stories might develop along the lines of fantasy or fable.

Wallace worked for several months with one adolescent boy at the Manhattan Occupational Training Center who had been very withdrawn, physically uncoordinated, and limited in speech skills. She encouraged him to play with a variety of ready-made puppets. When comfortable speaking through the puppets, he was asked by Wallace to build his own puppet characters and to tell their stories. Over time, the boy was able to create two simultaneous roles: that of Johnny, a real, everyday person, and Jack, an alien from another planet. In working with these two parts of himself, the boy created a formal puppet presentation, manipulating and speaking for both characters. His coordination and speech significantly improved as presented through the two puppet characters. His self-confidence was likewise elevated to the point that he could present his puppet show to others (Landy, 1982).

For moderately retarded, trainable individuals, the level of abstraction through dramatic action should be minimized, with attention to developing motor coordination, speech, social, and communication skills. Although formal psychodrama is not indicated for this group, basic role-playing techniques can be useful in exploring certain reality-based situations, such as a visit to the doctor.

Projective techniques involving concrete forms of play and puppetry are also useful, especially for adolescent groups. Some adolescents and adults can also work through storytelling and theatre, although there should be no pressure as to memorizing lines and blocking. Finally, in helping develop a greater sense of self-perception, video techniques can be introduced. In focusing upon his own image, the individual can be led toward a greater perception of who he is.

With mildly retarded, educable individuals, a greater level of abstraction and fantasy can be introduced. World technique objects can be used. Storytelling and story dramatization based in fantasy material can be enacted. Puppetry and mask work can also be extended into a range of character types, leading to a recognition of various roles one plays in everyday life. Further, extended dramatization can be used.

Several excellent examples of groups led by Dorothy Heathcote have been documented (Wagner, 1976). Although Heathcote considers herself a drama educator and not a drama therapist, her work with mildly retarded groups is exemplary in its attention to the social and psychological needs of her students.

Finally, more and more mildly and moderately retarded individuals are given the opportunity to perform through theatre. Within the school, such performances certainly can be valuable to affirm the accomplishments of the individuals involved. But the teacher/therapist should again exercise caution, asking himself: "Why performance?" If the answer is that the drama work seems to have led naturally to performance, that the context of the performance relates directly to the lives of the performers, that the group wants to perform publicly, and that public performance might well dignify their work, then theatre would most certainly be justified.

The criteria for choosing a drama therapy technique with a population of mentally retarded individuals within a special school setting are the same as those that apply to other special populations: the technique should help the individual arrive at a balance of distance, and should help the individual play a single role and range of roles competently. In fulfilling the educational goals of building communication, psychomotor, and social skills, personal hygiene, and verbal and cognitive skills, the drama therapist will use these criteria to inform his choice of technique and to evaluate its effectiveness.

The use of drama/theatre techniques with special populations in school settings does not necessarily imply that the teacher is a drama therapist. Many special education teachers have studied educational drama and theatre but not drama therapy. However, their use of creative techniques might well be therapeutic for their students. Many, presently untrained in drama therapy, unwittingly use drama therapy techniques in their classrooms. With the further development of drama therapy training programs and in-service workshops for such teachers, their therapeutic work can well be validated. And with further organization of the profession they will see themselves as part of a new community of educators/therapists committed to the therapeutic values inherent in the creative arts.

Chapter Nine

CLINICAL SETTINGS FOR DRAMA THERAPY

In many ways, the same techniques and principles apply to drama therapy with a disturbed or disabled population, whether in a special educational setting or a clinical setting. However, in a clinical setting, the clients will tend to be more acute in their symptoms and the focus of treatment will be upon psychological rather than pedagogical issues.

For many drama therapists, clinical practice, whether within an institution or in private practice, is the ultimate goal. Most will develop an approach based upon the political, social, medical, and psychological realities of the clinic. In most instances, the distancing model can be used as an aid in diagnosing clients, planning appropriate therapeutic strategies, and evaluating the results of the drama therapy.

One clinical setting for drama therapy is a public hospital that serves diverse populations. An example is Bellevue Psychiatric Hospital in New York City, which serves a psychiatric population of various diagnostic and developmental categories, including a psychiatric prison population and a transient short-term population of children, adolescents, adults, and elders with schizophrenic disorders, conduct disorders, organic mental disorders, and the like. The psychiatric clinic might also be part of a larger public general hospital that devotes several wards to individuals suffering from a variety of psychological disorders. Specialized hospitals, such as the Veterans Administration, also treat psychiatric disorders. Large public hospitals tend to carry the stigma of many bureaucratized institutions, perpetuating the inevitable dolor of green-gray walls, part-timers, and lack of support systems for patients and staff alike.

Private hospitals also serve psychiatric populations, either through special wards or through a total commitment to this particular group. Many have solved at least the cosmetic problems of institutions through the addition of wallpaper, furniture, and game tables. But the private hospital must also be willing to confront the deeper problems of staff burn-out, support and morale, innovation and change, if it is to be a viable alternative to the public system. Many psychiatric patients, however, do not have a choice. If one cannot pay the often exorbitant fees for a private hospital, they will, if needed, go to a public facility, green walls notwithstanding. Many private hospitals will have both inpatient facilities for a live-in population committed to a particular length of stay, and outpatient facilities for a population living elsewhere and receiving daily or weekly treatment at the hospital.

Drama therapists are also employed in regular medical wards of hospitals to help medical patients work through the anxieties surrounding their illness and hospitalization.

An alternative to the private hospital is the private clinic. There are many community mental health clinics throughout the United States that serve a wide variety of clients, including the individual going through a specific life crisis, the substance abuser, and chronic psychotic persons, living within the community. Few drama therapists are presently employed within small community mental health clinics. However, several innovative private clinics that view the creative arts as a significant form of healing, such as the Postgraduate Center for Mental Health in New York City, have continued to employ drama therapists.

The need for community-based outpatient facilities has been increasing given the trend toward the early release of psychiatric patients from public facilities. While many of these individuals are able to maintain at least minimal functioning on psychotropic medication, their deeper needs for social relationships, personal development, and productive activity remain unrealized. The innovative community-based mental health facility could address these needs through the employment of drama and other creative arts therapists.

Like its predecessors, art, music, and dance therapy, drama therapy will also become a primary treatment for some. As the profession develops, more and more individuals will choose to establish a private practice. Some may choose to become practitioners within a community, or a group of drama or creative arts therapists might establish a creative arts therapy center to treat individuals, families, and groups within a particular neighborhood.

The largest clinical population, many of whom require psychotherapy and productive recreational activity, include those elders who are unable to care for themselves and who are in need of community support. Presently, many live and are treated within public and private hospitals and nursing homes. Many creative arts therapists currently work with this group, and many more will be needed as the population of needy elderly increases.

Hospital wards and other clinical settings also house and/or treat the mentally retarded, the orthopedically disabled, substance abusers, and sexual abusers, among others, all of whom can potentially be treated through drama therapy techniques. We will, however, focus our attention upon two clinical populations, the emotionally disturbed and the elderly, and look at ways of treating them through drama therapy in public and/or private clinical settings.

THE CLINICAL TREATMENT OF THE
EMOTIONALLY DISTURBED THROUGH DRAMA THERAPY

Conduct Disorders

One large area subsumed under emotional disturbance is that of conduct disorder, defined in the *DSM-III* as "a repetitive and persistent pattern of conduct in which either the basic rights of others or major age-appropriate societal norms or rules are violated." This group includes both chronically aggressive, underdistanced types, characterized by violent acting out against others, and chronically antisocial, overdistanced types, characterized by withdrawal from others and/or non-aggressive violation of societal norms. When the conduct disorder becomes severe, psychopathic or sociopathic behavior can occur. The psychopathic or sociopathic person is one who experiences neither guilt nor any sense of social responsibility for his often criminal acts.

Society's response to sociopathic behavior is to incarcerate the violater of its norms. But the penal system has proven ineffective as reflected in the growing rates of recidivism. Conventional psychotherapy has proven limited, given its verbal nature coupled with the high levels of rationalization and verbal defenses of the conduct-disordered person. One radical approach adopted in the 1940s by Fritz Redl and David Wineman is milieu therapy. This has been effective with conduct-disordered children and adolescents in establishing a total therapeutic community to treat antisocial behavior in situ, as it is occurring within the life of the client (Redl and Wineman, 1951, 1952).

Within a therapeutic milieu, for example, a fight arises at the dinner table. Joe accuses Billy, a smaller, less powerful boy, of receiving more food than he. Rather than waiting until the next set therapy session, the counselor immediately intervenes and helps Joe work through his anger in relation to Billy.

The extended dramatization is, in many ways, a form of milieu therapy. The difference is that the milieu is a projected one, providing some distance between self and role. Such an approach might meet with initial resistance from a group of conduct-disordered individuals, but if a basic level of trust exists between the group and the therapist, many therapeutic possibilities can be realized. For one, through this approach, the individual is able to create several roles of self and thus begin to recognize alternative possibilities for action. For example, Joe, the impulsive, acting-out child, might create a mask character who is very frightened of doing something wrong and getting punished, and a puppet character who is a superhero, a savior of the weak and defender of justice. In working through an aggressive incident, such as the one at the dinner table, the therapist can get Joe to look at ways that the other parts of himself might have reacted. Within the extended dramatization itself, the therapist often sets up a dinner table scene, which frequently provokes transferences. Through the examination of the dramatized dinner table scene, the group works toward a recognition of their behavior patterns.

For those requiring even further distance, play therapy and world techniques are also significant means of examining the subjective world of the conduct-disordered individual. At times, the therapist will engage in the play with the client, especially with the acting-out person who needs to actively release an abundance of aggressive energy. In the aggressive play, the therapist will provide safe, distanced objects, such as soft foam rubber bats, puppets, and dolls, so that the client can hit or strike out with safety.

In working through world techniques, the therapist will provide a more quiet, internal activity, helping the client express his inner world through a still-life representation.

The power of drama therapy techniques with the conduct-disordered person lies not in talking about what is happening or what has happened but in symbolizing one's world through dramatic action. The ability to recognize and accept responsibility for one's aggressive and/or passive antisocial behaviors is a long-term goal in working with this group in a clinical environment. A more immediate goal is to help move toward a balance of distance so that the person is able to use the projected role as a means of seeing the self and the other toward whom one often directs his anger and rage. Seeing self and other is a large step toward feeling for self and other. If, through the use of properly distanced projective techniques, the drama therapist can help the conduct-disordered person take that step, then his work will prove quite significant.

Affective and Anxiety Disorders

Two other prominent forms of emotional disturbance are affective disorders and anxiety disorders. Although these disorders are primarily neurotic ones, they can also appear within the psychotic individual. Affective disorders are characterized in the *DSM-III* as "disturbances of mood, leading to protracted manic and/or depressive states of being." Mood is an emotional state that characterizes one's psychic life at any given time and when extreme, can control it. The manic state that may arise from a mood disturbance is an underdistanced one, characterized by hyperactivity, grandiosity, speeded-up thought processes, and distractibility. The depressive state is an overdistanced one, characterized by loss of interest in daily life events, withdrawal from activity and people, loss of energy, and feelings of hopelessness and guilt. Both manic and depressive episodes can be measured for severity depending upon the duration and intensity of the episode and the age of onset. Those individuals classified as manic-depressive will experience both disorders within a short space of time.

Anxiety disorders, marked by irrational responses to otherwise neutral stimuli, are generally of three types: phobia, panic, and obsessive-compulsive. Phobias are characterized by a chronic, irrational fear and avoidance of a particular object or situation, to such an extent that the fear can impede one's well-being. Panic attacks are characterized by sudden feelings of terror and helplessness, accompanied by such physical symptoms as palpitations, chest pain, choking sensations, shaking, unsteadiness, and faintness.

Obsessive-compulsive disorders are characterized by a recurrent, highly ritualized pattern of irrational thinking and/or action. Obsessions are disturbing recurrent thoughts or images that tend to occupy not only one's thinking but also to control one's behavior. Common obsessions include fantasies of violence, contamination, doubt, and guilt. Compulsions are repeated behavior patterns that appear to be purposeful but in fact are governed by an inner impulse to repeat the action over and over again. Common compulsions include counting, checking, touching, and hand-washing. Compulsions, like obsessions, are often irrational and excessive, although some forms of obsessive-compulsive behavior are necessary for completing an arduous task, i.e., proofreading a manuscript or training for an Olympic event.

Affective and anxiety disorders can be mild or severe and of long or short duration. In the mildest forms, the individual is often able to function within his everyday environments of work, play, school, family. In the most severe forms, the individual's daily routines are disrupted and either therapy or hospitalization is required.

Drama therapy is rarely the primary treatment in a hospital or clinic for an individual diagnosed as manic-depressive, phobic, or obsessive-compulsive. In most clinical situations, the drama therapist works under the supervision of a psychiatrist, clinical psychologist, or psychiatric social worker, who treats the client with other means of psychotherapy and/or drugs. However, drama and related creative arts therapies can become primary treatments within a private practice or creative arts therapy center.

Whatever the clinical environment might be, drama therapy can draw upon the model of distancing for both diagnosis and treatment. The distancing model is most effective in analyzing and treating the manic-depressive individual, as that dysfunction can be seen quite clearly as a disturbance in balance. Here again, projective techniques are useful, helping the person symbolize the different parts of himself through the construction and/or use of dolls, puppets, and masks. The question arises as to whether the manic person should work through a highly active process to cathart his excess energy or through a less active, more internal process that provides an alternative model in the search for balance. Given the distancing paradigm, it is advisable to provide a range of characters, objects, and dramatic situations so that the client may himself work toward discovering the proper balance of distance.

The phobic person might work toward systematically desensitizing himself (Wolpe and Lazarus, 1966); that is to say, gradually discovering a proper balance of distance in regard to the phobic object. In adapting Wolpe's behavioral technique, the drama therapist can help the client build or work with given projective objects that are overdistanced, then gradually introduce other objects that more closely represent the phobic situation until a balance is restored. Unlike the conduct-disordered client who is generally treated within a drama therapy group, the phobic person is generally treated individually. Those who suffer from forms of social phobia might begin individual treatment, working with safe representations of people in the forms of puppets and dolls, then gradually work toward a group therapy situation, in which their issues are examined in the social context of an extended dramatization or psychodramatic enactment.

The client subject to panic attacks also needs to work with safe objects in order to be free to approach fearful situations. Within a creative arts therapy clinic, the drama therapist would provide a range of projective objects for the client to play with. Through repeated dramatizations of dreaded situations likely to cause panic, the client imaginatively represents the conditions necessary for actual panic to occur. Given the distancing factor, he can begin to move toward balance and recognition of his dilemma.

The obsessive and/or compulsive client can work individually through several forms of projective play and dramatization. As an example, Jay, an obsessive-compulsive forty-year-old man worked with a drama therapist who combined psychodramatic and projective techniques. Through a series of world pictures and sand play, Jay discovered a repeated configuration. The objects he most closely identified with often appeared in groups of three. Following several sessions of sand play, the therapist questioned Jay about the repeated configuration. As Jay re-examined the photographs of his sand play taken by the therapist, he noted three books, lined up on a diagonal in the sand tray, three babies lying at the bottom of a water jar, and three tiny dogs, guarding the entrance to an unknown room. He related his obsession with the number three to magical thinking. When gambling, choosing numbers, or counting objects, he always chose three for good luck. He recalled chanting a particular jingle three times as a boy, fearful that disaster would occur if he varied the pattern.

Through further role play with puppets and masks, representing parts of himself, Jay became aware of three distinct roles: that of Jamie, the charming, happy child; Jay, the unhappy, self-critical, obsessive-compulsive adolescent; and Jason, the ambivalent adult, capable of holding a steady job and taking care of himself but incapable of finding the "perfect" job or the "perfect" relationship.

The obsession with three, though, still persisted. A breakthrough occurred when dramatizing a dream through play objects. Reflecting upon his play, Jay recognized that three was the perfect state of being in a family of himself, his mother, and his father. When a fourth person, a new brother, became a permanent part of the family, Jay's perfectly balanced world was crushed. He held onto three ever since.

Although this recognition was a key to understanding his obsession, Jay still needed to work on further issues of developing a more spontaneous personality, one in which the three roles of child, adolescent, and adult are fully integrated. Moving out from individual to group drama therapy, Jay continues to work on his issues in a less distanced fashion, proceeding through more reality-based psychodramatic techniques.

Schizophrenic Disorders

The most debilitating emotional disturbances are schizophrenic disorders. Although there is still much debate as to the cause, nature, and duration of schizophrenia, certain characteristics seem to be consistent among the different forms of the disorder.

One, according to the *DSM-III,* is the presence of psychotic features. These include bizarre behaviors and delusions, auditory hallucinations, in which the client hears voices or words repeatedly, disturbed speech patterns, ritualized movement patterns, and such mood disturbances as excessive anger, anxiety, and/or depression. Schizophrenics also manifest multiple psychological processes, characterized by disturbances in the content of one's thoughts. These disturbances include delusions of persecution, thought broadcasting (the belief that one's thoughts are broadcast directly into the world), thought withdrawal (the belief that one's thoughts have been removed from one's mind), thought insertion (the belief that one's thoughts have been inserted into one's mind), and thought control (the belief that one's thoughts are controlled by an outside force). A related symptom is a disturbance in one's form of thinking characterized by discernible lack of connectedness in speech. Ideas tend to be unrelated, and speech tends to be highly private and uncommunicative. In the extreme, speech becomes incoherent.

Other symptoms characteristic of multiple psychological processes include a loss of ego boundaries, leading to uncertainty as to the relationship between self and others; a loss of interest or motivation to work and/or play; and a withdrawal from the external world, accompanied by a preoccupation with one's own private, often bizarre fantasies.

The disorganized type of schizophrenia is extreme and chronic, occurring early in one's development. It is characterized by frequent incoherence in speech and gesture, inappropriate and peculiar emotional expressiveness, and extreme social withdrawal.

The catatonic schizophrenic is characterized by severely disturbed movement patterns involving a rigid body posture, excited, hyperactive movement for no apparent reason, and unusual posturing. The catatonic tends to withdraw into a stupor, becoming immobile and mute. At times, he will vacillate rapidly between the extremes of excitability and withdrawal.

The paranoid schizophrenic is noted for delusions and hallucinations of grandeur or persecution. This individual might also experience disturbances in affect, including an abundance of anxiety, anger, and violence. If his delusions do not lead to chronically inappropriate behavior, the paranoid schizophrenic can function within a variety of occupational and social circumstances. Total impairment of social, affective, and intellectual functioning is rare among this group. The disorder generally appears at a later point in life than the other types, and its characteristics remain fairly stable over time.

The undifferentiated type of schizophrenia is a classification that does not meet the characteristics of any other type or that combines elements of several types.

Schizophrenic individuals are treated in clinics as inpatients or outpatients. Most are treated through drug therapy; some experience traditional verbal psychotherapy which in many cases is ineffective. Some individuals are treated through the creative arts therapies of dance, art, music, and drama. The creative arts are a significant treatment strategy because they address the central issue of the schizophrenic disorder, that of the uncovering of identity through a symbolic, nonthreatening process.

Drama therapy is particularly useful in work with schizophrenics because of its focus upon the relationships between self, role, and other. From a dramatic point of view, the schizophrenic condition is one of a disturbance in the boundaries between self and role, one role and another role, and self and other.

David Johnson (1981) provides an excellent model for working with the schizophrenic through drama therapy. He looks at the relationship between two players in an improvisational role-playing situation from four perspectives:

1. Impersonal: the relationship between player A in role and player B in role; that is, the relationship between two dramatized or projected roles.
2. Intrapersonal: the relationship between player A (or player B) and his role; that is, the relationship between self and role.
3. Extrapersonal: the relationship between player A out of role and player B in role (and vice versa); that is, the relationship between self and the other's role.
4. Interpersonal: the relationship between player A out of role and player B out of role; that is, the relationship between self and other.

In observing an improvisational dramatic enactment, says Johnson, one can use this model to diagnose the degree of boundary confusion. As related to treatment, the model can help the individual recognize the distinctions between self, role, and other.

Johnson's approach is generally an improvisational reality-based one where he provides the individual a basic situation and character, then asks him to develop a scene spontaneously. He draws upon the psychodramatic technique of role reversal, as well as projective techniques of storytelling and video. In his approach to treating schizophrenic men within a Veteran's Administration hospital setting, he uses the projective format of a television news or interview show, videotaping, then playing back, the spontaneous enactments of clients. Further, he encourages his groups to create their own videotapes, based upon the everyday life of their ward, which again is played back to them. Through this work, Johnson allows the individuals to play roles and enact situations quite close to themselves, using humor, satire, and irony as distancing devices, and to receive direct feedback as to their dramatized behaviors. Often, the improvisations are enacted in dyads, either between two clients or between one client and the therapist. When role playing with his clients, Johnson works toward a recognition of boundaries and differentiation between self and role, one role and another role, self and other.

In his work with schizophrenics, Johnson (1980a) has been developing a highly promising diagnostic instrument, the dramatic role-playing test, to measure aspects of a client's role-playing ability when given a character and situation to enact.

Given the schizophrenic's need for reality-based enactments to counter the many flights of fantasy and delusional thinking, the question arises as to the appropriateness of the more distanced, imaginative techniques of puppetry and mask, for example, in uncovering one's search for clear boundaries. At present, we can only speculate, as formal research in this area is non-existent. However, it appears that the least severe paranoid or undifferentiated schizophrenics can be aided through work with puppets and other projective objects. At such clinics as the Postgraduate Center for Mental Health, drama therapists Galila Oren and Roberta Zito have been using puppetry and mask work to help schizophrenics make intrapsychic and interpersonal boundary distinctions. It is too early to speculate as to the results of their work.

THE CLINICAL TREATMENT OF THE ELDERLY THROUGH DRAMA THERAPY

In recent years, many residential and outpatient clinics have developed to meet the recreational, medical, and therapeutic needs of the growing number of people over sixty-five. The need for such clinics within hospitals, nursing homes, and senior centers becomes more pronounced when aging is coupled with deteriorating physical health, rejection by younger generations of family members, isolation, and loneliness.

In the film, *Citizen Kane*, the character of the aging newspaper editor, Mr. Bernstein, refers to old age as the one disease for which there can never be a cure. Like Shakespeare's King Lear, the elder is no longer as powerful as he was and is faced with certain inevitable realities. One is the onset of physical disabilities, which may include losses of hearing, vision, memory, movement, and language facility, caused by stroke or arthritis, Parkinson's or Alzheimer's disease. Another reality is the loss of relationships through the deaths of peers, friends, and spouses. Added to this is the changing relationship to one's children who, in many instances, experience a role reversal with their aging parents, themselves taking on a parental, care-taking role. Given the discontinuity of the family in Western cultures, many children resent the role reversal and, rather than burden their independent lives with an elder, they arrange for their dependent parents to be cared for in nursing homes.

A third reality of aging is the closeness to death. One may choose to deny or accept, to confront or withdraw from this inevitable reality. In choosing to look at one's dying, at the future, one invariably turns to the past, to a review of one's life, as a way of integrating meaningful experiences and justifying a life lived.

In clinical situations, groups of elderly are generally mixed as to age and disability. In working with the most severely disabled and disoriented elders, the drama therapist aims to connect with the individual and group through simple contact and movement exercises. He may create a movement to music and engage the person confined to a wheelchair by moving his chair in time with the music. Or he may connect the group with a large piece of elastic fabric, encouraging all to move rhythmically together.

In his work with a mixed group in a private nursing home, David Johnson (1985) states his aims as:

1. to serve as an orienting and socializing environment,
2. to be an arena for sharing reminiscences about important life events, and
3. to aid in the acceptance of one's physical limitations, interpersonal losses, and eventual death.

Johnson works primarily through psychodramatic and role-playing techniques, basing his improvisations upon issues that arise in the physical warm-ups. As the trust level of the group develops, Johnson notes that the therapist is able to explore deeper emotional issues affecting the group. As one example, an initial exercise, miming the movement of climbing a rope, led the group to the image of climbing a beanstalk. Through dialogue with the therapist, the group decided that they were climbing up to heaven to visit their parents. Taking his cue from the group, the therapist symbolically placed the parents in the center of the room and asked the group to speak out their thoughts and feelings to them.

During the exercise, varying degrees of distancing were evident. At times, to help the overdistanced person participate, the therapist took on the role of the parent. In doing so, he became a transferential object. In many ways, says Johnson, the therapist resembles the parent, as he is a "dependable protector," one who guides the more dependent client through a growth-oriented experience. In working through the child/parent transferences, Johnson uses further role playing, role reversal, and discussion to uncover the various projections. Through assuming the various roles of child, parents, and more neutral adult, the therapist helps the group see their issues of loss (i.e., the death and abandonment of a parent) and of rejection (i.e., the negligence or desertions of a child).

Further, in working through his own issues of countertransference, the therapist also examines his childlike dependency needs, his parental, nurturing needs, and his issues surrounding death and loss.

In Chapter One, we looked briefly at the work of Susan Perlstein in developing life history plays with elders for recreational purposes. Perlstein's work also has a strong therapeutic component and has led to insight and positive change in many instances. Her approach is to work through the process of improvisation and storytelling to arrive at a product, a script which will be publicly performed within a community center serving the needs of the elderly. The scripts, life history plays, evolve from two sources. The first is oral history, a process of examining the past by means of personal stories told by individuals who have lived through a particular historical moment. The second is life review, a form of therapy developed by the gerontologist, Robert Butler (1963) involving an examination of past conflicts in one's life and an integration of the past with the present. According to Butler, the process of life review can lead to insight and recognition of the cycle of life, to the development of positive relationships, and to a means of coping with grief, loneliness, and depression. Butler and others often use such devices as the photograph album to help the elder reminisce about the past and begin the process of life review.

Perlstein takes Butler's work one step further by working toward a dramatization of significant life events within a historical as well as a personal context. Like the oral historian, she aims (1981) to reveal cultural values "in the context of the circumstances that shaped them." Her view of history (1981) is that of "a complex process of a people's struggle for power, along with the ideas, myths, and rituals that shape a time and place." Perlstein aims toward a dramatization of the political, social, and mythic struggles of all human beings through focusing on particular moments in the lives of individuals.

In moving from life review to theatre, Perlstein works in six steps:

1. learning/teaching appropriate theatre skills,
2. selecting a theme,
3. collecting stories and other cultural and historical information,
4. selecting the historical information,
5. developing the scenario and rehearsing and setting the play, and
6. performance.

An example of Perlstein's work is in the play, *Blackout on the Boardwalk*, created by members of the Shorefront Y Senior Center in Brighton

Beach, Brooklyn, most of whom are East European immigrants and Holocaust survivors. The oral history component of the play concerned the experiences of the group between the years of 1939–1945. Many of the group members had never been able to reflect back upon their experiences and actions during the Nazi takeover of Europe and had developed "survivor's guilt," a sense of shame that they had escaped to America while many of their family members had perished in the Nazi death camps.

The life review component of the play came into clear focus in the case of Sophie, related by Perlstein (1983) in her clinical field notes, as follows:

> Sophie, a tall, slim, gray haired woman with a heavy German accent, quietly turned her chair away from the group circle. She usually set herself apart, but listened intently and seemed genuinely curious about the other members. She seldom offered information about herself. I was aware that she lived alone ... and never married.... Sophie came to the United States in 1939 from Danzig, Germany.... Her family owned a guest house in Danzig. First the children were forced to leave school because they were Jewish.... The Jewish people had their clothing and shoes confiscated, their house vandalized and finally the SS troups came in the middle of the night and arrested the guests.... So they wrote to Uncle Avram in New York to send affidavits for the family. Her uncle was able to help bring some of her father's family out of Germany. But her mother's family were all exterminated in the death camps. Sophie told the group this was the first time in years she spoke about those terrible times. She objectively told the story. She kept the pain hidden, holding and containing her anger and sadness.... At the end of this session, she came up to me and said that she would leave the group because she could not act.... I said she didn't have to act if she didn't want to. Her presence was important to the group and the development of the play. She replied that she didn't think so.... I asked her if she would return, not to participate, but to observe. She said, "maybe," but that she was different from the others and didn't really belong. In the following session, Sophie came late and watched.... I asked her if the group could reenact her story. She agreed. Essie, an American born Jew, volunteered to play Sophie. In the middle of the scene where the Nazi SS officer came to take the guests away, Sophie stood up and said: "That's not how it was done." With incredible strength, she burst forward in goosesteps across the stage to the guest house and knocked on the door. She symbolically beat a guest (a chair) and dragged it off the stage, cursing in German, "Dirty Jew, swine." Silence — fear — surprise, Sophie shocked herself as she relived those terrifying moments.... The group applauded her as a courageous heroine, rather than an outsider.... Through role play and discussion, Sophie shared her despair and guilt for having survived.

In living history drama, she found a safe place to give up the role of refugee and participate with people in a new and more intimate way. At 70 she is adapting to a new support network. It was Sophie's choice to rejoin the group.

Sophie had taken an overdistanced position in relation to the group. Through the gentle but persistent encouragement of the therapist, she was able to take the first step toward involvement by means of storytelling. Having experienced safety in the storytelling, she was then able to take a most dramatic step in re-presenting her past conflict through story dramatization. Because the experience was properly distanced and spontaneous, it released many years of guilt and isolation. Through the catharsis experienced in her role playing, Sophie was able to discover a balance and relate to others in the group for the first time. Her scene became a prominent one in *Blackout on the Boardwalk*, one which she performed with both dignity and abandon.

At the Hodson Senior Center in the South Bronx, Perlstein works with a different cultural group, many of whom are poor blacks. Bernice, a seventy-year-old black woman, appeared in the group in a state of physical disarray. She was incontinent, unkempt, and withdrawn. She demonstrated extreme inconsistencies in her appearance and behavior. For example, she wore a wig slightly askew to reveal the white, matted hair underneath, and a tight mini-skirt with a shapeless, bulky sweater. Her participation in the group would vary from total withdrawal to eloquent involvement in the storytelling process. Bernice lived alone in a nearby housing project and was supported by social security and medicare. Her mother, an immigrant Jamaican domestic, encouraged Bernice to improve her lot in life and study the piano as she, herself, never had the opportunity to do. Her father, however, who came from a poor, religious family, believed that music was sinful and wanted his daughter to become a traditional housewife.

In the drama group, Perlstein worked toward the creation of a collective poem about working hands. Within this structure, Bernice told the group of her conflict between developing the hands of a piano player and those of a secretary, a job that supported her during her working life. From the story arose a dramatization involving an argument between Bernice's parents. Assuming the roles of both her parents, Bernice dramatized the central conflict of her life. She revealed that in her adolescence she had rebelled against her father's strictures and played jazz piano at nightclubs, once accompanying Dizzy Gillespie. Yet, as a young adult, she had rejected the joyfulness of music, denying all pleasure and assuming an isolated, unattached life. According to Perlstein (1983a), she felt "caught between jazz and church music, the bad sexy girl and the good family woman, between choosing an autonomous, independent pathway different from her mother and the traditional feminine role."

Through her participation in the process of life history review, Bernice slowly began to feel accepted and valued and thus began to value herself more. Her physical appearance and health markedly improved as she took on the role of piano player for the theatre productions. At seventy, her creative skills are blossoming. And, at seventy, her isolation is rapidly diminishing.

In work with elders in clinical situations, most drama therapists avoid using puppets, masks, makeup, and world techniques, as these devices are often perceived as childish. Drama work with this group does not require as much distancing as with other groups, since the primary focus is upon re-examining reality-based experiences of the past. The use of photographs and video, as well as the use of storytelling, story dramatization, and theatre, appear to be the most effective dramatic methods of treatment. There is no need for a clinical drama group with elders to stay at the level of simple creative dramatic experiences and safe conventional theatre productions. For the drama to be more deeply therapeutic, the therapist must be willing to help his clients review their lives to discover a sense of purposefulness, to uncover some of the guilt and confusion caused by social circumstances as well as personal choice, and to move toward death, not with a sense of despair and regret, but with dignity.

THE DRAMA THERAPIST AS PRIVATE PRACTITIONER

In private practice, one can see clients on an individual, family, or group basis. In leading sessions with children, adolescents, adults, or elders, the drama therapist should consider the following:

1. the presenting problem and goal of the client,
2. the background of the client, including cultural, family, and personal psychological history,
3. the projected length of treatment and frequency of visits,
4. the cost of treatment,
5. the techniques appropriate for treatment,

6. the means of evaluation necessary to assess the effects of the treatment, and

7. the countertransferential issues that arise in interaction with a client.

Further, the drama therapist should be mindful of both his own therapeutic goals and his limitations. In confronting his limitations in meeting the needs of a particular client, he should be well informed as to alternative referral sources.

In the individual session, the therapist might choose to take the role of a more distanced observer or questioner, or that of a more active participant. In the former, he will draw upon the projective techniques of play therapy, world technique, mask, and makeup, among others, encouraging the client to play out his unconscious issues in relation to the dramatic objects. In the latter situation, he will move toward more psychodramatic enactment, choosing to play a complimentary or confrontational role in relation to roles chosen by the client. The active therapist can also work well through projective techniques. Selective interventions can be made through the mutual storytelling technique (Gardner, 1981), mutual play with puppets and/or masks, and participation in the play or world technique process.

The individual practitioner might also choose to work with a family. Many of Satir's notions of family therapy can be implemented using projective as well as psychodramatic techniques. The family structure can be represented through world pictures created by each family member, through puppet presentations, storytelling, and, in some instances, through extended dramatization, in which the actual family is asked to take on roles within a fictional family. Through an examination of the family dynamics during the dramatizations, the therapist is able to view the problems of the group and help them move toward alternate ways of conceptualizing their issues and relating to one another.

A group drama therapy session functions in ways similar to those of individual and family therapy. Through psychodrama, sociodrama, extended dramatization, and many of the projective techniques, the drama therapist proceeds to uncover issues of relationship and communication.

Private drama therapy sessions can be a form of short-term treatment with individuals needing to deal with a crisis or particularly stressful life event. Through focusing on that particular issue within a present time context and providing the appropriate distance, the drama therapist can offer a safe, supportive environment in which the client can recognize and release his feelings and move toward a resumption of his everyday life. With short-term clients, the therapist should take care not to open up larger issues based in the client's developmental history.

In working with the longer-term client, the drama therapist needs to take a more in-depth approach, working through a recurring pattern of images in dreams, world pictures, and role-playing situations. Imagery created through dramatization is related not only to the present moment in the client's life but also to his past history and strivings toward future integration.

A further innovation in private therapy is the formation of a creative arts therapy clinic. Such a center could draw upon a variety of techniques in music, movement, visual arts, and drama, all based upon similar conceptions of healing through the spontaneous moment of creative enactment. Given a support staff of physicians, nurses, and social workers, such a clinic could make a profound contribution to the welfare of individuals within a particular community. So many creative arts therapists who venture into private practice find themselves isolated from the mainstream, fighting many battles with often suspicious mental health professionals. Given a supportive group of trained professionals devoted to healing through a common process, their burden will at least be a shared one. Further, such a group could engage not only in practice but also in research activities that attempt to validate the effectiveness of the creative arts as therapy.

Chapter Ten

DRAMA/THEATRE FOR SPECIAL POPULATIONS WITHIN OTHER COMMUNITY SETTINGS

In looking at further settings and populations for drama therapy, we need to address an issue that was raised earlier: that of the often fine line between drama/theatre as art or recreation and drama/theatre as therapy. In writing about The Family, a theatre group whose roots are in prison settings, Steven Hart states (1981): "The difficulty with trying to make a program that is operated by artists offer the benefits of therapy and social work is that, in the final analysis, art is neither one of these things.... If The Family does not provide these services (therapy and social work), it does ... yield individual and social benefits as by-products."

When a drama/theatre program in a prison, church, or other community organization is operated by artists who have not been trained as therapists, we might safely say that the therapeutic and/or social benefits are by-products. But when the program is run by trained drama therapists, the social and therapeutic benefits become primary or can become primary if that is the focus of the group.

Theatre performance is the preferred form of drama/theatre when working with special populations within many community organizations. There are four basic approaches to working within the community:

1. a leader trained in the art form of drama/theatre works toward aesthetic and/or recreational goals,
2. a leader with the same training works toward social and/or therapeutic goals,
3. a leader trained in drama therapy works toward social and/or therapeutic goals,
4. a leader with the same training works toward aesthetic and/or recreational goals.

At times, these four positions will merge as, for example, a leader trained in both theatre and therapy works toward both aesthetic and therapeutic goals.

At present, most community programs in drama/theatre for special populations are run by those who fit into categories one and two. Let us look at several that are geared toward working with populations of prisoners and physically disabled people. Then we will turn to a rather unique social experiment—a theatre group in Latin America working with a particular peasant population. Although none of these groups are primarily therapy oriented, each would at least admit to tangentially working toward social, political, and/or therapeutic goals.

DRAMA/THEATRE IN PRISONS

The prison environment, like that of the mental hospital, is often a dehumanizing one. Rehabilitation in many cases is non-existent as inmates systematically lose all sense of dignity, self-worth, and positive social relationship. The education in prisons tends to be about developing better ways to beat the system and harden defenses against feeling. In most prisons, recreation consists primarily of competitive sports and endless hours of watching television.

In recent years, theatre artists have attempted to offer an alternative to the prison routine. Since 1967, Theatre for the Forgotten has penetrated the prisons of New York state, presenting more than 130 plays of varying form and content, including a sociopolitical dramatization of the trial of Sacco and Vanzetti, as well as the more conventional Broadway play, *Luv*, by Murray Schisgal. Taking a realistic position concerning the effects of theatre in prison, the co-founder, Akila Couloumbis, states (Hart and Waren, 1983): "People in jail need a hell of a lot more than just a theatre performance or a workshop. It has taken years to bend them into the shape that we've got them into. It'll take an equal number of years—with care, understanding, patience—to get them straight. Therefore, I take no credit for rehabilitating anyone. Entertaining a few folks, yes."

In contrast to Couloumbis, Marketta Kimbrell of the Street Theatre Caravan sees prison theatre as a revolutionary process to change the consciousness of prisoners, whom she sees as "those who have been politically and socially humiliated" (Hart and Waren, 1983). Kimbrell states her aim as follows (Hart and Waren, 1983): "I want to change the world, society, the system. We cannot blame the guards [for the effects of prison]. The [social] system cannot deal with the causalties it creates. . . . Entertainment is meaningless unless it combines with my deepest inner concerns."

The Street Theatre Caravan tours the United States with plays developed by the group which present a political message. The style of production is similar in intent and form to the epic theatre of Bertolt Brecht. Like Brecht, The Street Theatre Caravan inserts contemporary references to political realities in their plays, challenging prisoners to think about their predicaments and move toward change.

A third major theatre organization working with prisoners is the Cell Block Theatre, now defunct. The director, Ramon Gordon, began by directing inmates in plays within the prison environment. Then he developed an extensive workshop program for inmates and ex-offenders with the following goal: "to teach them to play the game of the middle class power structure" (Hart and Waren, 1983). Gordon's workshop approach was primarily improvisational, drawing upon basic role-playing techniques designed to break the impulsive, underdistanced, violent behavior patterns that often lead to antisocial acts and incarceration. Gordon used improvisation to solve specific reality-based conflicts. Three rules governed the enactments: each conflict would be resolved without recourse to violence, without calling the police, and without walking away. In exploring alternative solutions, Gordon's aim was to teach new ways of thinking and acting, so that the prisoner would be able to integrate himself within the straight world.

Gordon's approach was more directly therapeutic than that of most prison theatre artists, as he encouraged the expression and exploration of emotion and helped the person move toward catharsis and recognition. His work included a name game, during which a client stands in front of the group and shouts his name as loud as he can. In discussing the power of the name game, Gordon writes (Ryan, 1976): "At first, the workshop participant is shy and embarrased; . . . he has never had that much attention focused on him at one time in his life. . . . Many, in this first exercise, shift about nervously, unconsciously clutching at their genitals, as if to make sure they are still attached."

Gordon would also ask his clients to tell the story of their lives in three minutes. Most of the stories were told within thirty seconds and only concerned the crimes committed and the jail sentences doled out. Through time, Gordon would help the group focus upon more positive aspects of their existence.

The best-known group working with prisoners, The Family, does not subscribe to therapeutic goals, although it does address significant social issues of the disadvantaged. One of their stated goals is (Landy, 1982): "to develop training methods and mount productions that relate directly to the disadvantaged, providing positive alternatives to drugs and crime; to facilitate the re-entry of ex-offenders into society by providing opportunities for involvement in theatre both as actor and instructor, coupled with personal and job counseling."

In the early 1970s, The Family's director, Marvin Felix Camillo, led a series of workshops at Bedford Hills Correctional Facility in New York. There he worked with the inmates to develop the play, *Short Eyes*, concerning the emotional and physical brutality of prison life. The play was written by an inmate, Miguel Piñero, who has gone on to write many more plays that have been widely produced in commercial and regional theatres. Since the early 1970s, The Family has continued to develop workshop experiences and productions of particular relevance to populations of prisoners and ex-offenders. Their work incorporates the music, games, language, and rhythms of the streets. Through their commitment to the drama/theatre process, they have provided an alternative family for many. In response to the question, "Why is drama and theatre such a significant alternative to drugs and crime?" the actor Raymond Ruiz notes (Landy, 1982): "It gives you something to do, and it takes up a lot of your time. It puts a lot of that time into positive things. Right now, I don't know where I'd be if I wasn't involved with The Family. . . . The Family gave me a home to come to and keep my thoughts positive."

Most theatre-in-prison groups, then, shy away from directly therapeutic goals and techniques. Few work through the projective techniques of puppetry, mask, or other fantasy-based means of exploring personal issues in some depth. The favored projective techniques are storytelling, role playing, and theatre production. Most theatre workshops for prisoners stay within the parameters of reality-based enactment, with some distance provided by an improvised or scripted role in a play. Psychodramatic techniques have been used in prisons but sparingly and for specific purposes, i.e., to foster awareness between groups of prisoners and others in the criminal justice system. Richard Korn of the John Jay College of Criminal Justice in New York City has experimented with psychodrama and sociodrama as a means of putting the entire system of justice on trial and examining issues of responsibility and blame (Hart and Waren, 1983).

Many groups that are uncomfortable with a characterization of their work as therapeutic are most willing to admit to the social and/or political components of their efforts. In many ways, the very act of walking into a prison with a drama workshop or opening up one's doors to a group of ex-offenders is a revolutionary one. In offering alternatives to individuals brought up in broken homes and mean streets, such groups offer the hope "that you could get a better high off of your creativity than any of those cold, unnatural, deadly chemicals that [you were] addicted to" (Camillo, 1975).

Drama therapy applies equally to all classes and to all life circumstances. As is the case with other new disciplines, some people practice it unwittingly. That is not to say that all prison theatre artists are covert drama therapists. But those who subscribe to recreational goals could just as well be entertaining vacationers in resort hotels. Yet, they have chosen the bleakest of settings and the most despised of populations. Given such a choice, they appear committed, if not to healing through drama/theatre, then at least to offering a positive alternative to extreme conditions of physical and emotional incarceration described by sociologist Erving Goffman (1961) as "a series of abasements, degradations, humiliations, and profanations of the self."

A strong justification for drama/theatre in prisons was written by Gray Smith, founder of The Street Theatre (Ryan, 1976): "Inmates will tell you that they have been acting all their lives. What they usually mean is a highly developed repertory of appearances. The workshops break down the appearances and attempt to discover what is real."

Prison theatre artists, whether drama therapists or not, whether working through improvisation or theatre performance, utilize the natural drama of prisoners, the myriad masks, disguises, and roles, to help uncover the reality of the self, the family, the society. To the extent that they are successful in establishing a balance of distance between self and role, self and other, individual and society, they are, indeed, realizing therapeutic goals.

DRAMA/THEATRE WITH THE PHYSICALLY DISABLED

Bill is a severely physically disabled, bright, eighteen-year-old boy. His disability, an acute form of cerebral palsy, makes him dependent upon others for feeding, bathing, and personal hygiene. Bill's limbs are strapped to his wheelchair, because he has no control over their movement and can easily hurt himself or others with a wayward gesture. Bill's physical world is a kind of prison from which there are no reprieves. As a participant in a community arts program for disabled individuals, funded by a local school district in Southern California, Bill became interested in drama. When first confronted with Bill's disabilities, the drama instructor was at a loss. In conversation with Bill, he discovered the richness of Bill's imagination. Coming from a highly educated family, Bill had not only been exposed to many of the great works of literature and philosophy, but he had also learned several foreign languages. His rich fantasy life had taken him on many foreign journies.

Bill's drama work began with imagery-based warm-ups. The instructor asked him to visualize the muscles in various parts of his body and to tense and release them in imagination.

Although some of the one-to-one sessions with Bill concerned storytelling, much of the work remained imagery based. In one particular experience, Bill was asked to imagine himself floating on a cloud, slightly above ground level. As the cloud began to rise, Bill focused upon the sensations of sight, sound, smell, and touch. Once the cloud was high above the houses and trees, Bill's body began to transform into that of a bird. As the transformation was taking place, Bill was asked to imagine the shape, size, and physical characteristics of the bird. Once he had transformed into the bird, he left the cloud and began to explore his new environment—all in imagination. Adding more detail, the instructor asked Bill to utter a sound as the bird and to engage in a particular action. Then, the bird was coaxed into returning to the cloud and gradually transforming back into a person. Finally, the cloud was brought back down to earth, ending the exercise.

Following the experience, Bill felt exhilarated. He became a black crow, very sleek and beautiful. His action concerned a search for food, for earthworms. It wasn't the desperate search of a hungry animal, but a leisurely, natural journey. When it was time to return, he did so with no regrets. He was content to have taken such a free flight.

The drama instructor, trained in educational drama and theatre, was not a therapist. Yet, his work helped one person transcend his physical prison, at least temporarily.

Aside from various private workshops and classes led by theatre artists or educational drama instructors, several community-based organizations have evolved that work primarily with physically disabled individuals.

These groups funded by private donors or by such organizations as the National Committee, Arts for the Handicapped, include the Center for Independent Living in Berkeley, California, the National Theatre Workshop of the Handicapped in New York City, the Rolling Stock Company in Dayton, Ohio, the Rainbow Company in Las Vegas, Nevada, and the Access Theatre in Santa Barbara, California.

Edward, an orthopedically disabled man of twenty-five, confined to a wheelchair, joined such a group in the late 1970s. At first, Edward was terrified of performing any exercise in front of the group. His background included endless experiences in school and community of being hidden away, assigned a special "safe" place "for his own good." In the theatre workshop, he was asked to come out, to perform, to be seen. Over time, Edward gained a remarkable sense of self-esteem and began to take more risks in exposing himself through the exercises. In doing so, Edward moved from an overdistanced position to a balanced one. The primary technique that brought him there was storytelling.

One standard exercise in the group was to tell a personal story. At first Edward's stories were minimal, focusing upon external events of the day. But one day, he was able to share a story that brought about a significant change in both his theatre work and his self-esteem. The following is a re-creation of that story:

> "I went to a bar. I'd been alone all day and needed to connect to someone. At the bar, this man begins to talk about this and that. After a while, the guy invites me to his apartment. I tell him about my problems of getting around, about my chair and leg braces, but he says no problem, so I say OK, let's go. In the apartment I'm feeling tense. Something's going on. It's getting late. The man asks me if I'm tired. I say, yes. So he says, you want to sleep over? I figure why not. It's too much hassle to leave now. So the man helps me into bed and asks if he can take off my leg braces. I tell him, sure, why not. But he puts his hands on my legs funny. He's not turned off like most people. I'm feeling weird all of a sudden. So I tell the guy I just wanted the company, that's all. Just the company. He plays around some more and my mind is going a mile a minute. But then he gets tired, rolls over, and goes to sleep. I'm up all night, afraid to move or even to breathe too loud. In the morning I get myself dressed and into my braces and chair and, finally, home. The guy slept through the whole thing. I hope he was alright."

In telling the story, Edward transformed from overdistanced narrator to balanced actor. Through his story, he was able to make the past present, to relive a complex moment in his life. For the first time in the drama group, Edward was full of feeling without being overwhelmed. Following the story, he reported an awareness of simultaneously being in the past and present: the apartment and the performance space.

For some in the group, the sexual undertone of the story was threatening.

But for most, a great sense of identification and relief emerged. Many shared their experiences of loneliness and isolation and of early confusing encounters with the outside world. For Edward, the experience in theatre was indeed therapeutic. In discovering a confluence of feeling and thought and in taking a risk and being affirmed by a supportive group, Edward felt balanced and whole.

Both Edward and Bill's drama groups focus upon the art form of theatre. As we have seen, however, the therapeutic by-products often become prominent aspects of such programs, as individuals recognize significant life issues and move toward a more fully functional way of being.

Another experiment in community-based drama/theatre, geared as much toward recognition and change as toward entertainment, focuses more upon the audience than the actor, more upon the society than the individual. In examining this work, we turn to another culture and another political system: that of socialist Cuba.

TEATRO ESCAMBRAY—A COMMUNITY-BASED THEATRE FOR SOCIAL CHANGE

The Cuban socialist revolution of 1959 brought rapid changes in the areas of education, land reform, health care, and economics. But in the arts changes came slower. In the early 1960s, theatre companies began to produce more radical plays as well as radical interpretations of classics, and low ticket prices made theatre available for the first time to many urban, working-class people. The theatre, however, was not yet ready to speak directly to Cubans about the problems of living in a new, revolutionary society. Further, theatre artists were still tied to their theatres within the cities.

In the early 1960s, the Escambray region in central Cuba, a hilly, agricultural province, became known as a battleground for struggles between pro- and anti-governmental factions. In many cases, families were divided and men took to arming themselves, at times in pursuit of their own brothers. Towns in the Escambray came to resemble the old American West.

In 1967, Teatro Escambray was formed by a group of classically trained theatre artists from Havana committed to extending the purpose of theatre from that of pure entertainment to that of examining and solving significant social-political problems. The pioneering group, led by Sergio

Corrieri and Hilda Hernandez, both well-known Cuban theatre and film actors, moved into the Escambray region and began to learn of the struggles of the local campesinos (peasants). Focusing their research upon such problems as the continuing civil war, they created plays designed to engage the local audiences in discussions concerning those problems that were central to their lives.

Initially, Teatro Escambray planned to conclude each production with a discussion between actors and audience. Most of the viewers never experienced live theatre before, and during performances, audience members began to address the actors directly, breaking through the sacred convention of the fourth wall. The trained actors, unsure of how to respond, carried on with their performance. Upon analyzing the interruptions, the company began to alter the form of their plays, building moments of debate into their dramas. During the discussion and debates, the actors were to remain in role and respond to questions from the point of view of their characters.

The problem of continuing hostilities among families was addressed in the play, *La Emboscada (The Ambush)*, concerning the relationship between two brothers, a revolutionary and a bandit (counter-revolutionary). In a later play, *El Juicio (The Trial)*, based on an actual case, a man imprisoned for counter-revolutionary activity returns to his village after an extended time in prison. At the beginning of the play, several audience members are chosen as judges who will decide whether the man should be permitted to remain in the village. Throughout the play, the actors dramatize the effects of the man's counter-revolutionary activity upon others in the village. For the audience, these are particularly poignant scenes, as many had lived with the often painful consequences of political conflicts. Included in the performance are scenes that portray the social conditions that caused the man to become a counter-revolutionary.

Following the testimonies of the villagers, the judges and audience members ask questions of the witnesses to clarify the reasons why the man acted as he did. After the discussion, the judges meet to decide upon a resolution. Some opt for reconciliation; others for banishment from their village. One judge, whose father had been killed by bandits, wanted the man to be shot. But the majority ruled that he should be asked to relocate to another community.

Other plays have addressed issues of religion, education, sexuality, and feminism. The work of Teatro Escambray is clearly entertaining, incorporating traditional forms of music and stories well known to the campesinos; but it is difficult to know if the dialectical nature of the open-ended plays directly affect the lives of the audiences and lead to a change in social consciousness. According to several members of the company, one play did have an immediate consequence in social action. The play, *La Vitrina (The Showcase),* concerned the agrarian reform program of the Cuban government, which redistributed land to the campesinos and resettled them within new, self-sufficient communities. Within the Escambray region, there was much resistance among some peasants to moving from their old homes. The play raised the issues of resettlement, presented the advantages of the new communities, and encouraged the audience members to debate the issues. Following a long run of *La Vitrina,* the process of resettlement accelerated within the Escambray region. Further, residents of these new communities began to develop their own amateur theatre companies, modeled after Teatro Escambray, to further the debates around pertinent social issues.

Teatro Escambray is devoted to dialogue and productive social change. The plays and discussions are not intended to be morally and ethically prescriptive but, rather, dialectical. Teatro Escambray is often critical of the imperfection within the revolutionary process, noting the conflict between the individual's struggle for excellence and the system's demands for sacrifice, and noting the often unrevolutionary actions one is forced to commit in order to live up to one's revolutionary ideals. The latter is well represented in the play, *Molinos de Viento (Windmills),* in which three adolescent boys burdened by a work-study system that demands a 6:00 A.M. to 10:00 P.M. commitment are forced to steal an important examination from their teacher in order to maintain the grades necessary for admission to the university.

In raising significant issues and in addressing the inherent contradictions within socialism, Teatro Escambray is a revolutionary theatre. Its therapeutics are social and its aims are political as well as aesthetic. It is truly a community-based theatre, created by artists whose work embodies the ideals of the revolution. But in many ways, there is an imbalance between the group product, the making of the play, and the group process, the development of the individual players. In dismissing a psychological world view and embracing a sociological, Marxist perspective, the concept of personal development is often neglected.

Teatro Escambray solves practical problems with practical solutions. All company members work toward solutions through the construction of plays addressing a given problem. For Freud and other depth psychologists, the problems to be solved through therapy are the conflicts inherent in one's existence for which there are no tangible solutions. Although Teatro Escambray often takes an open approach, entering into direct dialogue with audiences, its focus is too generalized and too public, often leading to a diminishing of the particular and the private sphere.

During a drama therapy workshop with Teatro Escambray, the therapist used the sociodramatic exercise (referred to in Chapter Seven) involving identification and exploration of a particular social issue. In asking the group to identify social issues within their theatre company, the therapist discovered that most focused upon problems within the larger community which provided the themes of their plays, rather than issues within the group itself. In noting a repeated yet implicit theme — the tension between men and women — the therapist suggested that the group work on exploring gender conflicts. At first, many were highly resistant, having expected to solve more distanced, less personal problems. But when an inner circle of women was formed and each began to construct a personal story of a particular woman facing particular social circumstances, a therapeutic process was underway. No longer were the generalized problems of "the people" being addressed. Specific issues of individual women living in a communal theatre company five hours from home, separated from their families, some divorced and alienated from a productive sexual and family life, were addressed directly. The expression of personal pain within the sociodrama was also a revolutionary act. Women were speaking of themselves, not only collectively, but also individually. There was no script and no formal controls. The community of actors, that in its zeal to solve large social problems had turned away from the pain of individuals, was in a state of further possibility, balanced between Marx and Freud, the people and the person, women and the individual woman.

Teatro Escambray exemplifies the highest ideals of the Cuban revolution. Through a process of research and open discussion, the group helps people recognize and address difficult issues in their lives. Like the best TIE companies in England and America, they are devoted to constructive and positive social change. As such, Teatro Escambray is a therapeutic theatre. Yet, the social therapeutics will be limited unless the group members are willing to turn the mirror back on themselves and address the problems of their own lives as individuals.

With the exception of many groups mentioned above, much of theatre that aims toward therapeutic goals in the United States does so often in ignorance of social and political realities. To be most effective in treating prisoners, mental patients, elders, and others, the drama therapist or theatre artist working toward change would greatly benefit from an attention to the social and political realities that so significantly affect the lives of the clients. In discovering a proper balance of distance between the personal and the political, the drama therapist can move toward a deeper and more authentic examination of the human condition.

PART V
RESEARCH IN DRAMA THERAPY

Chapter Eleven

REVIEW OF CURRENT RESEARCH

Drama therapy is a new, emerging discipline. As the field is grounded in both a performance art and a social science, there exists a wide range of appropriate research methods and strategies. The researcher does not need to remain tied to either the quantitative, empirical bias of American social science research or the historical, critical approach of much theatre arts research.

But in its status as beginner, the field of drama therapy is experiencing its own growing pains. Early descriptive writing in the field has been too general and subjective, praising the effects of the techniques without any criteria or conceptual explanation for how and why they work.

Early publications have also tended to emulate research strategies in the social sciences, using traditional psychological instruments and statistics to determine the effects of the drama therapy experience upon clients. Such an approach is certainly respectable in terms of the trend to quantify and generalize, but, in following the lead of experimental psychologists, drama therapists could well lose sight of their unique nature as creative artists.

Much social science inquiry has come to mean quantitative, statistical research. In our age of accountability, mental health administrators often ask the same questions as corporate executives: How can we reach the most people in the quickest time by spending the least money? Numbers and percentages answer these questions. However, given a discipline that focuses upon non-observable, subjective phenomena—feelings, images, values, and creative processes—numbers of cases lose their meaning. Drama and therapy are both processes that defy conventional quantification. Drama therapy, as a hybrid discipline, needs to develop an identity in terms of significant research strategies that acknowledge this reality.

Research, like re-creation and re-presentation, implies a distanced action, a process once removed from reality. The researcher is taking another look at reality, from the point of view of an observer. In doing so, he creates some distance between himself and the event observed.

Research, however, can imply any number of levels of distance between researcher and the event researched. The scientist in a laboratory, observing the growth of cells through a microscope, exemplifies a highly distanced relationship between researcher and event researched. The theatre artist, searching for the effects ·of an acting technique upon his own development, represents a much less distanced position. In finding a balance between his two roles of actor and observer, he must achieve the objectivity necessary to generalize from the event and the subjectivity necessary to personalize the experience.

In his research, Freud often observed the effects of his therapy upon patients while engaged in practice with them. He could not always maintain a balanced position in relation to clients, as his own countertransferential issues would surface from time to time. In his self-analysis through dreams, Freud also drew upon evidence from his own unconscious life to confirm and/or modify his theories.

It has been argued that Freud's methods of research were not scientific but rather subjective and intuitive (Postman, 1984). Throughout the years, more scientific researchers have been unable to measure the dimensions of such psychoanalytical concepts as the unconscious and the transference neurosis, which have remained invisible to the eye of the observer and most difficult to translate into a set of observable actions.

Like the researcher of psychoanalysis, the drama therapy researcher needs to find a balanced position either within the therapeutic interaction or from without, observing other therapists at work. And, like his psychoanalytical counterpart, he needs to discover ways to characterize mental constructs without trivializing their complexity.

Most researchers, whether scientific or artistic, or a combination of both, look for answers to several common questions. These are:

1. What is the frame of reference or conceptual base of the research?
2. What general issues or specific questions are most significant to investigate?
3. How will the investigation proceed?
4. How will the findings be interpreted?
5. What are the results?
6. What is the significance of the results for the larger field of knowledge?

The first question applies to the choice of a theoretical model or models which will inform the research. The second concerns the formulation of research questions, problems, or hypotheses. The third is a question of methodology; the fourth, that of the means of analysis. The results and the conclusions are represented by questions five and six. Let us now look at past and present research in drama therapy based in these categories.

THEORETICAL MODELS

Chapter Four represents an early attempt to construct a theoretical model of drama therapy. The model is eclectic, drawing freely from concepts in psychology, sociology, and drama/theatre. At the heart of the model is the dramatic process which is viewed as representational and dialectical. The central concept that carries this notion is that of distancing. Within the field of drama therapy, there has yet to be research based upon a distancing paradigm. In the related field of social psychology, however, Thomas Scheff (1979) has been studying the nature of humor, anxiety, and pain through an application of the distancing model.

One of the most prolific researchers in drama therapy, David Johnson, has used several theoretical models to provide a frame of reference for his investigations. One is the developmental model based in the theory of object relations (see Kernberg, 1976) and that of psychological development (see Piaget, 1962; Erikson, 1963). For Johnson, the developmental model of Erikson provides a view of the full spectrum of human growth and development, from birth to old age. Further, it provides a progressive movement toward change and self-actualization.

Johnson has conducted substantial research into the effects of the drama therapy experience upon populations of schizophrenics. With this group, he has adopted a related model based in role theory. In this work, Johnson has developed a structural role model, which characterizes improvisational role playing by four conditions: impersonal, intrapersonal, extrapersonal, and interpersonal. As we have seen, this is an especially useful model in looking at the issues of boundary confusions among schizophrenics. Johnson and his collaborator, Quinlan, have used the role-playing model as a means of differentiating between groups of paranoid and non-paranoid schizophrenics (1980).

Johnson has also applied a sociopolitical model, that of communitas, to his research with psychiatric patients in a veterans hospital setting. He defines communitas (1984) as: "the feeling of belonging to a community, of recognizing the common bonds which link people together in a unit, with shared purpose." Johnson's notion of communitas is based upon the work of Robert Almond (1974) and others, like Fritz Redl, who have conceptualized the mental health setting as a healing community or therapeutic milieu, rather than a compartmentalized institution.

Eleanor Irwin and her collaborators have taken a different approach in their drama therapy research. They have adopted a psychoanalytic model, based in the play therapy work of Anna Freud, Melanie Klein, and Margaret Lowenfeld. Irwin's position has been that the psycho-analytical model is applicable to research in drama therapy, because it offers an explanation of how and why repressed feelings take on a symbolic form through playful, spontaneous enactment. Irwin (1983) writes: "The child's spontaneous 'acting out' of concerns in therapy is a kind of language to be examined and understood." Irwin's model leads directly into an exploration of the effects of such projective techniques as puppetry, sand play, and storytelling on various groups of emotionally disturbed and communication-impaired children.

The five models (i.e. distancing, development, role playing, communitas, and psychoanalysis), whether applied singly or in combination, are highly promising as means of guiding drama therapy research.

RESEARCH QUESTIONS

Drama therapy researchers drawing upon these models have begun to address several general issues and specific problems. In Johnson's work with schizophrenics, the main issue has been the relationship between improvisational role playing and the development of clear intrapsychic and interpersonal boundaries. In his present research, he continues to address the problem of the loss of the self and the potential of drama therapy in recovering it. Johnson has transformed this general issue into several specific, researchable questions. These include: can the use of improvisational role-playing techniques help in differentiating the behaviors of paranoid and non-paranoid schizophrenics (Johnson and Quinlan, 1980)? Can improvisational role-playing techniques help schizophrenic clients to recognize a "whole set of complex interrelationships" (Johnson, 1981)? What are the effects of theatrical productions on the lives of hospitalized psychiatric patients (Johnson, 1980)? Can a healing commu-nity approach (that of communitas) transform the behavior of severly psychotic individuals (Johnson, 1984)?

For Irwin and her collaborators, who have directed much of their attention to work with emotionally disturbed children, a primary issue has been the effects of projective techniques upon the development of the child's self-esteem. Specific research questions have included: How can dramatic play aid in the development of cognitive skills for the learning disabled child (Irwin and Frank, 1977)? How can drama and art be used reciprocally in a child guidance center for diagnostic purposes (Rubin and Irwin, 1975)? Can the drama experience positively affect the ability of the emotionally disturbed child to communicate feelings and to appropriately interact with others (Irwin, Levy and Shapiro, 1972)?

Further studies by Renée Emunah (Emunah, 1983, Emunah and Johnson, 1983), Nancy Breitenbach (1979, 1984), and others appear regularly in the international journal, *The Arts in Psychotherapy*, and the British journal, *Dramatherapy*. More and more of the research is based in solid theoretical models and raises significant researchable issues.

RESEARCH METHODOLOGIES

In his book, *Re-play: Studies of Drama in Education*, Richard Courtney (1982) makes a distinction between experiential and reflective research. In experiential research, the subject becomes the object of his own inquiry; he is both the participant and the observer. For example, the experience of the actor within a group is researched by that same actor. Experiential research is often a group process. Throughout the 1960s and 1970s, several prominent experimental theatre groups engaged in experiential research as a means of creating plays. Although the process of inquiry was usually led by a director, it was based in the collective experiments of the full group. Examples include the work of the the Open Theatre and The Living Theatre in New York and the San Francisco Mime Troupe and the ProVisional Theatre in California.

Experiential research is often the preferred method for artists. It functions to activate the creative process of making art. Although mindful of the past, the creative artist involved in experiential research focuses upon the here-and-now, the moment of spontaneity, in order to discover the appropriate form in which to embed his feeling. Experiential research often proceeds inductively, from the part to the whole, through a process of trial and error.

Courtney (1982) refers to reflective research as "inquiry about enactment." In this case, the researcher takes a more distanced position from the event. He is no longer a participant but purely an observer. In drama therapy, several forms of reflective research methods have been used. Some researchers have taken a descriptive approach, documenting experiences in clinical, community, or school settings with particular populations. Their descriptive research is usually based upon field notes written up following the observation of drama therapy sessions. This is valuable in delineating the kinds of techniques and strategies germane to the practice of drama therapy with clients in particular settings. However, descriptive research is rarely rooted in theory and tends to make claims based upon vague criteria.

Another method of reflective research is that of the case study or field study. Through this approach, the researcher focuses upon an individual or small group of individuals to illustrate a theoretical point of view or to elaborate upon the effects of a particular dramatic treatment strategy. In Johnson's "Drama Therapy and the Schizophrenic Condition" (1981), for example, reference is made to individual case studies which illustrate his structural role model. Similarly, Eleanor Irwin and Marvin Shapiro use case examples to illustrate the use of puppetry in diagnosis and treatment (Irwin and Shapiro, 1975). Elaine Portner's article, "Drama in Therapy: Experiences of a Ten Year Old" (1981), is a full case study of an emotionally disturbed child whose life is affected by drama therapy treatment.

When case studies are grounded in theory, as in these three examples, they can provide a complex view of the drama therapy experience. Although limited to a single subject or small group, the case study method takes an in-depth, qualitative look at the person. Researchers and theorists in the field of psychology, such as Freud and Piaget, have often relied upon the case study as a way to validate or refine their developing theory.

Quantitative, empirical methods have also been used in drama therapy research. Taking this approach, the researcher translates his research questions into observable, testable hypotheses, specifying the effects that may occur given a particular treatment strategy. He then chooses or develops an instrument in which to measure the effects of the drama therapy experience upon an individual or group of clients. The empirical researcher will often compare the treatment group to a control group. Further, he will employ statistics to analyze his data and to predict the probable effectiveness of a particular treatment strategy.

In two empirical studies of emotionally disturbed children (Irwin,

Levy, and Shapiro, 1972; Dequine and Pearson-Davis, 1983) and one of schizophrenic adults (Johnson and Quinlan, 1980), the researchers used psychological instruments to examine the effects of the drama therapy experience upon their subjects. The results will be reported below.

Empirical research tends to be linear and to show a cause-and-effect relationship between two variables. Yet, in the process of psychotherapy, in general, and drama therapy, in particular, there exists a complex range of human variables in the many changing roles of the client in relation to the therapist. Thus, often there is not a direct cause-and-effect relationship in evidence. Until these variables can be clearly delineated and quantified, empirical research methods will be limited in drama therapy.

A more qualitative research method, developed by Eleanor Irwin and her colleagues, is that of the drama and puppetry interview (Irwin and Shapiro, 1975; Irwin and Rubin, 1976). With this approach, the child subject tells or enacts a fictional story himself or through a puppet. During the storytelling or enactment, the therapist enters into dialogue with the subject, helping him elaborate upon the story. The story is then analyzed by the researcher in terms of its form and content. The analysis will provide the means of diagnosing the client and determining treatment strategies. Like the clinical interview often used by Piaget and his colleagues, the drama and puppetry interview attempts to uncover modes of thought and affect rather than specific behaviors. It is an in-depth approach in which the researcher engages in an open-ended dialogue with the subject.

A final reflective approach to drama therapy research is an analytical one, delineating concepts essential to the theoretical structure of the field. Thus far, such research is limited. In Chapter Four, several concepts were examined, all of which can provide the basis for further investigation.

ANALYSIS OF THE DATA AND RESULTS

In some cases, drama therapy researchers have been able to apply standard psychological instruments to the analysis of subjects' behaviors. When conventional approaches proved inadequate in measuring the effects of the drama experience, researchers have developed new instruments.

Irwin and her colleagues have used both old and new means of analysis. When first analyzing puppet stories presented by children,

Irwin and Shapiro (1975) examined the form and content of the stories. Their analysis was somewhat general and was reported anecdotally within the context of case studies. In subsequent work, Irwin and Kovacs (1979) developed more specific criteria for analyzing stories, breaking down the content into the categories of: main character, theme, setting, affective tone, and ending.

Drawing upon such standard instruments as the Rorschach Index of Repressive Style (RIRS) and the semantic differential, Irwin and her colleagues have also been able to analyze the effects of the drama experience upon emotionally disturbed children. In analyzing the form of children's stories, Irwin and Rubin (1975) turned to quantitative means of analysis, rating the stories according to nine categories, i.e., organized/disorganized, clear/confused, and complete/incomplete. In a complex study examining the effects of drama therapy upon emotionally disturbed children within a child guidance setting, Irwin, Levy, and Shapiro (1972) applied several standard instruments of analysis: the RIRS, the verbal fluency test, the semantic differential, and the parent competency scale. Their results affirmed several positive effects of drama therapy, as children with low RIRS scores proved less repressed and more expressive and imaginative in their language following the drama treatment. In terms of self-concept, however, there was no significant change between those in the drama group and those in the control group, as measured on the semantic differential. Further, there was no demonstrable change in the ways their parents viewed them, as measured on the parent competency scale.

Johnson and Quinlan (1980) developed new instruments to assess the behaviors of paranoid and non-paranoid schizophrenics on a role-playing task. Their instruments, the Fluid Boundary and Rigid Boundary scales, differentiated the paranoid group from the non-paranoid group and measured the distance between self and role, self and other, self and environment. Items on the Fluid Boundary Scale included: breaking role, fluidity, intrusion, self-reference, loss of distance, and fusion. The Rigid Boundary Scale included the following: perseveration, concrete replacement, entering/leaving (a setting in the improvisation), boundary, narration (speaking in the third person), and the use of telephone to interact with others in the scene.

The findings of the research confirmed their hypothesis that paranoid schizophrenics create more rigid boundaries in their role playing, while non-paranoid schizophrenics create more fluid ones. They concluded that improvisational role playing is an effective means to assess boundary behaviors and differentiate one diagnostic group of schizophrenics from another.

In a subsequent study elaborating upon the above findings, Johnson and Quinlan (in press) again used improvisational role playing to examine representational boundaries in schizophrenics. They applied an instrument developed earlier by Johnson (1980a): the dramatic role-playing test. The test assesses nine aspects of the subject's role playing: organization, action representation, integration of action, motivation, interaction, ending, accuracy, content, and movement. The dramatic role-playing test is particularly relevant to drama therapy research, as it is based in the art form of drama. It is close in intent to two non-therapeutic dramatic instruments. The first, the Assessment of Dramatic Involvement Scale, was developed by Sutton-Smith and Lazier (1971). The scale specifies nine behaviors to be assessed in a role-playing situation. They include: focus, completion, use of imaginary objects, elaboration, use of space, facial expression, body movements, vocal expressions, and social relationships. The second, the Inventory of Dramatic Behavior, developed one year later by Lazier and Karioth (1972), assesses improvisational role playing by an actor according to the following: time, space traversed, number of stops, dramatic incidents, novel dramatic incidents, dramatic acts, repeated scenes, and characters created.

Johnson (1980) has also conducted a study on the effects of theatre upon an adult, hospitalized psychiatric population. For this research, Johnson adapted two clinical instruments: the social contact scale and the clinical state scale. The nursing staff rated the subjects before, during, and after the presentation of two plays. Johnson discovered that patients in the first play had greater social contact and a more positive clinical state while in rehearsal as compared to a control group exposed to the regular recreational programs of the hospital. During a period of four weeks following the play, however, the experimental group became more withdrawn and clinically symptomatic. To remedy this regression, Johnson added a weekly support group following the production of a second play. He discovered that the clinical state following the performance of the second play markedly improved, even though social contact decreased during the same period of time.

For many artists and researchers in the field of drama therapy, the key to understanding how and why their techniques work lies in the artistic process itself. With this in mind, we turn to the future to speculate as to the directions that researchers can take in their search for the meaning and function of drama therapy.

Chapter Twelve

FUTURE DIRECTIONS IN RESEARCH

The artistic process is conceptualized by the British sociologist, Robert Witkin (1974), as an intelligence of feeling. For Witkin, the artistic process is dialectical, simultaneously cognitive and affective. Further, it is a means of making order, giving form to an essentially unformed state of sensation. Says Witkin (1974): "Feeling-form is the product of subjective-reflexive action in which the disturbances wrought within the individual are projected into a medium which recalls them." Should these "disturbances wrought within the individual" remain repressed and/or unexpressed, then dysfunctional behavior can result. The essence of the artistic experience, that of giving form to feeling, is, broadly speaking, therapeutic. Like the drama therapist who proceeds in his therapy and research through applying the distancing model, Witkin offers a paradigm of balance. The moment of creative expression is that of discovering a balance between feeling and thinking. Feeling becomes intelligent as it finds an appropriate form. And in projecting the feeling onto the form, the subject moves toward integration.

In formulating research strategies in drama therapy, the model of distancing, grounded in the artistic process of simultaneously thinking and feeling, of feeling intelligently and thinking feelingly, can well serve as a guide to the development of research problems, methodologies, and analyses.

THEORETICAL MODELS RECONSIDERED

Future researchers in drama therapy might continue to work from conventional psychotherapeutic models. As the field develops further, however, indigenous drama therapy models are likely to emerge. The distancing model, for one, holds much promise. It is dramatic, in that it conceptualizes the relationships between self, role, and other. The application of the distancing model does not imply a rejection of psychoanalytical, sociological, or developmental concepts. The concepts of transference, projection, identification, and imitation are well suited to the distancing model, as they are inherently dramatic, responding to the notion of a balance between dual realities.

Future research in drama therapy, then, should be based in theory derived from drama. If a conventional psychological or sociological model is applied, it should contain concepts which inform the dramatic process of representation.

RESEARCH QUESTIONS RECONSIDERED

In formulating future research questions and problems, one general focus remains constant: What is it about the dramatic, creative process that is therapeutic? Assuming that a satisfactory response can be given, there still remains the need to address the question raised in the introduction to the book: Why should the psychotherapy profession already overloaded with a plethora of artistic and scientific modalities admit yet another one? What can drama do that other therapies cannot?

These general questions need to be translated into more specific, researchable ones that explore the uniqueness of the drama experience in healing disturbed or disabled individuals. Johnson has already begun to demonstrate the directness and speed of role playing in diagnosing and treating schizophrenics. Irwin, likewise, has worked toward demonstrating the subtle power of puppetry and play therapy techniques in treating children. The questions both researchers pose are different from those of their psychoanalytical and developmental colleagues, in that their orientation is toward direct action, mediated by the role-playing process.

Many of the concepts delineated in Chapter Four can be applied to research with a particular population. For example, the concept of transference can serve as the basis for research with a group of emotionally disturbed children. As such, the researcher needs to formulate specific questions to inform his exploration of the transference that occurs due to the fact that the therapy is dramatic. Questions might include: How can transference be demonstrated directly and rapidly in drama therapy? What is it about the dramatic role structure that fosters transference? How can transference, once evoked, be resolved within the structure of role playing? How can the model of distancing be applied toward the resolution of the transference neurosis?

In developing research questions based in related concepts (i.e., projection, identification, and catharsis), the drama therapy researcher can move toward validating the conceptual basis of drama therapy. For this to occur, he must clearly demonstrate the inherently dramatic nature of each concept.

METHODOLOGIES RECONSIDERED

If drama therapy, although an interdisciplinary art and science, is most essentially an art, then its primary method of investigation should be an artistic one. The mathematician and philosopher, P. D. Ouspensky, has eloquently written (1971): "Like science and philosophy, art is a definite way of knowledge. . . . An art which does not reveal mysteries . . . does not yield new knowledge, is a parody of art. . . . "

When the therapeutic process is based in an artistic experience, that of drama, then we need to look at those dramatic methods of knowing that reveal mysteries and yield new knowledge. This implies a movement away from the most restrictive quantitative, behavioral research toward more qualitative, in-depth methods. The case study and clinical interview methods are highly promising in drama therapy. Both take an in-depth, open-ended approach. The case study method addresses not only the effects of the drama experience upon the person but also the historical and social factors that have contributed to. the person's development.

Yet, these and other social scientific methods still do not respond to Ouspensky's challenge. To create an artistic method means to move into the sphere of the creative act itself, to engage in experiential research from the inside. Thus, the researcher becomes a part of his own research, a participant observer, an artist making art while observing its process. The artist/researcher in drama therapy can assume several roles of actor, director, and designer.

As an actor, he might work alone, creating an autobiographical performance piece to examine a particularly difficult period in his life. While engaging in the process and searching for the appropriate media—puppets, masks, objects, makeup—through which to uncover his issues, he needs to create enough distance in order to document his moment to moment observations.

The creation of an autobiographical performance piece is a direct method of research. The documentation of the process is more difficult, as it interrupts the natural flow of the action and demands that the subject play the simultaneous roles of actor and observer and engage in the simultaneous modes of intuitive and rational thought.

Although the creative process varies significantly from subject to subject, certain elements can be noted which conform both to the model of distancing and to Witkin's notion of intelligence of feeling. In creating the autobiographical performance piece, the subject begins with a feeling state or a sensation. Filmmaker Ingmar Bergman describes this early stage of the creative process as follows (1960):

> A film for me begins with something vague—a chance remark or a bit of conversation, a hazy but agreeable event unrelated to any particular situation. It can be a few bars of music, a shaft of light across the street. Sometimes in my work at the theatre, I have envisioned actors made up for yet unplayed roles. These are split-second impressions that disappear as quickly as they come, yet leave behind a mood-like pleasant dream. It is a mental state, not an actual story, but one abounding in fertile associations and images. Most of all, it is a brightly colored thread sticking out of the dark sack of the unconscious.

The subject can document these sensations, feelings, or images and note how they provide the impetus to move toward the next stage: the search for a specific form in which to contain the sensations, feelings, images. Says Bergman: "This primitive nucleus strives to achieve definite form, moving in a way that may be lazy and half asleep at first. Its stirring is accompanied by vibrations and rhythms which are very special and unique to each film. The picture sequences then assume a pattern in accordance with these rhythms, obeying laws born out of and conditioned by my original stimulus."

The early struggles toward articulating feelings and discovering form in the autobiographical performance piece might well be accompanied by internal stirrings and the unearthing of painful feeling. For many creative artists, these primitive feelings are secondary, an occupational hazard, a familiar but rough terrain to get through as quickly as possible. For the experiential researcher in drama therapy, these feelings are primary, a main focus of attention. To document these feelings, the subject can draw upon several unconscious sources. For one, he can transcribe the dreams that occur during the time of his creative process and carefully analyze the imagery. He can also become aware of significant moments of projection, identification, and transference in his relationship to others that can further reveal the forms and themes he needs to explore through the performance piece. The subject can also draw upon conscious sources, noting his behavior, physical state, and social interactions as he is struggling to find the appropriate feeling-form.

As the creative process proceeds, Bergman notes several other stages: the transformation of rhythms, moods, and tones into words and sentences; the continuity or sequencing of images; and, finally, the realization of the scenario in its completed form—the showing of the work of art to an audience. For the experiential researcher in drama therapy, these stages, too, will be marked by moments of resistance and flow. In documenting the continuing process, he will again take note of these moments. Following the performance to a group of peers, he will reflect upon the experience, re-examining his documentation and directing it toward answering the question: How does the creation and execution of an autobiographical performance piece yield new knowledge about the dramatic process of healing?

As a director, the artist/researcher can work with a particular group, leading the participants toward the development of an extended dramatization or of a more formal theatre piece. Again, his focus would be upon illuminating a problematic aspect of his life through the creative process of shaping a representational world that reveals his own vision of reality. In playing the director role, the researcher would document the experience through writing or videotaping. If available, videotaping would provide an excellent means of documentation, as it would not directly interrupt the process of creation. Following the extended dramatization or performance experience, he would again reflect upon the psychological components of the creative process.

In the role of the designer, the artist/researcher can work through a personal experience in world technique. Through a series of world pictures, constructed over a period of time with a variety of objects, the subject can design many "sets" for plays, movies, or rooms in imaginary houses. Again, a process of documentation can occur during the set construction. This, too, would be best served by the use of a video camera that would not only reveal the final images created but also the process in choosing objects, arranging objects and space, and arriving at a finished picture. During the construction, the subject can articulate his thoughts which would also be recorded. Following an extended series of world pictures in sand and on other surfaces, the subject would review the videotapes, analyzing both the process of creation and the final images created.

ANALYTICAL STRATEGIES RECONSIDERED

In analyzing the data from world pictures and performance, the researcher needs to discover or invent instruments that are based in drama and/or useful in analyzing dramatic process. Johnson has already begun to develop the dramatic role-playing test to measure a subject's ability to engage in improvisational role playing. This means of analysis would be most useful in reflective research.

In analyzing experiential research, as well as those forms of reflective research which test the effects of a particular dramatic projective technique upon a group, the researcher might well develop a new instrument based in the distancing model. Such an instrument, similar to Scheff's model on page 102, would measure a subject's spontaneous creative process and performance according to a continuum marked by overdistance at one pole, underdistance at the other, and balance of distance at the midpoint. Criteria at each point would have to be carefully developed and tested. Yet, as the model is based in an artistic process, it will be difficult to delineate fully observable criteria, especially at the midpoint of balance. Again, the researcher may need to turn to non-scientific sources, such as literature and aesthetics, to validate the point of balance of distance. At the point of aesthetic distance lies Odysseus's outwitting of the Cyclops, Lear's discovery of love and truth through the death of Cordelia, Stephen Dedalus's moments of epiphany and initiation into the world of art, and Edward Bullough's (1964) notion of balance as "the utmost decrease of distance without it's disappearance." Although these moments cannot easily be translated into items on an analytical scale, they can be used as a means to guide the development of a qualitative analytical instrument.

In developing an evaluative instrument based in the distancing model, the drama therapy researcher can turn to both social scientific and artistic sources. Without the former, his instrument might become too vague, imprecise, subjective, and impressionistic. Without the latter, his instrument might become too superficial, objective, and mechanical. In combining the objective precision of the scientific method with the subjective feeling-form of the creative process, the researcher can move toward a means of evaluation that responds to the interdisciplinary nature of drama therapy.

THE TASK THAT REMAINS—DRAMA THERAPY
AS A MEANS OF RESTORING BALANCE

Throughout the book, the image of balance has been used repeatedly. In the drama therapy process it applies not only to diagnosis and treatment but also to theory and research. The aims of the drama therapy process mentioned throughout—to recognize experience, to increase one's role repertory, and to learn how to play a single role more spontaneously and competently—all spring from a common source: that of the balance of distance. The moment of balance is one that others have called insight, catharsis, spontaneity, faith, confluence, enlightenment, transcendence. It is a moment charged with infinite possibility. As a therapeutic moment, it is well suited to a dramatic method. For in drama, the self, the role, and the other are suspended in a fertile space, waiting to be impregnated, one by the other. For drama to occur, this impregnation must take place. The three agents will naturally strive toward balance, as the self learns who it is through taking on the role of another. But in the process of living, the balance will be disrupted over and over again. In Erikson's words, identity will struggle with role confusion. Significant others will change, roles will change in quality and quantity, and the self will disappear and reappear transformed, developed, regressed. When the inevitable process of change becomes highly threatening to the integrity of the self, that is, when the self is unable to take on and play out meaningful roles with a sense of commitment and fulfillment, then a form of therapy is indicated that can help restore a balance. Drama therapy, based in role theory and providing a clear model of balance, is well suited for this task.

The task that remains is to demonstrate the effectiveness of drama therapy in restoring balance within the individual, as well as between and among individuals. To reach this goal, several interrelated directions need to be explored. For one, treatment strategies and techniques need to be evaluated through trial and error, documentation, and precise research. These strategies must be tested with various populations within diverse settings to determine their effectiveness. Concurrently, theoretical models and concepts need to be specified that both point to treatment strategies and inform research methods. Research strategies should also be developed based in the healing potential of the creative art of drama.

Such organizations as the National Association for Drama Therapy must continue to develop rigorous but flexible standards for registration of drama therapists and certification of training programs. At the state and national levels, legislators need to become aware of the value of the creative arts in healing and enact legislation that paves the way for recognition of the creative arts therapist as a significant mental health professional, entitled to a position and a salary commensurate with his training.

Practitioners, lobbyists, researchers, and trainers of drama therapists need to combine their efforts in validating a new field that holds so much promise. The task that remains is an enormous one that, in many ways, demands a review and critique of the present mental health system. It is not enough to train drama therapists, publish research articles, and develop theories and techniques. All those involved must penetrate a system fraught with problems of dwindling funds, inefficient bureaucracy, political inequities, and methods that often only treat symptoms. And from the inside they must offer a viable alternative, one that addresses issues of imbalance within the person, between people, and among peoples.

Several years ago, an elderly man had a wild idea, a solution to the threat of nuclear holocaust. He began planning a global drama, a simulated nuclear war in which residents of selected cities and towns throughout the world would simultaneously enact the same scenario. Acting as if the dreaded bombs had fallen, they were to die, or attempt to rescue others, or get on with their lives based upon certain specified scientific facts of destruction and radiation. In working toward his goal of dramatizing the absurdity of the nuclear race, the man had contacted representatives in all corners of the world. To stage such a drama demanded the cooperation of Orientals and occidentals, capitalists and socialists, children, women, and men of all races and religions. But the demonstration never occurred. There were too many political and bureaucratic snags, too much resistance from too many people. That man has not given up hope, however. He and his colleagues are still organizing, still trying to use a dramatic method to critique the most profound threat of our age.

In many ways, drama is a viable alternative to the destruction of the self, the other, the world. If one's destructive impulses can be played out safely in imagination, thus restoring a balance, then there is little need to hurt oneself or another in reality. Although this formula is simplistic, it remains at the heart of the experience of healing through drama.

At a time when global peace seems so elusive and when the individual is so often at war with himself, the old solutions—negotiations, medications, and modifications—break down. Drama therapy is a new attempt to solve old problems—those of imbalance and protracted threat. Drama therapists are beginning to fashion powerful tools to solve the problems. They need now to encourage those entrenched in old methods to risk new solutions.

If a gun fires and a bullet is discharged, destruction can follow. If a gun fires and a flag appears that says "Bang!" the violent impulse is discharged in laughter. If we were all to enact our personal and political wars in play, perhaps we, too, could circumvent the actual consequences of destructive action.

BIBLIOGRAPHY

Almond, Richard: *The Healing Community.* New York, Aronson, 1974.

American Psychiatric Association: *Diagnostic and Statistical Manual for Mental Disorders,* 3rd ed. Washington, D.C., American Psychiatric Association, 1983.

Artaud, Antonin: *The Theatre and Its Double.* New York, Grove, 1958.

Axline, Virginia: *Play Therapy.* Boston, Houghton-Mifflin, 1947.

Bandura, Albert; and Walters, R. H.: *Social Learning and Personality Development.* New York, Holt, Rinehart and Winston, 1965.

Beck, Julian: *The Life of the Theatre.* San Francisco, City Lights, 1972.

Beckett, Samuel: *Waiting for Godot.* New York, Grove, 1954.

Bergman, Ingmar: *Four Screenplays of Ingmar Bergman.* New York, Simon and Schuster, 1960.

Bettleheim, Bruno: *The Uses of Enchantment.* New York, Knopf, 1976.

Bloom, Benjamin; Krathwohl, David R.; and Masia, Bernard B.: *Taxonomy of Educational Objectives, Handbook I: Cognitive Domain.* New York, David McKay, 1956.

Blumer, Herbert: Society as symbolic interaction. In Rose, A. M. (Ed.): *Human Behavior and Social Processes.* New York, Houghton-Mifflin, 1962.

Boal, Augusto: *Theatre of the Oppressed.* New York, Urizen, 1979.

Bolgar, Hedda; and Fischer, L. K.: Personality projection in the world test. *American Journal of Orthopsychiatry, 17:*117–128, 1947.

Bolton, Gavin: *Towards a Theory of Drama in Education.* London, Longman, 1979.

Breitenbach, Nancy: Secret faces. *Dramatherapy, 2:*18–23, 1979.

_____: Identity development during creative makeup sessions. *The Arts in Psychotherapy, 11:*101–107, 1984.

Breuer, Josef; and Freud, Sigmund: *Studies in Hysteria.* London, Hogarth, 1936.

British Association for Dramatherapists: Statement of goals. *Dramatherapy, 2:*19, 1979.

Brookes, J. M.: Producing Marat/Sade: theatre in a psychiatric hospital. *Hospital and Community Psychiatry, 26:*429–435, 1975.

Bruner, Jerome; Jolly, Alison; and Sylva, Kathy (Eds.): *Play—Its Role in Development and Evolution.* New York, Basic Books, 1976.

Bruner, Jerome; and Sherwood, V.: Peekaboo and the learning of rule structures (1975). In Bruner, Jerome, Jolly, Alison, and Sylva, Kathy (Eds.): *Play—Its Role in Development and Evolution.* New York, Basic Books, 1976.

Buber, Martin: *I and Thou.* New York, Scribner's, 1937.

Bullough, Edward: "Psychical distance" as a factor in art and an esthetic principle. In Rader, Melvin (Ed.): *A Modern Book of Esthetics,* 3rd ed. New York, Holt, Rinehart and Winston, 1964.

Butler, Robert: The life review: an interpretation of reminiscence in the aged. *Psychiatry, 20:*65–76, 1963.

Camillo, Marvin F.: Introduction. In Piñero, Miguel: *Short Eyes.* New York, Hill and Wang, 1975.

Chambers, E. K.: *The Medieval Stage.* London, Oxford, 1903.

Cooley, Charles: *Human Nature and Social Order.* New York, Scribner's, 1922.

Courtney, Richard: *Play, Drama and Thought.* New York, Drama Book Specialists, 1974.

————: *The Dramatic Curriculum.* New York, Drama Book Specialists, 1980.

————: *Re-play: Studies of Drama in Education.* Toronto, Ontario Institute for Studies in Education, 1982.

Dequine, Elizabeth and Pearson-Davis, Susan: Videotaped improvisational drama with emotionally disturbed adolescents: a pilot study. *The Arts in Psychotherapy, 10:*15–22, 1983.

Dewey, John: *Democracy in Education.* New York, Free Press, 1966.

Emunah, Renée: Drama therapy with adult psychiatric patients. *The Arts in Psychotherapy, 10:*77, 1983.

Emunah, Renée; and Johnson, David: The impact of theatrical performance on the self-image of psychiatric patients. *The Arts in Psychotherapy, 10:*233–239, 1983.

Erikson, Erik H.: Studies in the interpretation of play. *Genetic Psychological Monograph, 22:*557–671, 1940.

————: *Childhood and Society.* New York, Norton, 1963.

Ferri-Grant, Carson: *Sociodrama as a Technique for Developing Interpersonal Competence with Sex Offenders.* Unpublished M.A. thesis. Storrs, University of Connecticut, 1984.

Freud, Sigmund: The relation of the poet to daydreaming (1908). In *Collected Papers, IV.* London, Hogarth, 1953.

————: *A General Introduction to Psychoanalysis.* Garden City, Garden City Publishing Company, 1943.

————: *The Interpretation of Dreams.* New York, Avon, 1965.

Fryrear, Jerry L., and Fleshman, Bob (Eds.): *Videotherapy in Mental Health.* Springfield, Thomas, 1981.

Gardner, Richard: *Therapeutic Communication with Children: The Mutual Story-telling Technique.* New York, Science House, 1971.

Goffman, Erving: *The Presentation of Self in Everyday Life.* Garden City, Doubleday, 1959.

————: *Asylums.* New York, Doubleday, 1961.

Gregoric, Linda and Michael: Sociodrama: video in social action. In Fryrear, Jerry L., and Fleshman, Bob (Eds.): *Videotherapy in Mental Health.* Springfield, Thomas, 1981.

Hart, Steven E.: *The Family: A Theatre Company Working with Prison Inmates and Ex-Inmates.* Unpublished Ph.D dissertation. New York, City University, 1981.

Hart, Steven E., and Waren, Mark (Eds.): *The Arts in Prison.* New York, CASTA, City University, 1983.

Homburger, Erik: Configurations in play—clinical notes. *Psychoanalytic Quarterly, 6:*139–214, 1937.

Huizinga, Johan: *Homo Ludens.* Boston, Beacon, 1955.

Irwin, Eleanor C.: Drama therapy with the handicapped. In Shaw, Ann; and Stevens, C. J. (Eds.): *Drama, Theatre and the Handicapped.* Washington, D.C., American Theatre Association, 1979.

————: The diagnostic and therapeutic use of pretend-play. In Schaefer, Charles; and O'Connor, Kevin (Eds.): *Handbook of Play Therapy.* New York, Wiley, 1983.

Irwin, Eleanor C.; Levy, Paul; and Shapiro, Marvin: Assessment of drama therapy in a child guidance setting. *Group Psychotherapy and Psychodrama, 25:*105–116, 1972.

Irwin, Eleanor C.; and Shapiro, Marvin: Puppetry as a diagnostic and therapeutic technique. In Jakab, Irene (Ed.): *Transcultural Aspects of Psychiatric Art,* Vol. 4. Basel, Karger, 1975.

Irwin, Eleanor C., and Rubin, Judith: Art and drama interviews: decoding symbolic messages. *The Arts in Psychotherapy, 3:*169–175, 1976.

Irwin, Eleanor C., and Frank, Mary: Facilitating the play process with learning disabled children. *Academic Therapy, 12:*435–444, 1977.

Irwin, Eleanor C.; and Kovacs, Alberta: Analysis of children's drawings and stories. *Journal of the Association for the Care of Children in Hospitals, 8:*39–48, 1979.

Jackins, Harvey: *The Human Side of Human Beings.* Seattle, Rational Island, 1965.

James, William: *Psychology.* New York, World, 1948.

Janov, Arthur: *The Primal Scream.* New York, Putnam, 1970.

Johnson, David: Effects of a theatre experience on hospitalized psychiatric patients. *The Arts in Psychotherapy, 7:*265–272, 1980.

_____: *Cognitive Organization in Paranoid and Nonparanoid Schizophrenia.* Unpublished Ph.D. dissertation. New Haven, Yale University, 1980a.

_____: Drama therapy and the schizophrenic condition. In Schattner, Gertrud; and Courtney, Richard (Eds.): *Drama in Therapy,* Vol. 2. New York, Drama Book Specialists, 1981.

_____: Principles and techniques of drama therapy. *The Arts in Psychotherapy, 9:*83–90, 1982.

_____: Developmental approaches in drama therapy. *The Arts in Psychotherapy, 9:*183–190, 1982a.

_____: The arts and communitas. *Design, 86:*36–39, 1984.

_____: Expressive group psychotherapy with the elderly: a drama therapy approach. *International Journal of Group Psychotherapy, 35:*109–128, 1985.

Johnson, David; and Munich, Richard: Increasing hospital-community contact through a theatre program in a psychiatric hospital. *Hospital and Community Psychiatry, 26:*435–438, 1975.

Johnson, David; and Quinlan, Donald: Fluid and rigid boundaries of paranoid and nonparanoid schizophrenics on a role-playing task. *Journal of Personality Assessment, 44:*523–531, 1980.

_____: Representational boundaries in the role portrayals among paranoid and nonparanoid schizophrenics. *Journal of Abnormal Psychology, 94,* in press.

Jung, Carl G: *Man and His Symbols.* Garden City, Doubleday, 1964.

_____: *Analytic Psychology: Its Theory and Practice.* New York, Random, 1968.

Kalff, Dora: *Sandplay: A Psychotherapeutic Approach to the Psyche.* Boston, Sigo, 1981.

Kernberg, Otto: *Object Relations Theory and Clinical Psychoanalysis.* New York, Aronson, 1976.

Klein, Melanie: *The Psychoanalysis of Childhood.* London, Hogarth, 1932.

Klein, Melanie; Heimann, Paula; Isaacs, Susan; and Rivière, Joan: *Developments in Psychoanalysis.* London, Hogarth, 1952.

Kovel, Joel: *A Complete Guide to Therapy.* New York, Pantheon, 1976.

Krathwohl, David R.; Bloom, Benjamin S.; and Masia, Bernard B.: *Taxonomy of Educational Objectives, Handbook II. Affective Domain.* New York, David McKay, 1964.

Krauss, David; and Fryrear, Jerry L. (Eds.): *Phototherapy in Mental Health.* Springfield, Thomas, 1983.

Kris, Ernst: *Psychoanalytic Explorations in Art.* London, Allen & Unwin, 1953.

Kübler-Ross, Elisabeth: *On Death and Dying.* New York, Macmillan, 1969.

Laing, R. D.: *The Politics of Experience.* New York, Pantheon, 1967.

Landy, Robert: *Handbook of Educational Drama and Theatre.* Westport, Greenwood, 1982.

_____: Training the drama therapist—a four-part model. *The Arts in Psychotherapy, 9:*91–100, 1982.

_____: The use of distancing in drama therapy. *The Arts in Psychotherapy, 10:*175–185, 1983.

Lazier, Gil; and Karioth, E. J.: The inventory of dramatic behavior: a content analysis technique for creative dramatics. Theatre Science Laboratory, Florida State University, 1972.

Leaf, Linaya: Drama, theatre, and the handicapped: a review of the literature. In Shaw, Ann;

and Stevens, C. J. (Eds.): *Drama, Theatre and the Handicapped.* Washington, D.C., American Theatre Association, 1979.

_____: *Identification and Classification of the Educational Objectives of Creative Dramatics when it is done with Handicapped Persons Ages Five-Eighteen in the United States.* Unpublished Ph.D. dissertation. Eugene, University of Oregon, 1980.

Lippard, Lucy: Time will tell. *Village Voice, 102,* June 19, 1984.

Lowen, Alexander: *The Betrayal of the Body.* London, Collier, 1967.

Lowenfeld, Margaret: The world pictures of children. *British Journal of Medical Psychology, 18:*65–101, 1939.

May, Rollo: *Existential Psychology.* New York, Random House, 1969.

Mead, George H.: *Mind, Self and Society.* Chicago, University of Chicago, 1934.

Michael, J. C., and Buehler, Charlotte: Experiences with personality testing in the neuropsychiatric department of a general hospital. *Diseases of the Nervous System, 6:*205–211, 1945.

Miller, N. E., and Dollard, John: *Social Learning and Imitation.* New Haven, Yale, 1941.

Mitchell, E. D., and Mason, B. S.: *The Theory of Play.* New York, Ronald Press, 1948.

Moffett, James: *Teaching the Universe of Discourse.* Boston, Houghton-Mifflin, 1968.

Moffett, James; and Wagner, Betty Jane: *Student-Centered Language Arts and Reading, K-13: A Handbook for Teachers,* 2nd ed. Boston, Houghton-Mifflin, 1976.

Moreno, Jacob L.: *Sociodrama as a Method for the Analysis of Social Conflicts.* Beacon, Beacon House, 1944.

_____: *Psychodrama,* Vols. I and II. New York, Beacon House, 1946, 1959.

Mowrer, O. H.: *Learning Theory and the Symbolic Process.* New York, Wiley, 1960.

Murray, Henry A.: *Explorations in Personality.* New York, Oxford, 1938.

_____: *In Nomine Diaboli.* New England Quarterly, 24:435–452, 1951.

Ouspensky, P. D.: *A New Model of the Universe.* New York, Vintage, 1971.

Obeyesekere, Ranjini and Gananath: Comic dramas in Sri Lanka. *The Drama Review, 20:*5–19, 1976.

Opie, Iona and Peter: *Children's Games in Street and Playground.* London, Oxford, 1969.

Piaget, Jean: *Play, Dreams and Imitation in Childhood.* New York, Norton, 1962.

Piaget, Jean; and Inhelder, Barbel: *The Psychology of the Child.* New York, Basic Books, 1969.

Perls, Frederick S.: *Gestalt Therapy Verbatim.* Moab, Real People Press, 1969.

Perlstein, Susan: *A Stage for Memory-Life History Plays by Older Adults.* New York, Teachers and Writers, 1981.

_____: *Sophie's choice: a tale of adaptation.* Unpublished paper, 1983.

_____: *Social, cultural, psychological and biological factors in human behavior, a character study.* Unpublished paper, 1983a.

Portner, Elaine: Drama in therapy: experiences of a ten year old. In Schattner, Gertrud; and Courtney, Richard (Eds.): *Drama in Therapy,* Vol. I. New York, Drama Book Specialists, 1981.

Postman, Neil: Social science as theology. *Et Cetera, 41:*22–33, 1984.

Redl, Fritz; and Wineman, David: *Children Who Hate.* New York, Free Press, 1951.

Redl, Fritz; and Wineman, David: *Controls from Within.* New York, Free Press, 1952.

Reich, Wilheim: *Character Analysis,* 3rd ed. New York, Farrar, Straus, and Cudahy, 1961.

Rogers, Carl: *On Becoming a Person.* Boston, Houghton-Mifflin, 1961.

Róheim, Geza: *The Riddle of the Sphynx.* London, Hogarth, 1934.

Rose, Scott: Producing *Our Town:* therapeutic theatre in a psychiatric hospital. *Hospital and Community Psychiatry, 33:*1018–1020, 1982.

Rubin, Judith; and Irwin, Eleanor: Art and drama: parts of a puzzle. In Jakab, Irene (Ed.): *Psychiatry and Art,* Vol. 4. Basel, Karger, 1975.

Ryan, Paul R.: Theatre as prison therapy. *The Drama Review, 20:*31–42, 1976.

Sarbin, Theodore: Role theory. In Lindzey, Gardner (Ed.): *Handbook of Social Psychology,* Vol. I. Cambridge, Addison-Wesley, 1954.

Satir, Virginia: *Conjoint Family Therapy.* Palo Alto, Science and Behavior Books, 1967.

Schaefer, Charles E.; and O'Connor, Kevin J. (Eds.): *Handbook of Play Therapy.* New York, Wiley, 1983.

Schein, Jerome: Group techniques applied to deaf and hearing-impaired persons. In Seligman, Milton (Ed.): *Textbook of Group Psychotherapy and Counseling with Special Populations.* Baltimore, University Park, 1982.

Schattner, Gertrud; and Courtney, Richard (Eds.). *Drama in Therapy,* Vols. I and II. New York, Drama Book Specialists, 1981.

Scheff, Thomas J.: *Catharsis in Healing, Ritual, and Drama.* Berkeley, University of California, 1979.

_____: The distancing of emotion in psychotherapy. *Psychotherapy: Theory, Research and Practice, 18:*46–53, 1981.

Shaw, Ann: *A Development of a Taxonomy of Educational Objectives in Creative Dramatics.* Unpublished Ed.D. dissertation. New York, Columbia University, 1968.

Selman, Robert: Taking another's perspective: role-taking development in early childhood. *Child Development, 42:*1721–1734, 1971.

Skinner, B. F.: *Contingencies of Reinforcement.* New York, Appleton-Century-Crofts, 1969.

Slade, Peter: *Child Drama.* London, University of London, 1954.

Smith, Susan: *The Mask in Modern Drama.* Berkeley, University of California, 1984.

Spolin, Viola: *Improvisation for the Theatre.* Evanston, Northwestern University, 1963.

Stanislavski, Constantin: *An Actor Prepares.* New York, Theatre Arts, 1936.

_____: *Building a Character.* New York, Theatre Arts, 1949.

Sullivan, Harry S.: *The Interpersonal Theory of Psychiatry.* New York, Norton, 1953.

Sutton-Smith, Brian; and Lazier, Gil: Psychology and drama. *Empirical Research in the Theatre, 1:*38–47, 1971.

Wagner, Betty Jane: *Dorothy Heathcote — Drama as a Learning Medium.* Washington, D.C., National Education Association, 1976.

Way, Brian: *Development through Drama.* London, Longman, 1967.

The White House Conference on Handicapped Individuals, Vol. Three: Implementation Plan: Washington, D.C., Superintendent of Documents, U.S. Government Printing Office, 1978.

Witkin, Robert: *The Intelligence of Feeling.* London, Heineman, 1974.

Wolpe, Joseph; and Lazarus, Arnold: *Behavior Therapy Techniques.* New York, Pergamon, 1966.

Willett, John (Ed.): *Brecht on Theatre.* New York, Hill and Wang, 1964.

INDEX